MAKING POPULAR MUSIC

Musicians, Creativity and Institution

MAKING POPULAR MUSIC

Musicians, Creativity and Institutions

JASON TOYNBEE

A member of the Hodder Headline Group
LONDON

Co-published in the United States of America by
Oxford University Press Inc., New York

First published in Great Britain in 2000 by
Arnold, a member of the Hodder Headline Group,
338 Euston Road, London NW1 3BH

http://www.arnoldpublishers.com

Co-published in the United States of America by
Oxford University Press Inc.,
198 Madison Avenue, New York, NY10016

The advice and information in this book are believed to be true and
accurate at the date of going to press, but neither the author nor the publisher
can accept any legal responsibility or liability for any errors or omissions.

British Library Cataloguing in Publication Data
A catalogue record for this book is available from the British Library

Library of Congress Cataloging-in-Publication Data
A catalog record for this book is available from the Library of Congress

ISBN 0 340 65224 1 (hb)
ISBN 0 340 65223 3 (pb)

1 2 3 4 5 6 7 8 9 10

Production Editor: Julie Delf
Production Controller: Priya Gohil
Cover Design: Terry Griffiths

Illustrations on pages 41, 62 and 139: Bernard Gudynas

Typeset by Phoenix Photosetting, Chatham, Kent

What do you think about this book? Or any other Arnold title?
Please send your comments to feedback.arnold@hodder.co.uk

Contents

Acknowledgements

Lots of people have helped me write this book; to start with everyone in the Communication, Culture and Media subject group at Coventry University. My thanks go in particular to colleagues Peter Playdon for contacts and help with dance music research, to John Downey and Martyn Lee for excellent critical feedback on particular chapters, to Andrew Beck for invaluable assistance with sources written and recorded, and to Val Hill for the loan of useful books, but even more for hours of illuminating discussion about everything from psychoanalysis to country and western (and often both together).

The present study is based on my PhD. I have had three great supervisors over what has been a long project. Jim McGuigan got me started and helped with the formulation of the central argument. Dave Hesmondhalgh took over after Jim left Coventry. Dave's support, intellectual and moral, has been wonderful and very much needed. I doubt whether I could have finished without his help. Dave Laing has been reading chapters, discussing ideas and sharing his massive knowledge of things popular, musical and much else besides right from the start.

At the beginning, and at critical stages throughout the project, Simon Frith has provided generous advice and support. I have also talked a lot with Dai Griffiths who read a chapter and through his constructive criticism got me thinking that I might dare to write about 'the music itself' without being a musicologist.

It needs to be mentioned that popular music studies is a domain where internationalism and solidarity are alive and kicking: thanks to all friends in the International Association for the Study of Popular Music, both in Britain and throughout the world, for stimulating discussion and good times at conferences.

In Coventry two friends and experts on music culture from times past deserve acknowledgement: Kevin Buckley and Aiden Every. Amongst musician friends and colleagues thanks go in particular to Nick Buxton and

Kevin Mason. Two informants whom I met during the study were especially helpful, namely Mike and James from the Guardians of Dalliance, while for an introduction to clubbing *à la mode*, thank you, Cheryl Stott.

Writing this book was not easy, but the process has been facilitated by advice, patient understanding and also utterly appropriate chivvying from my editor, Lesley Riddle, at Arnold.

Finally, I should like to thank Chrissie, Georgia and Max Toynbee for keeping me going at some cost to their own lives. Georgia and Max have been great informants about music, and have freely shared their knowledge and astute critical judgement. Chrissie has cheerfully shouldered a lot of extra work and responsibility, not to mention dealing with a distracted partner. Thanks.

Introduction

Forget what you may have heard about Brian Wilson and the Beach Boys – this is the real thing: Brian Wilson's searingly candid autobiography.

(front notes, Wilson with Gold 1996)

David Hadju uncovers a fascinating but hitherto largely hidden figure, recalling to vivid life the man, the milieu and even, to a degree that is unusual in biographies, the music.

(*Scotsman*, front notes, Hadju 1997)

This book exists on the premise that somebody, somewhere, is interested in *who I am, how I got that way, and what the fuck I'm talking about.*

(Zappa with Occhiogrosso 1989: 13, original emphasis)

Popular musicians are popular figures in the media. Specialist magazines carry lengthy interviews and features on them, newspapers have shorter ones, television programmes scrutinize the lives of artists and there is a sub-genre of the biographical feature film which deals with singers and musicians.[1] Clearly, people want to know about music makers.

My particular interest, and an important source for this book, is the print (auto)biography. Titles here range from breathless accounts of the rise to fame of recent stars to considered reflections on the life and work of established performers or greats from the past. What they share, though, is an assumption that the meaning of the music can be found in the lives of its makers. These lives begin as ordinary lives, or at least they ought to do so. For the popularity of popular music is very much based on an ideal: popular musicians come from the common people but they make extraordinary music. Over the course of the book I want to take this archetypal myth at face value and explore its implications. In brief my argument goes that musicians are *exemplary agents* who make a difference, in the shape of different songs, sounds and styles.

However, that is not at all to invoke the romantic conception of the artist. The composer, novelist or painter is supposed to be a special kind of being whose creativity and imagination rise up above the banality of everyday life and the everyday psyche. Similarly, the social world inhabited by the artist should be an elevated one. Salon, loft, country retreat or literary enclave in the city – these all identify the artist as the member of a rare species which requires the sustenance and protection of an exclusive milieu. The popular musician, on the other hand, is exemplary just because s/he comes from the people and cleaves to popular values. Musicians have to 'pay their dues' and 'stay in touch with the roots', even (perhaps especially) in genres like independent rock which set themselves up in distinction to purportedly commercial sorts of music.

This suggests that the term popular is very much a matter of what Jim McGuigan calls 'populist sentiment' (1992: 13–20), rather than a precise sociological term. We cannot map the popular directly on to class or race, although it will overlap with these social formations. Instead the popular tends to be an *image* of the people, ranged in opposition to elite culture and privilege. Actually, it is this very imprecision which gives pop such enormous potency.[2]

First, it enables the music to function as a banner under which ordinary people can congregate and identify themselves as a community or group. In this context musicians tend to be representatives mandated by 'their' people. They ought, in the populist discourse of pop, to recognize this and have the common touch, acknowledging where they have come from even when they are stars. Second, and in contrast, popular music carries the promise of transcendence of the ordinary. As Jon Savage proposes, a basic tenet of pop is that 'overnight you can be transformed into something superhuman' (1996: 113). From this perspective musicians should shine in their abundant artistry. This applies even to 'cool' musicians like Miles Davis or Bryan Ferry who, despite being extraordinary, behave as though it involved no effort at all.

My argument is that the exemplary agency of musicians then arises in the need to negotiate between these two positions – that is, being ordinary, typically of the people, and being marvellous, showing what life could be like 'if only'. This is a large and rather abstract claim. It also has the implication that popular musicians always succeed in their role. In fact being a musician is fraught with problems which often arise from the very contradictions which I have been suggesting are so productive. It might be useful, then, to produce an initial specification in order to weigh up the potential value of musicians. In the table which follows the left-hand column is a credit account. It itemises the affirmative role of musicians, the ways in which they may indeed be considered exemplary agents. On the right are the debits, in other words a corresponding set of problems with the life and role of the musician. At the end of the table we will attempt a balance between the two.

Musicians are nomadic subjects. Transgressing the ordered time and space of everyday life and work under high capitalism, they tour and record in different towns and countries, stay up late and go to work when others are playing (Frith 1983: 77–9). More importantly, musicians have broken through racial and class barriers by performing in all kinds of hybrid combinations and reaching across to what were once segregated audiences. Above all, musicians are receptive to new people and ideas: they synthesize otherness.

Musicians are insecure subjects. The nomadic life produces enormous pressures and the cost of breaking through barriers of race and class is huge. A long list of casualties among musicians who have succumbed to drug abuse, depression and, all too often, early death suggests that nomadism is most often experienced as insecurity. The profit imperative of the music industry then exacerbates these problems. Musicians struggle desperately to be recruited. Most fail and most of the few who do succeed have the briefest of moments in the spotlight (Jones 1998).

Musicians make utopias. Sometimes these are explicit. For example songs like 'Blue Heaven', 'Woodstock' or 'One Nation Under a Groove' spell out what the good life might actually be like.[3] But there is a much more widespread and implicit utopianism which derives from the commonly held idea that music is a transcendental medium, and that it expresses something more than words can say (Flinn 1992: 9–11). In this sense all popular musicians, from Louis Armstrong to the members of Megadeth, are engaged in developing the utopian sensibility. In making music they get people to yearn for a better life, free from prejudice and oppression and full of beauty (variously 'swinging', 'funky', 'banging', 'it rocks' . . .).

Musicians make dystopias. The glossy, seductive utopia of the pop song conceals, and is therefore a sign of, social reality in all its horror and inequity. The presentation of the good life demonstrates bad faith, a form of ideological manipulation which serves to confirm the full extent of domination in advanced capitalist societies (Adorno and Horkheimer 1979). In the late twentieth century, musicians (NWA, Marilyn Manson . . .) have gone a step further by producing *overtly* dystopian texts which invite a puerile pleasure in the depravity, squalor and hopelessness of living in a modern urban society.

Musicians are popular creators. Their example suggests that ordinary people are creative too. Being a musician is a spur to action, a call to others to get involved in the social process of music-making. In this sense it is a validation of *doing* even in the most reactionary of times when the possibility of agency seems to be lost. Music-making is also structurally democratic. Not only does it tend to be organized on a mutual basis (the 'band' is the prototypical unit), but the means of production and distribution are relatively accessible and decentralized. Lots of people can and do become musicians.

Musicians are vainglorious. Far from being exemplary agents they are hyper-individualistic and motivated by greed and the need for adulation. Stars willingly turn themselves into commodities to be bought and sold by the music industry, while struggling musicians desire to become commodities. To the extent that musicians provide an example of the transformation of everyday life it is purely at the level of spectacle (Debord 1994).

Musicians make change. Although the rate has varied at different times and places, innovation is perhaps the most important defining feature of popular music. The musician's role is central here. S/he produces the new, both through combining the already heard to generate new hybrid forms, but also by appropriating technology. The popular musician is an opportunist researcher in sound who adapts instruments and technology so as to make them throw new voices in sublime ways. Musical innovation is thus a form of popular self-management within capitalism.

Musicians invent fads. Their key role is to produce novelty in order to supply a market-place where the new is at a premium. In this sense the facility to change and move on, far from being disruptive of social norms and capitalist routines of production, represents a key capitalist value ('flexibility'). Generally, the chronic innovation of popular music is symptomatic of a fragmented and anomic (post)modern world.

Musicians play a part in the public sphere. Popular music includes public debate, in the sense that musicians sometimes write and perform songs about political issues. But genres of popular music are also articulated with particular social movements and groups, what Nancy Fraser (1992) calls 'counter-publics' consisting, for example, of African-Americans and black British, gays and lesbians, eco-warriors, youth cultures in conflict with the repressive state. Often it is the secretly coded or oblique nature of musicians' performances which resonate most strongly with counter-publics.

Musicians fail to represent social movements and subaltern identities. In an important sense the history of popular music is the history of exclusion: of African-Americans and Caribbeans whose intermittent success in popular music markets only serves to underline their systematic exploitation and repression in economy and polity; of women who have either been ruthlessly pushed into 'women's quarters' (diva, girl group . . .) or forced to deal with the essential misogyny of pop through varieties of masquerade and caricature (Reynolds and Press 1995).

How can we possibly make a judgement about these debits and credits of popular musicianship? In an obvious sense we cannot. This 'balance sheet' is only a heuristic device and none of the entries can be given a numerical value. Moreover it is too early to say. We are at least the length of the present study away from reaching any conclusions. However some working assumptions can be extracted. First, musicians, and the system of musicianship, are produced by a brutalizing and distorting social system. No matter what heights of sublime invention they reach, musicians never escape from the constraints of living under capitalism.[4] A persistent strand of musical populism keeps alive recognition of this fact: musicians must, in the interest of truth to the people, understand that they belong to a world where the utopian values of music do *not* count. We can hear this in the downbeat and self-deprecating vocabulary used by music makers to describe what they do: 'twanging', 'tweaking', 'knocking it out'.

On the other hand some of the negative attributes listed in the right-hand column derive from placing an unreasonable burden on musicians. So long as we do not expect them to change the world on their own then prima facie the credit column would seem to support the following, cautiously optimistic, thesis: popular musicians show in a limited, but none the less substantive, fashion the transforming power of human agency, first as producers of desire for a better life, second as exemplars of autonomous action. Over the course of this book I want to test this position through an examination of popular musicians from a number of different perspectives, and in a range of periods, places and genres. In doing this, though, it will always be necessary to keep the warnings from the right-hand column in mind. For unless a rigorously critical approach is brought to bear it will be difficult to claim any validity for the investigation.

Before we start, one preliminary issue needs to be addressed. Important criticisms have been made of the concept of creativity and indeed of the significance of cultural production more generally. These arguments are powerful and have considerable currency in cultural studies, so we ought to respond to them now, before taking the concrete analysis of musicianship any further.

Two critiques of production

The first argument from this quarter might be described as author-icidal. It attacks the idea of an all-powerful author in whose personality and intentions the meaning of works should be found. Rather, the significance of cultural artifacts must be located in the text alone. The key work here is the essay by Roland Barthes, 'The death of the author' (1976a). Barthes talks mainly about literary authors but the argument is equally applicable to musicians and their work. His charge is that '[t]he image of literature to be found in ordinary culture is tyrannically centred on the author, his person, his life, his taste, his passions' (143). Barthes responds with an exposé – he will show up the cult of the author for the illusion it really is.

> We know now that a text is not a line of words releasing a single 'theological' meaning (the 'message' of the Author-God) but a multi-dimensional space in which a variety of writings, none of them original, blend and clash.
>
> (146)

What we are presented with here is the liberation of the text. Once separated from the prescriptive hand of the author it becomes wildly productive and resistant to closure, a state of which Barthes clearly approves. Indeed at some points the text actually seems to acquire a perverse agency of its own: 'writing ceaselessly posits meaning ceaselessly to evaporate it' (147).

This argument for the autonomy of the text is associated with a strong objection to self-expression on the part of the author. 'Did he wish to *express himself*, he ought at least to know that the inner "thing" he thinks to "translate" is itself only a ready-formed dictionary,' Barthes says (146, original emphasis). Again the primacy of language is asserted, but now it serves to emphasize the crassness of the author-subject. His arrogance in pretending to authority is only matched by his stupidity in mistaking what is actually the common stock of language for his own expression. What's more, far from mitigating this conceit, any attempt by the author to demonstrate conviction just makes things worse. As Barthes sneers in another essay, 'the sincerity of the enunciation – veritable "cross" borne by literary morality' (1976b: 161).

Barthes' attack on authorship has had a widespread and lasting influence on cultural studies. In particular, the notion of textual, rather than authorial, productivity has been crucial in postmodern theory, underpinning arguments about fragmentation, simulation and the loss of the referent in contemporary culture (see for example Lyotard 1984, Baudrillard 1988, Jameson 1991).

However I am more interested here in the specific charges made by the anti-author position. In particular its radical scepticism about romantic conceptions of the sovereign and omnipotent artist carries substantial weight. The 'Author-God' characterized by Barthes is a real social institution, and one which needs to be attacked not just in high art, but also in those areas of popular music which have imported it. I am thinking mainly of jazz and rock where the author cult has been renewed with a vengeance. Many of those biographies which I mentioned at the beginning of this Introduction fall into the trap of hearing music as an expression of the soul or psyche of the complex/sensitive/tortured/heroic artist. Moreover this is almost invariably a great *man* approach which celebrates masculine energy and drive, and conflates these qualities with creativity.

Having said that, it seems to me that anti-authorism goes much too far. Rigorously applied it contradicts any notion of agency, or the idea that music might be made by people. What's more, it contradicts itself. Its preferred alternatives to the author as source of meaning – the productive text or born-again reader – are just as mysterious in their self-generation *ex nihilio* as any romantic artist. Barthes does pose the notion of intertextuality (that is the citation and passage of discourse between one text and another) as a way of accounting for movement and change. Yet as Seán Burke points out, 'intertextual currents open up between [various authors] . . . precisely because there is influence, continuity, succession and revision, withal, an act of strong reading between their work' (1992: 155).

This idea that authors are mediators in the intertextual process is crucial for the present study. I want to argue that popular musicians, are first and foremost, engaged in exchanging sounds, styles, musical ideas and forms. They are designers and assemblers who take pieces of what is already heard and recombine them. As such they are not expressive, that is they do not generate music from within. Instead their materials are located outside in the field of the social. As I suggest in Chapter 2, we need a new term for this function: 'social authorship' seems appropriate.

There is another way in which authorship can be reclaimed, though, namely by considering it as speaking position. A powerful criticism of the romantic conception of the artist is that he is white, ruling class and male. Clearly such criticism has a strong counter-hegemonic thrust to it. To show up authorship as a myth is to damage an institution of class, gender and racial domination. But might not the reading of texts which are implicated in relations of power depend on attributing a certain authorial intent? So asks Kobena Mercer (1994). Mercer is concerned with the question of what Robert Mapplethorpe's photographs of black male nudes mean. Having initially read these images as racist and the fetishization of black bodies by a white man, Mercer changes his mind. Recognizing his own identification with the homoerotic gaze inscribed in the photographs, he also reckons that the very coolness of Mapplethorpe's vision produces a reversal. When he looks a second time the images deconstruct the objectification at stake in the whole western tradition of 'the nude', not to mention the objectification which goes in the process of producing a racialized, eroticized Other.

These complex issues of point of view (by very close analogy we can add point of audition in music) mean that authorship must be reconsidered. As Mercer puts it:

> [t]he contestation of marginality in black, gay and feminist cultural politics thus inevitably brings the issue of authorship back into play, not as the centred origin that determines or guarantees the aesthetic and political value of a text, but as a vital question about agency in cultural struggles to 'find a voice' and 'give voice' to subordinate experiences, identities and subjectivities.
>
> (1994: 194)

Given the enormous importance of black music and musicians in pop, not to mention the widespread absence of women as authors, this point is absolutely vital for the present study too. We will return to it.

There are good reasons, then, not to discard authorship so much as to revise it. We need a more modest conception of creative intention and control which can be adjusted according to the particular text–power relations prevailing in a given musical environment. So far so good. However there is another variety of argument in cultural studies, a related one, which would dispense with consideration of cultural production altogether. Usefully described as the 'consumption orthodoxy' by Georgina Born (1993) this tendency locates the significance of culture in the process of consumption. We need to respond to arguments here too because they pose important questions about the nature of popular culture in general, and music in particular. The focus will be on the work of two of its chief protagonists, John Fiske (1989a, 1989b) and Paul Willis (1990).

Broadly, these writers propose that popular culture is coterminous with consumption, not only of texts and performances which have customarily been considered cultural like music, but of every kind of consumer product available in the market-place. Culture is thus defined precisely in its ubiquitous commodification. As Fiske puts it 'all industries are cultural industries, to a greater or lesser extent' (1989a: 4). The trouble with this is that it cuts off too quickly discussion of cultural work in production itself, in other words prior to the market transaction. In effect Fiske and Willis foreclose such a discussion with an analytical move. These post-Marxists transfer the labour process from production across the threshold of exchange to the domain of consumption.

In *Capital* Marx lauds the worker as an exemplary human subject who weaves the material fabric of the social world from nature's bounty (Marx 1976: 283–92). In an analogous way the consumption orthodoxy treats the consumer as quintessentially productive, making meaning through 'symbolic work' on the commodities obtained in the market-place (Willis 1990). Like minerals which consist in a fructuous combination of elements, commodities are resources containing, as Fiske puts it, 'both the forces of domination and the opportunities to speak against them' (1989b: 25). In this schema, then, the market takes the place nature had in Marx's conspectus. The worker–consumer makes sense and pleasure out of the symbolic raw material extracted from the shopping mall.

The other side of the consumption orthodoxy is its explicit hostility to the analysis of production – in the more traditional sense. Willis makes his position clear on this when he talks of 'a ludicrous (actually crude Marxist) emphasis on production and what is held to be initially coded into artifacts' (1990: 20). There are two problems here, it seems to me. First, the complexity and conflicted nature of cultural production is blithely ignored. Far from music just turning up in the market-place it is the outcome of intense competition and struggle between, for example, record companies and musicians, radio stations and music publishers, disc jockeys and club owners. As well as affecting the economic well being of the actors involved, these struggles have cultural outcomes. They have an impact on what kind of music gets made.

This brings us to the second point. I would suggest that 'what is held to be initially coded into artifacts' *does* count, not on the basis of absolute determination of meaning but rather as the subject of negotiation between producers and audience. In the case of popular music this produces surprising results. The currency of authorship discourse, not to mention the ideal of a popular music community in which musicians are representatives (Frith 1983: 75), means that audiences of jazz, rock, rap and dance want artists to be independent of market relations. In this sense consumers have helped music makers to gain a certain degree of autonomy from industrial control: the market has insisted on the amelioration of market relations. We will explore this theme further in Chapter 1. For now I simply want to note that it suggests that consumption, of music at least, includes an intense interest in the terms and conditions of production. People want their music to be 'initially coded', but only in ways of which they approve.

So far we have encountered arguments for sealing off production completely from the consideration of popular culture. However in Paul Willis's work a rather different, and almost contradictory, case is made in a chapter on music. Here Willis and collaborator Simon Jones discuss the reggae sound system. They suggest it is 'an institution where the activities of consumption merge into and become intertwined with more conventional forms of production' (Willis 1990: 72). This involves rather an uneasy shift in emphasis, first towards community and roots. The work of constructing speaker bins, for example, is an 'informal process' which embraces 'sound technology, electronics and carpentry'. Yet at the same time the sound system is also 'one of the key institutions in an autonomous commercial infrastructure' of black music (72). Such an economy is a product of young black people's 'disenfranchisement and marginalisation by the mainstream leisure industry' (73). The point is that it is simply not clear whether reggae sound systems belong to the sphere of consumption or production. Certainly one can agree that, along with other black music in Britain, the systems have been marginalized. But my argument would be that to the extent it *is* produced and disseminated then black music is very much a commodity and we ought to treat it as such.

This becomes clear when we examine the history of the sound system. Emerging in Jamaica during the early 1960s as a large mobile discotheque with powerful amplifiers and banks of speaker cabinets, by the mid-1970s systems in both Jamaica and the UK were playing a new form, dub, with 'MCs' live on the microphone 'talking over' specially recorded instrumental tracks (Davis and Simon 1983, Hebdige 1988b: 82–9). Sound systems provided a testing ground for new music, and their disc jockeys (DJs) became pivotal figures in the Jamaican music industry acting as entrepreneurs and record producers. A special record format, the 'dub plate', was also developed for sound systems. It is still used in reggae as well as the new British dance music genre called jungle (see Chapter 5). Pressed up in very limited quantities and made out of soft acetate, these records have a short life but an extremely good frequency response, especially in the bass register (Willmott 1998). And that is precisely the point. If the dub plate looks like an ordinary consumer good – the vinyl record – it is actually an instrument made for exclusive use by the DJ and marked as such by dint of its cost, rareness and special performance qualities. In the classical music world the analogue of a dub plate is a Stradivarius.

The 'consumption into production' argument used by Willis and Jones thus falls down because it does not engage with the professional, craft dimension of the sound system. As I argue in Chapter 1, there is a continuum of music-making activity in popular music as a whole which stretches from the small scale and local to the global and fully industrial.

But, crucially, the connection between the two levels derives from the fact that local music scenes constitute a labour market, or in Howard Becker's phrase, a 'resource pool' of musical talent (1982: 77–92). By treating youth involvement in music-making purely as an 'expression and celebration of sociability' (81) Willis and Jones fail to grasp the extent to which young musicians at every level of competence also desire fame and fortune in the music industry. They want to be recruited.

Researchers in cultural studies who argue for the priority of consumption and its redemptive powers are surely driven by a love of the common people. They wish to present fecund consumption as the engine of a new cultural movement which is *already* transforming everyday life. The politics of this position are admirably democratic, yet at the same time the perspective is blinkered. Clearly audiences want ready-made music and they like to hear and see spectacle or virtuosity. In this context we need to acknowledge the gap between producer and consumer, and see it not as an unequal relationship so much as a condition of musical performance and an integral part of the popular aesthetic.

The banal but essential point is that both production and consumption are important, and should be considered together, rather than one side or the other being taken. In the present work the emphasis will be on musical production and musicianship. However the notion of intertextual exchange, of musicians reading influences and idioms from different musical texts and other musicians, is a key theme. Moreover, as we will hear, popular music makers listen to themselves. In an important sense they must cast themselves as an audience for their own work as it takes shape. Thus, even within the sphere of production, consumption plays its part.

Popular music's short twentieth century

We looked briefly at the notion of the popular at the beginning of this Introduction, but it might be useful to say something more about how the term 'popular music' will be applied in the present study. For, as Richard Middleton (1990: 3–7) suggests, it has acquired different, and often contradictory, definitions. We can start with a structural approach. Popular music may be distinguished from other kinds of music and in particular from folk music and classical music. Folk music flourishes in pre-industrial societies and lingers on in more economically developed ones. It often carries a ritual or quasi-ritual function. It is not commodified and does not depend on media technology. Rather it is reproduced through an oral tradition of repeated performance with slow changes in form and style. Classical music is the art music of the western middle classes. It is characterized by a sharply drawn division of labour between composition/inscription on the one hand and performance on the other. The repertoire now consists largely of works composed between 1750 and 1950. In social terms classical music serves to mark the 'distinction' of its listeners' taste (in their ears at least) over and against the mass cultural predilections of the popular classes (Bourdieu 1984).[5]

Popular music differs from both folk and classical in that it developed historically in and through the mass media. Its symptomatic artifact, the record, represents at one and the same time a type of performance and a means of communication. Composition methods vary in pop, from prior inscription as in the case of classical music, to different kinds of integrated composition and performance involving the use of reproductive technologies. The latter has virtually replaced the former in the last 35 years of the century. Socially, popular music has a mixed constituency which includes large sections of the middle class (Frith 1996: 34–5), as well as working class and diasporic communities. Class and ethnicity are articulated in complex ways in popular music. However we can note two divergent tendencies. On the one hand styles within pop serve to identify and represent *particular* social groups in their resistance to exclusion and dominant cultural values – black people, gays, certain youth subcultures and, much more infrequently, women. On the other there is a strong hegemonic thrust towards a mainstream, a desire for popular music which would sing for *all* the people.

This approach to popular music, which defines it both in distinction to other kinds of music and in relation to popular social formations, also suggests a certain periodization. In his incisive study of recent world history Eric Hobsbawm (1994) uses the term 'short twentieth century' to refer to the period 1914–1991. The phrase can be productively applied to the more limited field of popular music too. However, more appropriate dates in this case would be 1921–1999. The beginning date is suggested by the fact that it was the moment record sales in America exceeded 100 000 000 (Gellatt 1977: 212), as well as the year of the first regular radio broadcast, from station KDKA in Pittsburgh (Head *et al*. 1994: 33). The independent record company Gennett, the most significant of the 'race' labels of the 1920s, also won its protracted legal battle for the right to produce phonograph discs without a licence, so breaking the majors' long-established stranglehold on the record business (Kennedy 1994: 25). The short twentieth century is thus inaugurated at the intersection of key technological, economic and cultural developments, developments which come to characterize popular music as form and institution over the next 80 years or so.

The year 1999 represents a chronologically neat, but rather less precise, terminal year. At the end of the 1990s there are signs that the constitution of popular music is undergoing considerable change. Partly this is because the demarcation between high and low culture is becoming less clear in the West, with taste communities and markets for music now being organized in complex and often overlapping ways (Peterson 1994). Partly it is because of processes of globalization. During its short twentieth century, pop has been predominantly Anglo-American, that is, it has been music made in Britain and America, shaped for those same markets and then sold on internationally.[6] Increasingly, however, the hegemony of the Anglo-American bloc is breaking down as regional networks of production and consumption emerge around the world. Sometimes these are based on hybridized 'folk' musics, sometimes, in the case of European dance music, on instrumental sounds which, in their absence of lyrics, carry no national markings and so can become the focus for new kinds of international musical alliance (Laing 1997).

The present study does not ignore these changes. Indeed the last chapter is a case study of British dance music and its makers. There are good reasons to suggest that this music scene belongs to the new paradigm of the regional network. There are indications too that it encapsulates a new way of making music. Thus the book ends by posing the question of change – how much and in what direction – now, at the *end* of 80 years or so of continuous development. In doing so it challenges the commonly held view that 'rock and roll' (Friedlander 1996) or the 'rock formation' (Grossberg 1991) represented a decisive break in popular music history some time in the 1950s. My position, rather, is that rock and roll/rock (henceforward rock), constituted the popular music mainstream in a particular period, from around 1965 to 1985. Mainstreams require a powerful discursive rationale in order to weld together a popular alliance (see Chapter 4). In the case of rock this alliance stretched across class, but only to a limited extent across race and gender – and it only prevailed for around 20 years. However the power of rock discourse in academic popular music studies has been such that rock is still read in some quarters as though it *were* popular music, or it least its crowning glory. A major effect of this has been to marginalize other kinds of popular music, especially jazz. Jazz has also suffered from being lifted out of popular culture by jazz lovers and treated as art (Horn 1991). Over the course of this book jazz and jazz musicians are pulled back into the frame of the popular. So, from beneath as it were, are other 'despised' genres like easy listening music. In short, the aim is to provide an inclusive if not exhaustive set of examples of musicianship, and to present a relatively *longue durée* which transcends the local history of rock.

Argument and methods

This book has five chapters. The first deals with economic organization and the market. The central argument is that the logic of the music industry's own structure as a capitalist cultural industry has, paradoxically, pushed it into conceding a degree of creative control to musicians. This theme is approached first through a review of key literature on popular music and the market, namely the now classical work of Theodor Adorno on the culture industry, analysis of the music industry by the 'production of culture' school of sociologists, and approaches to the cultural commodity from the critical political economy perspective.

Despite manifest differences in politics and theoretical orientation there is a degree of consensus between these positions about the music industry, particularly its instability, the special nature of its products and the exceptional routines needed to produce them. It is argued, however, that none of them has a proper account of the material conditions of music-making, in other words of what happens to musicians *within* the industrial apparatus.

The substantive proposal, then, is that a certain institutional autonomy (IA) has developed here which enables musicians to exert a large degree of creative control. The historical origins of IA are traced in the emergence of three kinds of music-making in the 1930s: the cross-media singing star, radio and film studio orchestras and the peripatetic swing band. IA is most strongly developed in the last of these modes. Here it derives mainly from the lack of dependence of the bands on any single media outlet – radio, record company, live circuit. Later, in rock and after, autonomy is assured more by audience demand. Now consecrated as authors, musicians are expected to be relatively free from industry control. The other key aspect of IA is the institution of the proto-market in local and small-scale music scenes. The industry cannot ignore them because this is where new talent and styles emerge. But the proto-market in all its anarchic voluntarism is extremely difficult to control. The notion of institutional autonomy as outlined above is crucial for the rest of the book. In particular it explains how the material conditions have arisen for musical creativity – the topic of the second chapter.

In Chapter 2, a theory of creativity in popular music is developed. In contrast to the way it has been used in romantic conceptions of art, creativity is understood as small scale and limited. Drawing on Bourdieu's (1993c, 1996) work on cultural production it is suggested that the musician–creator (individual or collective) stands at the centre of a radius of creativity. The creator identifies and selects musical possibles within this radius according to her habitus, but also the rules of the field of musical production – conventions, techniques and so on. Crucially, options here are tightly constrained in that the radius of creativity traverses a limited set of possibles.

What are possibles? Turning to Bakhtin's (1981) discussion of heteroglossia in the novel it is suggested that the possible is nothing less than voice, a musical equivalent of the utterance, in other words an idiomatic musical unit. Voices have two attributes: a site, which may be textual, social or in the body of a particular performer or instrument; and a sound-form, which will consist in syntactic and parametric aspects. It is the articulation of these two attributes – site and sound – which yields voice. Just how musical voices might be selected and combined is shown in a case study of the work of band leader and bassist Charles Mingus. Mingus provides an ideal, if not typical, example of social authorship in that his main technique is citation – of players, genres, places, periods. In the rich heteroglot texts that result Mingus conjures a cosmopolitan alliance of subaltern voices ranged in opposition to a monovocal culture of dominance.

As well as being manifested in social authorship, creativity has a strong performative aspect. Performance in popular music needs to be considered in two ways. First it refers to process, the ongoing making and remaking of music across media and through different versions. Second, performance is theatrical: musicians not only 'show off' but also try to reach an audience, in recording as much as in live concerts. Reference is made here to the work of Jacques Derrida (1991) on writing and context. Derrida argues that writing, and by extension all 'communication', is premised on absence in that the addressee is not here. No amount of 'context' can make up for this. There is thus a fundamental uncertainty, even impossibility, about musical communication which, I suggest here, fragments performance. Musicians tend to take up positions around the broken pieces, identified as expressionist, transformative, direct and reflexive modes.

In an important sense the aesthetics of performance consist in negotiating this permanent crisis. For if performance, in its impossibility, can be seen as a limit to creativity, it is by the same token the most significant domain in which it might be carried through. This bears strongly on the subject of the next chapter – the role of musicians as technologists.

The third chapter examines how popular musicians research, develop and perform technology. Crucially, mediation poses the crisis of performance (how to 'get across') in a new kind of way for musicians. It is suggested that a technosphere is constituted with the advent of recording and broadcasting, in other words an imagined space of communicative potentialities and constraints. Three overlapping periods, each characterized by a distinct method of imagining and navigating the technosphere, are then identified.

In the first, lasting from 1920 to the present, musicians develop techniques of ventriloquism, or, 'throwing the voice'. Such techniques include scat singing, crooning and the vocalization of instruments, particularly the saxophone which in jazz and rhythm and blues becomes an instrument of neophonic experimentation. With the arrival of tape recording it is argued that there is a shift in focus towards what becomes a second phase in the performance of technology, namely the construction of virtual musical space. Sam Phillips' recordings of Elvis Presley constitute an early example, but the phase reaches its apogee with Phil Spector's 'Wall of Sound' at the beginning of the 1960s. By means of microphone placement, echo and instrumentation, listeners are enveloped within a new and capacious sonic environment.

Rock's use of multi-track recording represents a transitional moment as the technosphere is now rendered in the imagination of musicians as layered and linear. Multi-tracking enables the re-emergence of what Richard Middleton (1986) calls the 'narrative-lyric' form in popular music, with hierarchical structures and a sense of narrative closure which can be heard, to fullest and most grandiose effect, in album-oriented rock. Finally, in the most recent, third phase, inaugurated at the start of the 1980s, there is a return to a two-stage sequence of composition–inscription and performance. Computers enable music to be represented graphically in the manner of a score. Meanwhile in dance clubs a separate cadre of performers emerges – the DJs – who are virtuoso creators of mood and marvel. This mode consolidates forms of spatial and temporal manipulation which emerged earlier.

In the last two chapters a longer focus is taken with the role of musicians being located in the social structure and cultural formations. Chapter 4 deals with 'genre-cultures'. It is argued that generic coding is inevitable. Even in the limited case of free music, which purports to be pure expression, a matrix of conventions delimits what musicians can and cannot play. Generic convention is partly a matter of the regulation of repetition and variation (Neale 1980), a psychic function which involves the compulsion to return to the same. But it is suggested that genre also has a social function when it is mapped on to community, in other words a social group which identifies itself in its difference, and usually its opposition, to dominant culture and power relations. The case is then made for a return to the notion of the structural homology, albeit in a heavily revised form. In the second half of the chapter the question of the relationship between musical style and social formation is opened out to include questions of mediation and market. With these additional factors included in the analytical frame it becomes possible to set out a typology of genre-cultures: race music, crossover, mainstream and the remote canon. The key point which emerges from examining these forms is that musical communities are neither wholly manufactured nor wholly authentic. Rather they emerge through struggle and negotiation in a space between the private sphere of the commercial and civil society.

The last chapter tests arguments developed earlier in the book through a case study of the British dance music which has emerged since 1988. The question is, do the concepts of institutional autonomy, creative agency and the performance of technology stand up here? Or is it rather the case, as has been proposed by some writers (Gilbert 1997, Eshun 1998a, Reynolds 1998), that dance music represents a paradigm shift in the nature of popular music and musicianship? Beginning with an examination of the nature of generic change in dance music it is suggested that a new kind of hyper-innovation can be identified. This is based on 'abduction' (Eco 1976) – the quasi-intuitive re-coding of musical materials, and intensification – the selection and intense development of limited aspects of a generic matrix. Both processes are assessed in a study of the progress of the sub-genre 'hardcore' as it mutates into 'jungle' over the period 1992–94.

If hyper-innovation challenges the model of the radius of creativity (the radius traverses a relatively *stable* field of musical production) so does the vaunted immediacy of dance music because it threatens to supersede the *reflexive* work of creativity. However in an examination of house music's repetitive 'four on the floor beat' it is argued that the sense of timelessness constructed here is always inflected by 'participatory discrepancies' (Keil 1994c) which serve to mitigate immediacy and subvert the endless present demanded by the beat. The point is that such discrepancies are creative tropes, but modest ones. Given the organization of the dance floor and dance scene as a 'flat' network this modest version of creative agency seems entirely appropriate.

My conclusion is that dance music does represent a significant change in the steady state of popular musicianship. Crucially, it is difficult to identify particular authors (groups or individuals) responsible for innovation. Rather, this is collectively induced. The strong contrast here is with the heroic mode of rock or jazz. Such change in the process of innovation has been underpinned by the reintroduction of a division of labour in production and performance (between producer and DJ). Musical creators have become craftspeople again. Meanwhile the organization of clubs in a flat network structure, spreading out across continental Europe, means that dance music makers no longer look across the Atlantic for ultimate recognition. Dance presages the collapse of the Anglo-American bloc. None of this means that creative agency disappears; far from it. It is just that creativity must be sought in other dimensions and across other spaces.

A note on methods: this book is interdisciplinary in its approach. It applies theories gleaned from economics, sociology, semiotics and cultural studies. There is limited use of terms and concepts from music theory, although none of the musical analysis should be considered musicological.

As for sources, many of them are secondary, that is to say books and articles written by academics from the various fields. The exceptions to this are music journalism, including interviews with musicians, musician biographies and music industry journalism. Some published economic statistics have also been used and there is quite extensive textual analysis of recordings. Two personal interviews with musicians are referred to in Chapter 5. Finally, in thinking about music-making I have drawn on my own intermittent experience as a rock singer and song writer between 1969 and 1989.

1

Market: the selling of soul(s)

Well, along came a man wanting me to join a show called the Tidy Jolly Steppers. He offered me ten dollars a week, and that was exciting. Ten dollars a week, you know, that was alright. So I would just put on a dress again and sing, and it was alright.

(Little Richard, quoted in White 1985: 35)

We were each making fifteen dollars a night, and there was a lot you could do with fifteen dollars. We would play three, four nights a week – that's fifty dollars. And sometimes we would play at a place on the outskirts of Macon at a midnight dance. That would pay ten dollars and all the fried chicken you could eat.

(Little Richard, quoted in White 1985: 49)

The river was running. The river of loot. And I was on the bank at the time. ... Most often we would walk out with maybe ten thousand or fifteen thousand dollars as our part of the total gate receipt.

(Little Richard, quoted in White 1985: 90)

In this chapter we examine the market in music and musicians. There are two reasons for starting here. First, market organization is the most significant factor in explaining how a certain institutional autonomy has developed in popular music. By this I mean a tendency for the music industries to cede control of production (writing, performing, realizing) to musicians themselves; towards spatially dispersed production in small units (such as the rock group in concert tour or recording studio); and for a strong continuity between consumption and production (often within an over-arching subculture). Such institutional autonomy from corporate control establishes the terms and conditions for the creative agency of musicians. It also sets limits on what they can do. Although institutional autonomy is found in other cultural industries, it is developed in popular music to a much greater extent.

The second reason for treating the market at this initial stage is because it represents an ambivalent, but supremely important, threshold of success. Musicians aspire to enter market relations, to make large amounts of money, to become stars, and therefore commodities, themselves. Yet at the same time the market is held to corrupt the non-commercial values to which successive corps of music makers from swing to techno have subscribed. The tension between such conflicting attitudes to the market suffuses the discourse and practice of music-making.

The approach I take to these issues is based on the assumption that the production of commodities for the market, including music, serves to valorize capital. According to Marx (1976) labour, bought with money, is applied to an existing commodity (that is raw material or means of production) in order to produce something new. When it is sold in the market the new commodity realises more value than the cost of its production. The surplus is then appropriated by the capitalist, be this an individual person or, as more often today, an institutional owner. Two points need to be emphasized here. First, exploitation of labour is crucial in the sense that surplus value is created by labour but taken away by other agents. Second, capitalism is a dynamic system with an imperative to accumulate; because the surplus is fed back into the production cycle ('invested'), successively larger surpluses are yielded over time. Immanuel Wallerstein (1995) usefully calls the world instituted by this system 'historical capitalism' and he describes its chief characteristic as 'the commodification of everything'.

If the capitalist system has these properties, one aim of the chapter is to show how, none the less, the valorization of capital assumes an exceptional form in the cultural industries, and the music industry in particular. To understand this we need to consider the profoundly 'asymmetrical' impact of market relations on culture (Williams 1981). On the one hand, as Raymond Williams suggests, culture making 'has been increasingly assimilated to [the market]' (50). The popular musician is generally self-employed, with a fixed-term recording contract and publishing deal. The advertising copywriter is most often employed by a corporation. But in both cases the artifact produced takes the shape of a commodity to be bought and sold. Culture is the limit case for the formula, 'the commodification of everything'. On the other hand, as Williams insists, 'any full identity between cultural production and general production has been to an important extent resisted' (Williams 1981: 50). This can be seen most clearly in two ways: first, the maintenance of artisanal roles among cultural producers (50), and second in the fact that 'even where the cultural work is quite clearly a commodity it is almost always, and often justly, also described in very different terms' (67) – as art, craft, the best hard bop album ever made and so on.

Thus, while culture belongs to capitalism, there is also something antithetical to capitalism in it. In fact I would want to go further and suggest that in an important sense, if to a limited degree, popular culture perverts capitalism. It does so by producing a radius of creativity, that is a space in the economic field where precisely non-economic goals are pursued. Certainly capital continues to be valorized here, but by a paradoxical twist this depends on the reduction of the system imperative towards accumulation. To put it another way, in order for culture to be sold it must be shown to be (partially) external to the economic system. This thesis turns upside down the commonly held view that art is the defence-less victim of commerce. Strangely enough, popular culture also perverts capitalism in the opposite way. Those workers who cross the threshold of success and become stars effectively commodify themselves (Dyer 1987: 5–6). Such a move contravenes that liberal code in capitalism which ostensibly keeps the categories of labour and property apart (Callon 1997).

A major aim of the chapter is, then, to test these propositions and assess their implications by examining market organization, and closely linked to it, the mode of production in popular music. In the first half this takes the form of a critique of some of the literature on popular music markets. Later on I set out my own approach, an analysis of institutional autonomy in popular music. I then define institutional autonomy in a further way – as an institutional bulwark which encompasses the radius of creativity.

Adorno, equivalence and the market

Theodor Adorno inflicts a serious wound on the study of popular music even as he inaugurates the research tradition in this field. Time and again scholars have returned to his writings in an attempt to repair the damage caused by his deeply pessimistic assessment. In a limited way I want to do this too, by reassessing his conception of the market in culture and music in particular.

Writing mainly in the 1930s and 1940s Adorno sees the conflict between culture and capitalism as the central issue of the twentieth century. Culture, that is to say the realm of autonomous expression, is being crushed under 'the absolute power of capitalism' and its drive to produce acquiescence and identity (Adorno and Horkheimer 1979: 120). In the vanguard of this process of domination is the 'culture industry'. Adorno and Horkheimer are here talking about the new mass media of film, radio, records and magazines.

If culture, both potentially and historically, encapsulates autonomy then in the culture industry all traces of autonomous expression have been eliminated. Adorno insists that radio broadcasts, records and films 'are no longer *also* commodities, they are commodities through and through' (Adorno 1991b: 86, original emphasis). Crucially, these commodities are imposed not chosen. Whereas the cultural industry would have it that 'the

spontaneous wishes of the public' determine media content, in fact such
content is 'inherent in the technical and personal apparatus which, down to
its last cog, itself forms part of the economic mechanism of selection'
(Adorno and Horkheimer 1979: 122). Thus there is no market as conventionally understood, in the sense of a means of choosing among different
goods. Rather the culture industry forces a preordained and technically
prescribed series of cultural commodities on consumers.

None the less the market does have a crucial ideological function.
Adorno takes from Marx the concept of commodity fetishism and enormously enlarges it. For Marx the exchangeability of goods yields a fundamental misrecognition of capitalism. There seems to be a social relation
among the delightful array of commodities in the market when in fact it is
production which is socially constituted in the form of people working
together as wage labourers (Marx 1976: 163–77). Adorno adopts this idea
but changes its emphasis in a significant way. Now, as well as disguising
exploitative and alienating relations of production, fetishism obfuscates all
aspects of experience under capitalism (Adorno and Horkheimer 1979: 126,
Adorno 1991b: 55).

Fetishism derives from equivalence, the miraculous power of goods to be
exchanged through the medium of a universal commodity, money. In its
embodiment of equivalence the cultural commodity has a special power
though. On the face of it, culture promises immediacy and a unique relation
with the beholder. However, 'it is this appearance in turn which alone gives
cultural goods their exchange value' (Adorno 1991c: 34). In other words
Adorno is suggesting that the very thing which seems to mark off the
cultural artifact as different – an incommensurability which elevates it
above exchange – actually guarantees its commodity form, and hence its
essential sameness (1991c: 33–5).

Now it seems to me that Adorno is entirely wrong to conceive cultural
markets in such a bleak and pessimistic fashion. I want to criticize both
aspects of his thinking which we have just examined, that is the arguments
about preselection and about equivalence. These notions of the powerful
market need to be challenged not least because my thesis about institutional
autonomy rests on a contrary premise, namely that consumers and producers can enter relations within the purview of the market which are relatively
direct and non-instrumental.

First, then, Adorno's idea that the market is a means of transmitting to
consumers that which has already been selected goes against the empirical
evidence presented in various places in his own work. As Adorno and
Horkheimer point out, '[d]emand has not yet been replaced by simple
obedience' in the culture industry (1979: 136). In the case of popular music,
for example, consumers seek novelty and so there is a constant drive to
produce new songs, records and stars in response (Adorno 1990: 311).
Adorno also notices how the music industry uses its own sales data as a
marketing tool through publishing the 'Hit Parade' – the public display of a

market in constant and rapid transition (Adorno 1945: 215, Adorno 1967: 124).

In passages such as these Adorno presents a picture of an industry which has to win its audience. Far from being monolithic, cultural domination involves constant adjustment to psychological states which are always being undermined by the need to stimulate jaded palates. As he concedes, '[i]n this situation the industry faces an insoluble problem' (Adorno 1990: 311). How does it control the very instability which it promotes? Such a dilemma seems to be inherent to the cultural market-place. Of course the key thing for Adorno is that despite this the culture industry always wins the game. However I would suggest that his emphasis on volatility is actually much more significant. Indeed, as we will see, the idea that cultural markets are inherently problematic for the industry comes to play a key part in subsequent research as well as in my own argument about institutional autonomy.

Adorno's observations concerning instability clearly go against his claims about the mechanistic preselection that occurs in the culture industry. The question is why should constant change, even if cosmetic, be necessary if cultural commodities are so technically well matched to their consumers. In the end, though, such a difficulty does not upset his overall case. This is because the second function of cultural markets, the dissemination of equivalence, is actually more important for Adorno. It is this aspect of his thinking we will examine now.

Adorno considers that music is the most autonomous of aesthetic forms. As Andrew Bowie suggests, '[f]or Adorno music, and by implication the subject, is confronted with the contradictions between "expression of what goes on inside human beings", which is inherently individual, and "convention"' (1990: 261).[1] Through this dialectic serious music can, at the cost of immense difficulty of form, still present the truth about the modern world – its suffering and subjection (Adorno 1973: 18–20, Adorno: 1978a). By the same token, however, popular music is a particularly powerful instrument of ideological domination, able to organize perception and, ultimately, constitute the listening subject. It does this because musical convention has here become utterly formulaic, or standardized. The individual is thus subsumed.

Standardization is the materialization in the fabric of popular music of that equivalence which derives from its commodity form. We can hear it in the structure of the pre-war popular song – the repetitive 32-bar pattern, prescribed harmonic sequences and limited melodic range (Adorno 1990, Adorno 1991c). But equivalence is also manifested in 'pseudo-individual-ization', or apparent differentiation within and between songs. Improvization provides the 'most drastic example' (1990: 308), although all manner of stylization from 'dirty notes' to generic labels like 'swing' and 'sweet' belong to the same category (1990: 309). Up crops the figure of the fetish again, working to disguise standardization through a spurious appeal to difference. Now there is an important case to be made against standardization and pseudo-individualization in relation to the musical text. At its core is the notion that, notwithstanding their pejorative connotations, the two terms actually get at key aesthetic attributes of popular music; its repetition and reflexive rhetoric. The problem is that Adorno fails to valorize them, or, to put it another way, he can see funk but he can't hear it.

We will return to these issues later in the book.[2] For now, though, I want to concentrate on Adorno's argument about the market and commodity form. The key problem is its generality, we might even say a metaphysical aspect. For once the commodity has been endowed with such a powerful homogenizing logic that any amount of degradation can be attributed to it; there is no end to its reach. There is also a difficulty over causality, actually inherent in Marx's original formulation. If the market is premised on equivalence between commodities in terms of their literal exchangeability (against the indexical commodity, money), it does not follow that commodities necessarily embody equivalence in any other sense. It is unclear, for example, just how *musical* standardization might emanate from the commodity form.[3] Finally, I object to Adorno's suggestion that the cultural commodity is the quintessential commodity because it appears not to be a commodity (see above and Adorno 1991c: 34). This is dialectical thinking taken to an extreme of abstraction. In fact people resolutely cleave to the promise of autonomy in popular music. This may be ideological in its effect – it can serve established relations of power, for example when people fetishize the notion of an immediate relationship to music. However it always has progressive consequences as well. For instead of being a '[commodity] through and through' (Adorno 1991a: 86) popular music takes on a diminished commodity form just because people insist on an authentic connection to it. Such a discourse (distilled in the phrase 'our music') helps to push back industrial control over music activity.

So far I have been discussing Adorno's ideas about the market in relation to the consumption of music. By and large I have rejected them (although we will return to his observations about the endemic volatility of the popular music market later). At a general level we can sum up the problem as a gross overestimation of the industry's ability to control markets. My own assessment would be that rather than popular music audiences being cowed and incorporated by the industrial apparatus, they are extremely difficult to assimilate. This independence of audiences, and, just as important, their ideal independence, is a precondition for institutional autonomy in pop. Fans claim a direct link to musicians, and subcultures, from jitterbug to speed garage, wrap 'their' creators in an embrace which, initially and relatively but always significantly, protects these musics from corporate control. One consequence is that the music industries rely on marketing categories which have already been created. Adorno's examples of the terms 'sweet' and 'swing' are actually evidence of this, being coined first by fans and musicians rather than publicists (BBC 1999).

That brings us to the last aspect of his analysis which I want to discuss: the way in which the cultural market impinges on cultural producers – the musicians. Again there are both abstract and more grounded sides to his argument. In the first case Adorno seems to be suggesting that the logic of the commodity infiltrates the producer's psyche. We get a strong sense of this in a passage where Horkheimer and Adorno characterize the routinized technique of a jazz musician who 'playing a piece of serious music, one of Beethoven's simplest minuets, syncopates it involuntarily and will smile superciliously when asked to follow the normal divisions of the beat' (Adorno and Horkheimer 1979: 128). There is an almost heroic scepticism about this. Whereas according to conventional wisdom the jazz musician is a supreme spontaneist, in fact, the writers argue, he is possessed by the objective spirit of the commodity. He has become an automaton implanted with a grotesque belief in his own agency.

In this passage, then, the market operates on the musician at a remove, through the fetish character of music. My objection here, along much the same lines as before, is to the attribution of almost mystical powers to the commodity form. Elsewhere, though, Adorno observes the insidious pressure of the market being exerted in a more direct fashion, from the bottom up. As he puts it, '[e]ven cultural products introduced and distributed with the maximum display of expense repeat, though it be by virtue of impenetrable machinery, the public-house musician's sidelong glance at the plate on the piano while he hammers their favorite melody into his patrons' ears' (Adorno 1978b: 196).

What Adorno seems to be criticizing here is a correlation between (anti)aesthetics and exchange. The musician plays while watching neither keyboard nor audience, but rather an accumulating pile of cash. Moreover there is an implication that the intensity of the performance (the 'hammering in') can be explained by this. Adorno is always fascinated by popular music's potency, how it engulfs the audience and the way in which musicians throw themselves into their work under the thrall of the market. I think he has an important point here. One significant aspect of the memoirs of certain popular music stars is how much they remember about money earned – dates, places and amounts. Little Richard's recollections, which the quotations at the head of the chapter come from, are particularly vivid in this respect. Richard gets across very well the link between cash, success and the exhilaration of performance.

Still, in relation to production, just as much as in the discussion of consumption above, I want to distinguish what I am saying from Adorno's position. Where he sees the energy of the market and its action on musicians as demonic, I would argue rather for the ambivalence of the phenomenon. The intense desire for money is also a desire to be adored. Indeed to be a star-commodity (people buy you) is to be invested with a magical fullness of being which is a tragic illusion and a rightfully utopian dream at one and the same time. Anyway, the money imperative constitutes only one drive. The urge to autonomy, to be free from the economic system is just as important, perhaps even more so.

Entrepreneurs and innovation

Beginning in the early 1970s a group of young American sociologists began to research and write about the popular music industry in a very different way to Adorno. Their theoretical background is in functionalism and organization theory, rather than critical Marxist thought. This brings both benefits and disadvantages. The biggest benefit lies in the fact that in place of relentlessly negative and one-dimensional critiques of the cultural commodity we are presented with a picture of the music industry as a complex system. Furthermore, where Adorno had dismissed the market as a confidence trick the new approach takes it seriously. In fact the main objective is to understand the way that the music industry interacts with its market and the organizational consequences of this. I want to suggest that such factors are absolutely critical for understanding the nature of institutional autonomy in popular music. We will need to explore their implications in some detail. Having said that, the perspective also has real limitations, mainly because there is no conception here of capital, culture or their strange relationship. We ought to explore what this lack means too.

Richard Peterson and David Berger (1972) set the new agenda nicely by way of a contrast. They suggest that the 'outspoken rock lyric of the 1960s (and the counterculture it animated) were largely unintended by-products of earlier mundane changes in technology, industry structure, and marketing' (283). The new genre of rock should not, then, be considered as expressive, or an efflorescence of Zeitgeist in the way subcultural ideologues proclaimed. Rather it stemmed from a series of organizational contingencies within the record industry. In the work which follows – by the mid-1970s assembled under the heading 'production of culture' and now concerned with all kinds of cultural production (Peterson 1976) – a number of themes begin to emerge. First, the record industry is conceived as a 'system' within an 'environment', whose most important aspect is the market.[4] The market is characterized by extreme 'turbulence' which arises from 'the rapidly changing style preferences of millions of predominantly young buyers' (Peterson and Berger 1971: 97).

In this unstable milieu record companies want as far as possible to check innovation in music and reduce competition in the market. Partly this is because companies are bureaucratic and routinized. Partly it is because culture producing organizations seek to avoid the expense and risk of developing and selling new styles in an uncertain market. The result is a pair of complementary tendencies, towards oligopoly and the control of innovation (DiMaggio 1977, DiMaggio and Hirsch 1976, Peterson and Berger 1990/1975). If these are inherent to the music industry system it none the less has a feedback mechanism which allows for compensation. In the end the market-environment wins out. Peterson and Berger (1990/1975) demonstrate this in a historical survey of the American record industry. Taking the period 1949–1973 they compare, year by year, the market share held by the largest record companies with the turnover of records and artists in the Top 10 singles chart. What emerges is a series of cycles in the ratio of market concentration which can be broadly correlated with the number of new records and new artists in the charts each year.[5] Thus, in the period 1948–55 when the 'big four' majors dominated there was relative stasis. Then, as smaller, independent record companies entered the market, innovation and diversity in music increased. Crucially, this began to happen in the second half of the 1950s when rock'n'roll took off. The concentration ratio then bottomed out in the early 1960s, only to build back up again. By the early 1970s it was approaching pre-1955 levels once more.

The cycles thesis *qua* cycles is revised in a later series of publications (Rothenbuhler and Dimmick 1982, Burnett 1990 and 1996, Lopes 1992, Christianen 1995). However I am more interested here in the way it can help to throw light on the role of the popular music market at a more general level. Above all it vindicates the market. Against Adorno who suggested that monopoly had replaced competition in the music industry (1990: 306, see also Note 3 in this chapter), Peterson and Berger propose that market openness prevails – or, to use the language of organization theory, the system adapts to the environment. Two key concepts underpin their thinking on this. As they are important for my argument about institutional autonomy I want to critically examine both of them. The two concepts are innovation and entrepreneurship.

In an important sense 'innovation' provides the rationale for the cycles research. However there is a problem with it in that while innovation is taken as an index of aesthetic value little argument is offered about how we should consider it a musical good. Nowhere, for example, is Adorno's criticism that a high turnover of records constitutes 'novelty', a despicable illusion of difference, addressed. Peterson and Berger do cite several papers from the tradition of mass culture critique (including Adorno's own 'On popular music' (1990)) which attack the homogeneity of 'Tin Pan Alley' output before 1950 (1972: 285, 1990/1975: 145). But this is hardly a sufficient rationale for their heavy investment in the concept of innovation in the post-rock'n'roll era – especially since they are concerned to repudiate the mass culture approach.

An implicit aesthetic can perhaps be discerned in the measures used to assess innovation. These are the number of records, cover records and number ones; and the percentage of new, established and fading star performers in the weekly top ten singles chart, year by year (Peterson and Berger 1990/1975: 146).[6] Two evaluative criteria seem important here. First, velocity – the speed at which a record passes through its popularity cycle – is to be judged positively. The faster a record goes in and out of the chart the better. Second, institutionalized fame – the length of time a successful performer has been selling records – is to be evaluated negatively. 'Established' performers, and especially 'fading stars', are bad.

The question remains though. How did speed come to be such a central (if unproblematic) value in the work on popular music cycles? My contention is that Peterson and Berger like rock'n'roll and its quality of bustle. They consider fast turnover to be an intrinsic part of the rock'n'roll aesthetic. The institutional arrangements which have produced rock'n'roll in the mid-1950s are then 'backwardly' valorized. What are these arrangements?

The first is the advent of pop format radio. This was actually premised on the rise of television and the consequent demise of network radio in the early 1950s. Local stations, programming cheap recorded music, then filled the radio 'gap', while audience survey methods tended to skew airplay towards teenagers. One other key factor is that the reliance on records gave disc jockeys a new celebrity status and gatekeeper role as they vied with one another to discover artists and play new songs first (Peterson and Berger 1990/1975: 149).

The second institution for increasing speed is the record popularity chart (noted by Adorno as we saw earlier). The entertainment industry magazine *Variety* had published a sales list in the 1930s (Sanjek 1988: 154–5), and from 1940 the music trade paper *Billboard* issued a chart based on radio play and direct sales of records. But this only became important for consumers in 1958, two years into the rock'n'roll boom, when *Billboard* turned it into a national 'Hot 100' hit parade, intended for wide circulation and use by radio stations (Parker 1991: 207). Martin Parker argues that quite apart from their function of monitoring the market for the industry, the charts played a crucial role in building a culture of consumption in rock'n'roll and after; in effect a community which was also a 'democracy of taste' (210).

The important thing here is visibility, that the choice of the individual buying a record or tuning in to a radio station is registered by the audience on a collective basis. And because the charts are presented in serial form, letting everyone know what is new each week, the music fan's communitarian impulse works to privilege innovation.

As Peterson and Berger argue it was a combination of the above factors which ratcheted up velocity to such an extent from the mid-1950s. DJs would heavily rotate a small number of songs from a chart-based playlist and this greatly shortened the life cycle of records (1990/1975: 149). Innovation, the aesthetic of the cycles thesis, was thus born in a particular set of institutional relations between the record and radio industries which the writers identify in the mid-1950s.

I am sympathetic to this idea. It points to the democratic and autonomous implications of popular music markets and the way in which change in modes of production and dissemination can foment explosions in creativity and new musical cultures. In Chapter 5 I make a similar point about British dance music in the 1990s. The limitations, however, are that it is too tightly identified with a 'Book of Genesis' story of rock'n'roll in which the mid-1950s are eulogized as heroic and special. In fact, as we will see shortly, developments in media technology and industry organization also had a major impact on the growth of institutional autonomy before the Second World War. Even in a notoriously 'slow' period like the mid-1970s, an intensely innovative subculture such as disco could thrive in the centre, as it were, of the mass market (Straw 1990).

Although Peterson and Berger affirm the importance of the market for the production of popular music they do not posit a direct response by the record industry to signals from the market. Instead independent companies tap latent (or 'unsated') demand among consumers (1990/1975: 146–7). This calls for special expertise and initiative, encapsulated in the term 'entrepreneurship'. In the 1930s the economist Joseph Schumpeter had identified these dynamic qualitites in the managers of large manufacturing firms (Peterson and Berger 1971: 98). For the later writers, however, the key thing is that in the record industry entrepreneurship is segregated from functions such as manufacturing and marketing which can be organized bureaucratically (98–9). This is because the tasks which the entrepreneur supervises – recruiting of artists, origination of material, recording – are the ones which are most sensitive to change in a turbulent market. In effect uncertainty about the environment pushes the record company into ceding control to experts. These experts combine a special understanding of the volatile market, with the skills necessary to coordinate production for it (103–4).

Developing his own closely related concept of cultural 'brokerage', Paul DiMaggio (1977) makes an important addition to this line of inquiry. He suggests that what distinguishes the cultural market is that there are no professional standards for judging the competence of work done. As a consequence '[a]rtists, and often brokers themselves, can only be evaluated post hoc on the basis of success, or on the basis of reputation and track record' (442). In other words the brokerage system is one where culture coordinating and distributing organizations insist on short-term autonomy for brokers. The commercial quality of results determines whether or not they continue to be hired.

The concept of cultural entrepreneurship (or brokerage) is crucial for the present argument. I am particularly interested in the way it is predicated on a decentralizing imperative which derives from the music industry's encounter with the market environment. In other words institutional autonomy is 'built into' the system. However, just because it is constructed according to the terms and conditions of organization theory, entrepreneurship remains quite faceless in the production of culture literature. Peterson and Berger (1971) mention record producers. Clearly the independent record companies which pioneer rock'n'roll are entrepreneurial too (1990/1975), but we have little idea of who the entrepreneurs are or how they operate. This matters because the social relations of entrepreneurship have important implications for the extent and quality of institutional autonomy, in other words how much room for manoeuvre musicians have and what form it takes.

I want briefly now to fill in some of these gaps and characterize entrepreneurship in the same rock'n'roll moment privileged by Peterson and Berger. The entrepreneurial type which emerges in this period has been usefully described by Simon Frith as 'the huckster' (1983: 92). He is a petty capitalist who has an eye for the quick buck. By the same token, though, he can think creatively and knows how to mould talent for the market-place. (I use the male form intentionally here – this is almost always a male role, often an aggressively macho one.) At the turn of the 1960s two influential books provide, for the first time, an 'archaeology of rock'. The huckster has a central role in both.

For Nik Cohn (1989/1969) the rock'n'roll moment in the 1950s was demotic and brash. Crucially, the unprecedented buying power of teenagers caught the record companies unprepared. 'All they could do was release noise by the ton and see what caught on best' (1989: 60). In effect teenage desire triggered a correspondingly wild and unfocused commercial energy. In this environment the strongest performers were the ones who most thoroughly internalized the rampant imperative to novelty. What mattered now was sheer output.[7]

Behind the scenes, orchestrating the rock'n'roll maelstrom, was a new kind of entrepreneur. In a section on the Rolling Stones, manager Andrew Loog Oldham appears as the impish animating spirit of the band (Cohn, 1989/1969: 128). Elsewhere Cohn develops a sort of trash aesthetic for the late 1950s – 'faceless spotted groups' are manipulated by 'fat cigar smoking agents [and] crooked managers' (1989/1969: 92).

Charlie Gillett (1983/1970), the other early chronicler of rock'n'roll, is more earnest. He sees the market for music as the site of a musical uprising by consumers during the 1950s. '[O]nly by determined resistance to this fare [the prevailing sentimental pop song] did the audience of the mid-fifties force the music industry to provide something else: rock'n'roll' (1983/1970, p. xii). It was independent record companies which responded to the new demands. Like black rhythm and blues on which it was based, rock'n'roll was a regional, grass-roots phenomenon. In this context the 'indies' had the necessary local knowledge to recruit raw talent and respond quickly to new trends in the market. They also found a direct promotional channel to their teenage audience through the new, local Top Forty radio stations which depended on music programming.

Like the men in Cohn's account, Gillett's entrepreneurs are mostly sharp practitioners. Often they are the opportunist owners of short-lived record companies. A few of them like Syd Nathan, owner of King records in Cincinnati, build up long careers, but do so out of dubious practices like claiming authorship rights on the releases of their writers and artists

(Gillett 1983/1970: 158). Yet another class of entrepreneur is the peripatetic producer or 'record man'; Huey Meaux, for example, who recruited talent and made records around the Southwest, and had an intermittent series of hits from the late 1950s through to the early 1970s (175–8, 316–18).

What the rock'n'roll histories of Cohn and Gillett have in common is that against the common-sense of mass culture critique they endow the huckster with an aesthetic function. The encounter between aggressive petty capitalism and popular music is fecund; it produces great music. Such accounts certainly flesh out the sociological analysis of entrepreneurship. But there is a contradiction here of which the writers rarely speak. On the one hand the huckster is autonomous in the sense that he operates at the margins of the music business. Moreover, he often cedes decison-making over repertoire, style and sonority to musicians. On the other hand he is out for himself and will tend to extract as much as he can for the least payment possible from the musicians contracted to him. A number of accounts of the 1950s and 1960s have emphasized the prevalence of exploitative contracts, nonpayment of musicians and fraudulent usurpation of composition rights. Sometimes enforcement of terms involved violence or the threat of violence. Frequently such abuses were carried out by white entrepreneurs at the expense of black musicians (Chapple and Garofalo 1977, White 1985, Berry *et al.* 1992, Otis 1993, Dr John 1994, Dixon and Snowden 1995, White 1995).

These observations point to the limits of both the rock'n'roll chronicles and the sociological approach to entrepreneurship. With certain qualifications the former tend to endorse the huckster, yet do not explain how he comes to occupy his position as a harsh and self-serving taskmaster. The latter at least has a theory, namely that entrepreneurship is a system function. It represents the need of relatively large and bureaucratic organizations to contract out the management of origination given a turbulent environment. As I have stressed this is an extremely productive idea. It takes us some way down the road to understanding the conditions of institutional autonomy in popular music. However it never shows the implications of this for the working lives of musicians. In other words it takes no account of the material conditions of creativity.

There are similar problems with the concept of innovation. It can be explained as a function of the market environment – turbulence makes for a fast turnover of records and artists within the system. But we do not find out why the market takes this form nor therefore how the system is constituted in relation to it. Above all, the most salient characteristic of the music industry – the drive to accumulate capital – goes unremarked. In the next section we attempt to redress the balance by examining another approach, the political economy perspective. It treats cultural production for the market precisely as though it were a part of capital. This is a system with an interest – in capital accumulation.

Music markets and the political economy of popular music

Immediately, though, it has to be admitted that capital is a more problematic term, and subject to more criticism, than might have been suggested in the introduction to this chapter. I therefore propose to take a short excursion in order to defend and clarify its further use in the book. In the first place we can note criticism of the theory that capital is a process of accumulation based on the exploitation of labour, in other words arguments against the idea that there is an 'endogenous logic of capitalism' (Laclau and Mouffe 1985: 75–85). Laclau and Mouffe insist that far from possessing 'a primal economic contradiction' (77), capitalism has persisted in historically variable forms and that modern societies consist in an 'ensemble of social relations' which cannot be reduced to relations of production (85). Such a critique has been taken up recently in a discussion of the formation of people's identity at work. The case made is that the capital–labour dualism of Marxist accounts fails to account for a host of contingent and discursive factors which bear on the subjectivity of workers. We therefore need a social constructionist approach in order to analyse the sphere of production (du Gay 1997). Actually, I would want to go along with this line of argument quite some way. My point is that it complements rather than contradicts a capital–labour perspective

For example, the term 'exploitation' is certainly discursive and contingent. There is a rap tune from 1987, 'Paid in Full' by Eric B and Rakim, whose import is that black musicians are not normally so paid. This theme, if rarely made explicit in songs, none the less circulates widely among musicians. Many music makers believe that the industry systematically pays them less than the true value of the work they put into making records or writing songs. They frequently use the word 'exploitation' for this. In fact the evidence suggests that exploitation discourse has loomed large in production cultures in many different times and places (see the last series of citations in the previous section). Record industry personnel also use the word 'exploitation', often in the limited sense of making money out of intellectual property in music. But there is also a bigger discourse – it has more statements – to the effect that the general function of such personnel is to 'make a profit', 'look to the bottom line', 'move product' and so on. I use the term 'exploitation', as we have seen, with yet different emphasis. I conceive exploitation as being an aspect of an economic system in which there never is such a thing as 'paid in full'. All work must be deemed exploitative because a surplus is invariably appropriated by capital. The discursive aspect of this is that, along with other Marxists, I say it. It is academic discourse in that, asserting it to be true, I call on evidence and authority in an academic way to support the assertion. Although all three discourses of exploitation (musician, management, academic Marxist) and the practices which they inform are organized by different interests there is a strong correspondence between them concerning the nature of exploitation. In Bourdieu's terms we have here a 'field' (Bourdieu 1993c: 72–7).

But there is another issue. The post-Marxist critique posits that in the capital and labour conspectus all social and cultural phenomena come to be explained by the economic. In other words it is reductive (du Gay 1997: 292–4). This is certainly not my position, nor that of most contemporary Marxists.[8] In my view the capital and labour duality (the economic field) is very important. Actually, as I suggested at the beginning of the chapter, I hold that it is the most important field in the context of the present argument. But it co-exists with other fields whose rules intersect, yet do not necessarily coincide, with its own (Bourdieu 1990: 66–8). We will return to this issue of fields and their interrelationship in the next chapter. For now, though, I hope to have established that it is possible to carry on speaking about capital and asserting that the economic field, traversed as it is by conflicted interests, remains highly significant for cultural production.

To resume the argument, then, Marxist approaches to cultural production since the 1970s have shared with Adorno the idea that there is an antinomy between culture and capital (I will be referring to Garnham 1990a and 1990b, and Miège 1989). However there are significant differences in the later work. At the most general level, the later writers have shifted the focus away from the cultural commodity per se, towards the particular conditions through which capital is valorized. These can be grouped under three headings.

CONTRADICTION

The contradictions of the 'cultural industries' are much more strongly emphasized.[9] In particular, rather than being considered an entity in which contradiction has been eliminated, the cultural commodity is held to be difficult to valorize and to require exceptional routines in its production and circulation.

LABOUR PROCESS

Where Adorno saw cultural workers as automata there is a much fuller understanding of the complex nature of cultural work, its special status and the way that creators tend not to be directly controlled by capital. Attention is also drawn to a split between the functions of creation on the one hand and reproduction or distribution on the other.

EXTENSION OF THE CULTURAL INDUSTRIES

Notwithstanding the first factor above, capital is seen to have extended its reach much further into the cultural sphere since the 1970s. In fact the cultural industries have become a leading sector of capital.

How do the neo-Marxists reach this position? Their point of departure is the nature of the use values of cultural commodities. In contrast to other goods which are not primarily symbolic, it is extremely difficult to assess the extent to which any particular cultural good will be found 'useful'. In culture, then, use values are unstable (Garnham 1990a: 161, Miège 1989: 25). I would add that if all cultural products have this quality, popular music is especially unstable. Associated with this is a second key use value, novelty. People want lots of different and constantly changing cultural products (Garnham 1990c: 160, Miège 1989: 42). Again, popular music seems to possess this characteristic in more abundance than films, books or television programmes.[10]

If the market is uncertain and given to novelty then this feeds back into cultural production which shows a related set of idiosyncrasies. First, in order to meet the demand for innovation, the music industry (we will keep to musical examples from now on) has to produce a constant stream of new prototypes in the form of master tapes or 'first copies'. The costs of making the prototype are high. For a traditional rock band they will cover writing, rehearsing, recording and, perhaps most importantly, the (prior) acquisition of status through repeated performance and image building. Garnham's point is that this process of creation is always more expensive than that of reproduction, in other words the manufacture of finished sound carriers (CDs, cassettes, vinyl etc.). High costs of origination then mitigate in favour of high volume sales because marginal profits from each extra sale are large once 'first copy' costs have been met (Garnham 1990a: 160). Second, because of the instability of their use value it is difficult to anticipate which of the records will sell. The market is inherently uncertain. Record companies therefore seek to spread the risk of market failure across a large range of different titles, in other words a 'repertoire' (Garnham 1990a: 161) or 'catalogue' (Miège 1989: 43). Such overproduction serves the demand for innovation too.

The implications of uncertain market and endemic overproduction extend in two directions; 'downstream' towards marketing and distribution, and 'upstream' towards origination. We are interested in the second of these with its economic logic of decentralized production, but we ought to deal with the first area too because it bears heavily on how music-making is organized. Nicholas Garnham makes the crucial point that given uncertainty and the need for a repertoire, '*cultural distribution, not cultural production, ... is the key locus of power and profit*' (1990a: 161–2, original emphasis). This is certainly true for the music industry. The major record companies all own large distribution divisions which make money from distributing an aggregate of records and are therefore much less susceptible to the vagaries of an uncertain market than the production side. Distribution is also capital intensive and this tends to reduce competition and increase concentration.

As Garnham suggests, the structural importance of distribution can hardly be overestimated. It suggests a major weakness of the production of culture work which, while recognizing the 'bureaucratic' and stable nature of distribution, fails to comprehend the power that a small number of large companies continue to exert, both over the market and over producers, through their control of the distribution function. This power persists, no matter what point has been reached in a 'cycle of symbol production'.

If the organizational sociologists miss the crucial dimension of power there has none the less been some very useful analysis from this quarter of the way record companies manage to mesh overproduction with the regularities of distribution. Paul Hirsch (1990/1972) points to the 'differential promotion' of records, both before they enter the market and then again in the period after release as initial sales information and responses from the media become available. Typically those titles which show early signs of success are heavily promoted in order to maximize sales. This is a sophisticated form of 'intra-market' testing which enables manufacturing and distribution to be adjusted to emerging demand.

Yet in the end it must be considered as a coping strategy, a defensive position. For compared to other media the record industry has much less control over the means of reaching its market. True, record companies are often owned by conglomerates which also own music-using television and film companies. However the media which disseminate new records – radio, dance clubs and, increasingly, Websites and telecommunications – are not so thoroughly integrated. Nor generally are the retail outlets. Through a series of historical contingencies, which we will come back to in a moment, the record industry has become relatively isolated from channels of communication 'downstream'. I want to suggest, then, that the political economy approach needs to be inflected in the case of music. Distribution is pivotal, yet records companies do not have direct contact with their markets. This contributes to institutional autonomy, because it allows music makers to find alternative channels for reaching audiences.[11]

Having examined the political economy approach to distribution we ought to turn back 'upstream' now and examine creation. Like Raymond Williams (1981), Garnham (1990b) points to the prevalence of an artisanal mode of production. It can be attributed to the design intensiveness of cultural production, the need to make many different prototypes in response to the demand for innovation. However Garnham is quite pessimistic about such a trend. While he recognizes that cultural production can be a focus of resistance to capitalist values, he none the less emphasizes its regressive form. Artisanship may keep the workforce divided and, in an uncertain market, it enables capital to pass on the costs and risks of production to the producers themselves (37). As a consequence cultural workers are often very badly paid (39).

This is as true in the music industry as elsewhere in symbol production, something which all musicians know of course. Their discourse of exploitation represents an expression of outrage about the power of record companies and publishers to insist on one-sided and onerous contracts.

Again, though, and particularly in the case of the music industry, it strikes me that Garnham is too pessimistic. For if musicians are exploited, the music industry also finds considerable difficulties in dealing with them. Their 'turbulent' nature calls for the firm hand of the entrepreneur. Actually, Bernard Miège understands this well. He uses the term 'éditeur' to characterize the entrepreneurial role in cultural production, a role which combines the capitalization of production with 'inserting cultural labour'. This latter phrase means, in the case of music, persuading musicians to address markets, collaborate with promotions divisions and so on (Miège 1989: 27–30). It is evidence of contradiction and the stubborn resistance of musicians and audiences to succumb easily to routines of accumulation. In short, entrepreneurship represents both exploitation and institutional autonomy.

The political economy of culture approach yields important insights into the market for music and musicians. Most importantly it shows how the imperative to valorize capital is articulated, often through quite contradictory forces, in the cultural industries. For this reason I want to use its vocabulary and methods. However if the economic does not here strictly determine cultural outcomes, the complex processes of cultural production are always suffused by the animus of accumulation. In the end, and despite the sophistication of the analysis, it is this pessimistic assessment which wins out. And therein lies the problem. In research informed by the political economy approach it has proved difficult to treat cultural workers as creative agents, always much easier to see them as drudges, as permanently put upon.[12]

Yet, if we hold that popular culture has meaning and value, we ought to account for the way in which those (enigmatic and unstable) use values of cultural commodities are produced. I would suggest that the way forward here is to look for the material conditions of creativity, not as an alternative, but as a necessary complement, to the critical examination of capital. We have already examined some of the factors at work here, in particular innovation, entrepreneurship and overproduction. In their analysis of these factors both the organizational and Marxist-critical perspectives tend to emphasize system properties; a propensity to adapt to the environment, or the imperative to valorize capital in difficult conditions. As I have suggested, this is an extremely productive way of understanding how the music industry is forced to cope with *inherent* contradiction and, in turn, how it devolves a degree of creative control to musicians. However where the sociological approaches to cultural production fall down is in their lack of attention to history. Even Peterson and Berger (1990/1975), who examine 25 years in record sales and ownership data, do not really account for the specificities of the mode of production within their period.

By way of compensation, and in order to show how quite divergent creative milieux have emerged in popular music, we turn to the inter-war period now. Here we can trace not only different kinds and degrees of institutional autonomy, but also significant counter-tendencies, towards integration and centralized control, too.

Growing up broken up: the emergence of institutional autonomy

The singular form, music industry, is actually a misnomer. From the 1920s, when a mass market in records first emerged,[13] until today the chief characteristic of popular music production and dissemination has been its disintegrated structure. In other words the functions of publishing, exploitation of rights, record production and distribution, the broadcasting of music, live performance and record retailing have not generally been owned and controlled by single corporations. Instead different institutions have become involved in different stages in the process of the valorization of pop. Often these institutions have been divisions of other cultural industries – historically cinema and radio, but more recently electronic hardware manufacturers.

The contrast here is with cinema. As Tino Balio suggests, '[b]y 1930, the motion picture industry had become, in economic terminology, a mature oligopoly' (1976: 213). Not only was there concentration of ownership, but also intense vertical integration in the American industry. The Big Five companies owned huge production facilities and contracted armies of writers, actors, producers, directors and technical personnel. Christopherson and Storper suggest that the Hollywood studio was set up 'as an assembly line for large-scale production of a standardized film product'. Production crews 'carried out discrete, well defined repetitive tasks' (1986: 306–7). This integrated studio system upstream was complemented by control of distribution and exhibition downstream. The Big Five owned cinemas which in 1930 'accounted for nearly 70 per cent of the nation's box-office receipts' (Balio 1976: 213).

Christopherson and Storper (1986), among others, claim that the integrated structure collapsed during the early 1950s, partly due to competition from television. In the new, more competitive environment an increasing number of production tasks were outsourced, while a 1948 court decision forced the majors to sell off their theatre chains. However, criticizing the notion that the majors are a spent force as a 'caricature' of film's industrial history, David Gordon (1976) argues that the major Hollywood companies have consistently maintained control over film-making since the 1940s. More recently, researchers have argued that integration has actually increased since the 1970s, with the corporations which control the key distribution function buying back into exhibition and producing more films in-house (Aksoy and Robbins 1992, Wasko 1994; for an overview of this contested terrain see Hesmondhalgh 1996a).

Notwithstanding the differences between these accounts of the post-war period it is clear that the history of the American film industry overall has been one of cycles in the level of integration. The argument is about particular levels at particular moments. In the case of popular music, on the other hand, the tendency has always been towards fragmentation in the era of mediated sound. There never was (*contra* Peterson and Berger 1990/1975) a mature oligopoly. Another way of putting this is to say that the history of the popular music industries consists in cycles of disintegration. How can we account for such a major divergence from the institutional development of film?

Perhaps the most significant factor has been the absence of a medium specific textual form on the model of the 'classical Hollywood narrative' (Bordwell *et al.* 1985). Crucially, the film is a long text unit (at least 60 minutes in length), depending on a large production unit (the studio with its cast and crew) and with a discrete mode of dissemination (the movie theatre). Popular music, however, is realized in a small text unit (the song or tune), made by a small production unit (the peripatetic band or studio group) and delivered by a variety of media (by the 1930s the phonograph, radio broadcast, film soundtrack, or combinations of these) or in performance with a co-present audience.

The lack of a unified commodity form also has to do with the ubiquity of music as a phenomenal form. Music is environmental, tending to surround the listener. Partly because it does not demand a uni-directional focus, it has been subordinate to the image in a long-established aesthetic hierarchy in the West (Silverman 1988). The portability and extensiveness of the particular technologies which were developed to carry music, especially microphone–loudspeaker systems, has then reinforced the dispersed aspect of popular music.

This adaptability for use in different contexts and the small-scale 'song' text together explain why popular music has never been constituted as an industry on the scale of film or broadcasting. Always used by other media, music has been a permanent junior partner. In the inter-war period, however, musicians were able to claim a degree of independence as a result of this very attribute. Rather than being employed by a single apparatus they sold their services to several buyers. Sometimes this involved musicians taking more control over creative decision-making. In other situations the fragmented nature of musical production and dissemination resulted in colonization by other, more centralized media. As music became more and more a mass-mediated phenomenon in the 1920s and 1930s both currents – towards musician autonomy and centralized control – became increasingly pronounced. I would suggest that we can identify three modes of musicianship in this period which show these divergent institutional tendencies at work.

The first is cross-media stardom. Bing Crosby, the best-known singing star of the time, launched his career as 'vocalist' with the Paul Whiteman

Orchestra in the late 1920s. Providing no more than an extra musical voice, band singers like Crosby had a relatively low status on a par with instrumentalists, and were definitely subordinate to band leaders (Lees 1987). Still, Crosby was able to break the mould and establish his own name. By 1929 Americans could hear him sing with Whiteman on record, in a simultaneous network radio broadcast from a hotel ballroom – called a 'direct hookup', or indeed in person at the venue itself (Whitcomb 1972: 112, Hamm 1979: 383–4). In 1930 Crosby made his first screen appearance in a showcase for Whiteman, *The King of Jazz*. The same year millions listened to the Whiteman band in a weekly programme on network radio sponsored by a paint manufacturer (Sanjek 1988: 89). Then, in 1931, Crosby left Whiteman to launch a highly successful solo career. His first leading film role was in *The Big Broadcast* (1932) based loosely on his 'real life' persona as the singing star of a weekly radio show (Gammond 1993: 139). One of the songs from the film, 'Please', was released on record and became a best seller (Deutsch 1992).

Crosby is the case *par excellence* of a new type of cross-media promotion (and stardom). As Marsha Siefert (1995) points out, this was premised both on developments in media technology and the emergence of a new type of film narrative, the musical.

> In the 1930s and 1940s, single songs introduced in films could be remarketed through record sales, radio play, and juke-box hit status. Once the various sound technology developments in radio, music recording and film had been incorporated into their respective industries by the early 1930s, the successes of hit songs were mutually beneficial, especially during dips in the business cycle for film musicals and recording during the Depression. In fact their separate domains of performance – the home and the movie theatre – provided an intertextuality of song performances from which all benefited.
>
> (50)

Two points emerge here, I think. One is that the vigorous and rapidly growing film industry assumed a key role in directing popular music through the vehicle of the screen musical. During the 1930s the film companies commissioned songs from song writers, set up their own music publishing divisions and contracted their own orchestras and arrangers. They also introduced the practice of 'song dubbing' whereby a leading actor would mime on camera to a prerecorded musical soundtrack on which the vocal had been laid down by a professional, but anonymous, singer (Siefert 1995). The other point is that singing stars, like Crosby, who did break through were able to present themselves across different communication channels on their own terms. Stardom was premised on a virtuous circle in which celebrity increased media attention which increased celebrity and so on. The cross-media careers launched in the 1930s also provided the matrix for later kinds of stardom, most notably in rock'n'roll where singers were able to utilize film and television. Elvis Presley provides the obvious example, but in fact most of the major rock'n'roll stars appeared on big or small screen. As Simon Frith points out, cross-media promotion of a relatively small number of music stars returned during the 1980s through films, film soundtracks and music videos broadcast on television (1988a: 18).

As well as the cross-media star, the rise of Hollywood and network radio as major music-using media generated a second type of musician: the studio session player. In the 1920s the rapidly expanding network of movie theatres provided the largest single source of employment for American musicians. James P. Kraft (1994a, 1994b) estimates that by 1927 there were approximately 25 000 musicians in film theatre orchestras supporting silent movies six or seven days every week. That same year around 2000 musicians were working in America's 500 radio stations (1994a: 294). Then, quite catastrophically, developments in each medium decimated these workforces. The coming of the film soundtrack in 1927 and the advent of regular coast-to-coast broadcasting a year later very quickly eroded demand for musicians in movie theatres and local radio stations. Between 1928 and 1933 about 20 000 musician jobs disappeared, as much as a third of all musical employment at the time (295).

Production now shifted to the metropolitan centres, and particularly Los Angeles. By 1935 film studio or network radio orchestras in that city employed around 1000 musicians (296). Although hired on short contracts for particular sessions the union, Local 47 of the American Federation of Musicians, was able to ensure continuity of employment for many players by exerting tight control over the labour market. The 'contractors' who supplied the film studio orchestras could take on personnel only after they had served one year's membership in Local 47 (299). Beyond the film studios, musicians were also employed in the orchestras maintained by the larger Los Angeles radio stations which supplied the networks with much of their broadcast music. In radio as in film, Local 47 made sure that members were kept on from session to session (305–8).

The eclipse of the pit orchestra in movie theatres, and the rise of the film and radio studio as a major source of employment for musicians bring up several issues. To begin with the changes represented a quite brutal form of the capitalization of cultural production. Large numbers of livelihoods were lost across the country and replaced by far fewer jobs in metropolitan centres, all in the space of four years or so. Many of the musicians who stayed in work only managed to do so by migrating across the continent to the west coast. Still, once this had happened the studio regime did offer new kinds of opportunity for music makers and also, through the bargaining power of Local 47, a better standard of living. In Hollywood 'contractors' with relatively little musical knowledge hired and administered the orchestras (299–305), while at the radio stations brokerage was carried out by orchestra 'leaders' who were musicians and often conductors too (305–8). But whatever the particular type of entrepreneurial regime, the studio system of musical production was built, as Robert Faulkner observes, on relations of interdependence between broker and musician. Each looked for competence in the other (1971: 49–50).

Studio production in Los Angeles in the 1930s and 1940s was as close to an integrated model as popular music-making would come during the twentieth century. However it only represented a short moment. By the early 1950s musicals were in slow decline and radio broadcasting of music increasingly took the form of record play. As Top Forty formats were introduced the role of the big, media orchestras was overshadowed by dispersed regional centres producing rock'n'roll.

Just as the contractor system was becoming established in Hollywood during the mid-1930s, a third form of music-making appeared which exemplified much stronger tendencies towards autonomy: swing. Swing inaugurated a peripatetic mode of production in which bands combined performance in the new media of radio and the sound film with extensive touring. Microphone–loudspeaker technology was crucial here – it enabled the big bands to play in a number of different contexts. In live performance singers used public address systems to lift their voices over the riffs blasting from the reed and brass sections. At the same time radio 'hookups' could carry the sound of the whole ensemble from hotel lounges or dance pavilions across the radio networks to a national audience. The most notable case was the vaunted launch of swing by the Benny Goodman Orchestra in its live network broadcasts from the Palomar Ballroom in 1935 (Collier 1989, Lees 1987). But there were also broadcasts from radio studios, and often big band music was recorded on transcription discs for distribution to local radio stations (Collier 1989: 87–8). Bands appeared in films too. By the summer of 1941 more than 11 swing orchestras were filming in Hollywood (Simon 1981: 67). Finally, swing in recorded form benefited from the economic upswing. Total shipments of records in America had fallen from 104 million in 1927 to 6 million in 1932, the trough of the Depression (Gellatt 1977: 255). However by 1939 output was up to 50 million, of which around 85 per cent could be accounted for by swing. Many of these records filled the new jukeboxes which had been installed in drug stores, cafés and other public spaces around America (Collier 1989: 257).

For all the media activity live performance continued to be the primary mode of dissemination. Swing was dance music, its main market being the ballroom and dance hall circuit. At first this was organized on a local basis, but by the mid-1930s it was rapidly becoming a national system (Driggs 1959, Lees 1987). The pioneers here were bands from the Southwest which took to the road to travel across the whole 'territory'. By the early-1930s they 'would work possibly two nights in one city, then travel by bus or car, often several hundred miles, to their next job' (Driggs 1959: 194). Bands from the metropolis went on the road too. In 1935 the Goodman Orchestra had gigged its way west from New York, playing at remote locations, often to a hostile reception, before the breakthrough residency at the Palomar in Hollywood. Then, in considerably more salubrious circumstances, it gigged its way back (Schoenberg 1991).

In this context the big bands' mediated performances were always an adjunct to their live work. Local radio play and early record sales played a large part in Goodman's initial success on the West Coast. But the relationship was precisely that way round: broadcasting and record sales boosted live performance (Collier 1989, Simon 1981: 58). For black bands like Jimmie Lunceford's, which were generally excluded from broadcasting, promotional channels remained limited. They depended on 'advance men' sent into towns ahead of the gig to build interest and get the band's records into local jukeboxes (George 1988: 17). The reliance on media promotion did mean that a certain degree of industrial discipline could be exerted. The Goodman Orchestra, for example, was almost thrown off its first network show, 'Let's Dance', because an advertising executive thought the music 'too loud and jazzy' (Collier 1989: 131). And band leaders sometimes complained about interference in musical direction from the agencies which booked their live dates (Simon 1981: 46–9). Still, the general point to make is that the swing bands maintained a considerable amount of independence from the media industries just because of their multifariousness – the fact that they could be 'plugged into' a series of disseminating media from ballroom to radio studio.

Another important factor contributing to swing band autonomy was independence from songwriters and publishers. Most bands used a standard repertoire of pop tunes. This freed them from relying on publishers for new material. What mattered in swing was not access to the latest hit songs so much as arrangements which would give a distinctive sound and a competitive edge. Arrangers, unlike song writers, did not belong to the Tin Pan Alley edifice and their books could be bought relatively cheaply (Lees 1987). In many cases band members or leaders provided their own arrangements. Some, like Duke Ellington, wrote their own material too (Collier 1987: 168–9).

The self-reliance of the swing band as a producing and performing unit was matched by a certain amount of self-management. Generally the leaders were entrepreneurs, negotiating contracts with booking agencies, sponsors and record companies on the one hand, on the other hiring and firing musicians and choosing the repertoire (Simon 1981). Benny Goodman was one of the most autocratic. The musicians he fell out with were invariably sacked. But in the Fletcher Henderson Orchestra decision-making devolved to several members (Collier 1989), while the highly successful Casa Loma Orchestra was effectively a cooperative with no named leader (Carr *et al.* 1987: 80).

The swing band thus inaugurated a new kind of autonomous production unit in popular music. Crucially, many aspects of its modus operandi reappear in the rock group in the 1960s, in particular the flat structure, self-reliance and constant touring. Like the rock group too, the swing band depended on the notion of a direct relationship between audience and musicians. The ideology of 'authenticity' which Simon Frith (1983) proposes is at the core of rock aesthetics was in fact already well developed in swing. It tended to focus on the virtuosic skills of the instrumentalist, skills which purportedly distinguished her/his music from the merely commercial (Collier 1989: 171). Swing thus established a key principle in popular music marketing, namely that the audience may have a special knowledge of musicians and musicianship which, when invoked, will transcend market relations.

To summarize the argument of this section; in the inter-war period three distinct modes of production emerged in response to the mediatization of popular music and the creation of new kinds of market. One, the quasi-integrated film and radio studio system, took off in the 1930s, but despite its initial importance failed to become a hegemonic form. The other two, cross-media stardom and the self-reliant band of musicians, have now emerged as the dominant models of making and selling music in the contemporary period. In contrasting ways, each provides a considerable degree of institutional autonomy and independence from corporate control.

Proto-markets and author-stars

The swing band and the singing star were not only institutions. As I have already hinted each was built on a distinct logic of the market. Simply put, from the 1930s onwards music could be made in many places and distributed along many channels. On the one hand this allowed for centralized production, broadcast dissemination, intense selection of artists and repertoire, and a relatively slow rate of innovation. On the other hand the new music media enabled decentralized production, dissemination via flat networks, wide access to the means of production, and a relatively high rate of innovation. The cross-media star exemplifies the first logic, the swing or rock band the second. Of course in practice there has been considerable overlap between the different types. Swing band musicians sometimes played in studio orchestras, rock guitarists may do sessions between their 'own' gigs, while singing stars like Bing Crosby or Elton John often begin their careers as band vocalists. Bands can become stars too; for example the Count Basie Orchestra, The Beatles or U2.

Crucially, this link between flat networks and centralized apparatus has become a structural one, embedded in the organization of the music industries. It takes the form of a continuum between dispersed music-making and highly capitalized production. We can note in particular a constant 'upward' passage of musicians, songs and styles from the first sphere to the second. Most innovation goes on in the first where young musicians hone their skills and develop new styles. This is often conceived as a form of apprenticeship, and the constant expectation and desire is towards moving up to the second sphere in order to achieve the maximum recognition and income. For record companies, conversely, developing new products depends on being able to look and listen down into the first sphere. A&R personnel must select artists and identify trends here, at the commercial margins of music-making.[14]

As I have suggested, changes in the means of production provided the conditions for the persistence of dispersed music activity. The development of small-scale and comparatively affordable technologies has been particularly important. Record decks, amplifiers and drum kits can be bought in every city; while clubs, pubs, radio stations and now the Internet provide access to low-level dissemination (see Chapter 3). But there is clearly something more at stake here than means of production. What we are confronted with, it seems to me, is a continuous insurgency of music-making.

To understand it we need to return to the endemic overproduction of the cultural industries or, as Bernard Miège (1989) describes it, the creation of a catalogue. Miège argues that producing a wide range of artifacts (in response to demand uncertainty), 'requires direct access to cultural workers and implies their rapid renewal and rotation according to the swings of fashion. Hence the interest in having ... an important reservoir of workers ready for work without the need to pay them wages' (1989: 30). In popular music the great majority of band members, computer music makers, song writers, DJs and rappers constitute such a reservoir. They all seek record contracts, publishing deals, gigs – in short, recruitment. Reservoirs (Miège mentions actors and journalists too) depend on the high status of cultural work. Many people want to be artists, and are prepared to put up with long periods of under-employment in order to stay in their chosen milieu.

But in popular music there are some important extra dimensions to the chronic oversupply of labour. For one thing few people exclude themselves on the grounds of lack of competence. It is possible to become a 'musician' with relatively low levels of economic and cultural capital, and little or no specialist training. Moreover professional status is quite vaguely defined. In, say, photography or fiction writing the threshold of 'consecration' – the term Bourdieu (1993a: 76–7) uses to describe the dual process of entering the market and being invested with artistic prestige – is sharply delineated at the point of exhibition or legitimate publication. On the other hand there is an enormous domain of low-level production and performance in popular music which ranges across genre and degree of competence, from the short-lived and palpably hopeless to the coruscating and apparently irrepressible. Music-making is ubiquitous; it goes on everywhere – in small clubs, pubs, portastudios, home MIDI suites, across the Internet ...

Thus when the record industry looks for new material it is confronted with an anthropological morass, an excess of creators and encompassing genres. Of course in one sense this oversupply of human and musical resources is in the 'interest' of capital, as Miège (1989: 30) puts it, because it enables constant adjustment to changing demand. Yet, crucially, it also complicates the recruitment of musical labour. In popular music, unlike the other cultural industries, there is a field of production which remains unassimilable to the firm and its regularized discipline of accumulation.[15] Instead of being subsumed under corporate control, the development of new forms (that is of popular music to come) takes place in a series of 'proto-markets' which are poorly connected to the capital intensive sectors of packaging, distribution and the exploitation of rights.

What distinguishes proto-markets is that they bring together performer and audience in arenas which are not fully commodified. Examples include local rock scenes, dance music networks, or jazz performance by players taking time out from regular session work. Commodity exchange does go on in cases like these. Records are bought and sold, audiences pay to enter clubs and pub back rooms. But the defining characteristic of the proto-market is that the level of activity cannot be explained by economic factors alone. People are engaged in music-making sometimes for the love of it, sometimes for the esteem and sometimes because they expect in the future to enter the music industry proper.

Just because the proto-market exists at the edge of the sphere of commercial music production there is a high degree of ambivalence towards the industry. In many cases success is equated with 'selling out'. This may be because the proto-market constitutes a 'field of restricted production' (Bourdieu 1993b: 115–20). The imperative in such a field is for artists and audiences to distinguish themselves from the values associated with the mass market. Accordingly, the disdain for commercialism amongst disenchanted dance band musicians (Becker 1952) or 'underground' club-goers (Thornton 1995) represents a strategy of distinction, a means of exerting symbolic power over and against the culturally dispossessed. Another explanation is that the repudiation of success constitutes an insurance policy, a sober recognition of the likelihood of failure. The many musicians who are not selected (see Jones 1998) can always explain their lack of success as a consequence of having stuck to non-commercial principles.

But there is a third factor mitigating against commercial values in proto-markets. This is the emergence of popular music as an expression of solidarity in youth or ethnic subcultures. From swing to techno, musicians and audiences have seen themselves as belonging to a community which precedes market relations. Whereas the mass media separate the moments of production and consumption, music communities restore a sense of intimacy and mutual affiliation. This usually depends on the assertion of community values in opposition to a more or less instrumental mainstream. As we shall see the notion that music might be an expression of community has come under intense and sceptical scrutiny.[16] Against the criticism I will argue that community has a vitally important and persistent role in music production and consumption (see Chapter 5). For present purposes, though, the coherence of community is less important than the fact that industry has deferred to the community idea. Subcultural credibility and therefore market share depend on evidence about the site of production being made available. Music-making must be seen to go on outside the industry, at some moment before the imperatives of exchange take over.

Labour supply push in proto-markets, together with the ambivalent attitudes towards success which are bound up in it, are a crucial aspect of music industry economics. Indeed, such factors go a long way towards explaining the prevalence of entrepreneurs at the 'input boundary' (Hirsch 1990/1972) – artist managers, independent producers, owners of small labels. Given the degree of contradiction which abounds in proto-markets they need to have a complex array of skills. First, popular music entrepreneurs must be adept traders, able to buy low – by recruiting artists before their potential is recognized elsewhere, and then sell high – usually to the next agent in the production-dissemination chain, although sometimes, in the case of small record companies, directly to the public. The crucial decisions here concern 'exactly what professional competence is or who may be expected to possess it' among music makers (DiMaggio 1977: 442). To make this kind of judgement the entrepreneur has in some sense to become an ethnographer and go among 'the kids' on 'the street' (Negus 1992: 58–9). But if familiarity with the more or less alien culture of proto-production is vital, the entrepreneur also needs to be a vulgarizer, able to turn 'unique and contingent (so far as their chance of success is concerned) cultural use values into products which can be exchanged on a market' (Miège 1989: 28). Finally the entrepreneur needs to adopt the role of protector and build relations of trust with the artist on the basis that s/he will *not* be turned into a mere producer of commodities (Stratton 1982: 95–7).

Clearly these terms and conditions apply just as much to entrepreneurs who work directly for major record companies, in other words the A&R personnel. Keith Negus says that managers of A&R departments, 'usually require staff to justify their choice of an act by having an overall "vision" of an artist's musical and visual direction, the audience they might appeal to and how they might develop in the future' (1992: 48). In other words A&R staff have to be able to conjure a presentiment of the commodity from the 'raw talent' which they encounter. They must then sell the marketability of potential recruits to the rest of the firm, in particular the marketing department (48–51). The interesting thing is that this rhetoric of the plan and known demand gets combined with a quite contradictory emphasis on '"following hunches", "gut feeling", "intuition" and "instinct"' (Negus 1992: 51).

It seems, then, that entrepreneurs in the major record companies are pulled in two directions. The first is towards the construction of the potential recruit as an *ideal* producer of commodities for the future market. Paradoxically, the pitch for this must be couched in tough, empirical terms. The second direction is aesthetic. Record company personnel focus on the *specific* and immanent qualities of a particular artist, but none the less fail to translate their reaction into the instrumental language of business. As Clive Davis of CBS Records puts it, '[s]omething happens in your chemistry, in your blood, when you hear the record – a tingling, a certain electricity, a sense that audiences will grab onto this song and take off with it' (quoted by Negus 1992: 52).

Negus recognizes the tensions at work here, but suggests they are overcome in a 'synthetic ideology of creativity . . . a combinatorial approach to both acts and material' (55). However it strikes me that the discourses of power and knowledge which he documents in record companies are not really synthetic at all, at least not in the sense that they resolve contradiction. Rather, differences in the way that A&R personnel talk about new artists on the one hand, and their imagined marketability on the other, suggest that risk-taking and regulation are to a great extent irreconcilable. It is just that record company personnel pretend they are not.

So, proto-markets are relatively autonomous zones and difficult for record companies to colonize. We can identify two main reasons for this: first, because the rampant over-supply of musical labour generates cacophony and makes it extremely difficult to spot future stars; second, because there may be ideological objections from musicians and audience to 'going commercial'. In this situation, record company A&R people have to speak different languages. By turn they will talk up their skills as backers of big winners, produce plans which assess and reduce risk on a rational basis, reassure the musician who cannot abide the prospect of selling out.

In this sense proto-markets reflect the real contradictions of capital in the sphere of musical production. Yet immediately one has to concede that there is an extraordinary *anticipation* of commerce, even in ostensibly anti-commercial music scenes. Contradiction flourishes here too. For as music makers enter small scenes they are, in effect, making themselves available for stardom. Thus, whatever expressions of resentment and doubt they come across, A&R people also encounter a ravenous desire among music makers to be recruited and gain wider acclaim. This is not only a matter of the material trappings of stardom. As Simon Frith suggests, commercial success is an index of artistic success. In a cultural form which is also a cultural industry failing to sell records and reach audiences through the medium of the market means failing as a musician (1983: 61). Frith's point is persuasive as far as it goes, but it seems to me there is more at stake here. Successive generations of musicians have been able to reconcile commercial and artistic success because they have subscribed to a certain ideology of authorship.

In the Introduction to this book I argued that we need to recover some notion of authorship in order to understand musician agency (more on this in Chapter 2). Crucially, however, the industry has also embraced the cult of the author. In an important sense it is an ideological embrace because although presented as an affirmation of autonomy, authorship also provides another way of valorizing capital. There are several aspects to this. Historically, authorship has helped to build markets and, in particular, extend middle-class consumption of popular music. The paradigmatic shift here occurred during the late 1960s with the advent of rock. Rock authorship also encouraged music makers to acquiesce to 'commercial' routines on the grounds that their creative expression called for, indeed demanded, public recognition. Bluntly put, authorship brought music makers into the fold, precisely at the moment when autonomy came to be valued in popular music cultures. How did this come about?

From the late 1960s groups began to build long-term careers around periodic album releases and synchronized, promotional tours. If not quite a new form, the rock album was certainly a new kind of extended textual unit, and as such became the central element in an emerging rock aesthetic. Successive album releases were now seen to constitute an oeuvre, and the album itself was rendered as a substantial art work. Authorial genius was both inscribed in the record-text – the realized sound of the composition, and in accompanying discourse – sleeve notes and credits increasingly referred to the creative process and identified the contributions of individual music makers. A new style of journalism then deepened and reinforced the legitimacy of this mode of *auteurism* (Toynbee 1993: 290).

Rock authorship significantly increased musician control over the means of production, extending institutional autonomy along a new dimension. In the 1970s rock musicians utilized a burgeoning and ever more expensive studio apparatus for longer and longer periods in order to make albums (see Chapter 3). In some cases this meant sharing control with a producer-entrepreneur. None the less big studio productions were premised on the notion of musician control over heavily capitalized resources. Crucially, this mode of production dovetailed with a new market regime. As the gap between album releases grew larger so unit sales were pushed up and the life cycle of the album was extended (Straw 1990). To put it another way innovation slowed and marketing became more predictable. Meanwhile those rock groups that had already crossed the threshold of success were able to lever up the size of advances and royalty rates from record companies (Frith 1983: 83–4); these cost pressures then worked to further entrench the longevity of artists.

Will Straw (1993b) has traced the decline of the rock market regime, and its replacement by a 'new pop mainstream' in the 1980s. Although celebrity persisted, it was no longer important as a way of interpreting music. Citing the cases of Culture Club and Madonna he suggests, '[t]here is little of the two-way passage between a performer's worldview and the meaning of his or her recordings which existed a decade previously'. Furthermore the rate of innovation increased significantly in the same period, so that by the mid-1980s there was a rapid sequence of stars (11). In the period since, this trend has continued. For example, there has been an ostentatious reversal of the authorship cult in British dance music. As far as possible the identity of the performer is disguised here, sometimes through the use of a different *nom de disque* for each record release (Hesmondhalgh 1998 and Chapter 5). It seems, then, that there may be a dip in the fortunes of institutional authorship.

In common with other aspects of its political economy, authorship in popular music is a contradictory phenomenon. On the one hand it does yield a degree of independence from corporate control for musicians. Crucially, meaning is invested in the text at the moment of its production by the author. This depends on visibility (Lury 1993: 54, Miège 1989: 25–6). The author must be seen to make great music by means of her/his exceptional faculties, while the music should in turn bear traces of the author's persona. The market thus guarantees the terms and conditions of authorship. What's more, even in the current period when it seems that the author cult has evaporated, it is really more accurate to say that authorship has been rearticulated. For connoisseurs of dance music the anonymity of the producer is a mask which when pulled away reveals a creator all the more beguiling for her/his modesty. And in British 'teen pop', where entrepreneurs appeared to have taken control at one point, there is now a struggle by the artists to assert their authority. The Spice Girls sacked their manager in the name of autonomy, while East 17 have changed their name to E17 and insist on writing their own material. There is a rhizomatic quality about authorship in pop: like couch grass it grows back from the merest shred left in the ground.

This is partly because authorship has become inextricably bound up with stardom. Discussing cinema, Richard Dyer suggests that '[s]tars are involved in making themselves into commodities; they are both labour and the thing that labour produces' (1987: 5). In other words stars have to assemble an image and persona, expending time and energy to do this. But once established the star becomes a means of production, 'something that is used with further labour (scripting, acting, directing, managing, filming, editing) to produce another commodity, a film' (6). The implications of Dyer's analysis of stardom are particularly interesting for popular music where the conjunction of authorship and stardom has produced quite divergent outcomes in the era of rock and after.

In one version, rock naturalism, authorship consists in disavowing stardom and attempting to revoke one's own commodity status. It is perhaps best exemplified by Bruce Springsteen. As Simon Frith (1988b) points out, in performance Springsteen presents his (ostentatiously hard) labour to the audience as though it were bereft of an outcome, as though it were pure work. Conversely those stars who, as authors, amplify and dwell on their construction as stars are not only true to their standing, they also undermine the ideology inherent in naturalism (Frith and Horne 1987). Examples here include David Bowie and, more recently, the Pet Shop Boys. I think there is something to be said for this critique of authenticity.

Yet ultimately it is not enough. To return to the point where I began this section: modern popular music is traversed by two axes. One is horizontal and links music makers organized in small music scenes, or proto-markets, in places like Cucamonga, CA or Wythenshawe, Manchester. The other is vertical and connects proto-markets to the heavily capitalized packaging and distribution sector at the apex of the music industries. The latter depends on small-scale music scenes as a source of new products, and yet finds them difficult to tap. This is the first element of what I have been calling institutional autonomy; the massive oversupply and indiscipline of musical labour. The second derives from the cult of authorship. When audiences demand that music makers are creators the music business must guarantee minimum conditions of independence for them. This condition comes into effect precisely as musicians are selected by the industry and begin to move up the vertical axis. The third element in the institutional autonomy of popular music is stardom. When musicians become extremely successful they commodify themselves. There is a solipsistic logic to this; the star makes herself a star and this renders her untouchable. Yet, at the same time, the very act of conversion from human subject to shiny object is an example to us all. It shows us that we could lead altered lives.

Thus in the case of stardom and authorship the issue is not so much one of authenticity versus artifice (Simon Frith's formulation), but rather of utopian potentiality. As Richard Dyer has argued the beguiling thing about stardom is 'the business of constructing/performing/being . . . a character' (1979: 24). This promise of transformation derives from the dialectical encounter between agency and commodification that occurs as musicians reach the threshold of stardom. Of course it can produce tragedy – some music makers die because they cannot live with the extraordinary alienation of being a thing. But, such is its ambivalence, pop stardom also offers the possibility of possibility. It is a resource of hope.

Conclusion

The account of the market I have been presenting in this chapter has been optimistic in tenor. But it is also a sober account, based on observation of the way in which popular music has been organized under capitalism in its short twentieth century. Above all, it strikes me that to explain how and why sublime music is produced on a daily basis is an urgent task in the critical analysis of culture. For that reason I have concentrated on examining the material framework in which this might occur – what I have called 'institutional autonomy'. However this is not because its counterparts, exploitation and inequity, are unimportant. Clearly, the bleak and onerous conditions of artisanal labour in the cultural industries identified by researchers like Nicholas Garnham (1990b) and Colin Sparks (1994) are found in popular music too. Musicians often work for low, or no, wages. Arguably the situation is worse than in other sectors of cultural production.

Evidence from America suggests that since 1945 musical labour has become increasingly casualized – more musicians have less secure incomes (Seltzer 1989: 221–39), while a recent ethnographic study in Britain shows that the predominant experience of rock musicians is of failure (Jones 1998). This perspective is important, not least because it brings to the fore the important notion that the music industry, like all cultural enterprise, is rapacious and exploits labour by keeping alive vain hopes of glory.

But in the end I feel compelled by the evidence to fall back on a resolutely optimistic position. In the case of music the drive to accumulation has actually helped to undermine the system imperative of capital and opened up space in which musicians can make lovely music. In the next chapter we turn to the question of how they do this by examining forms of creative agency and strategies of performance.

2

Making up and showing off: what musicians do

In the early 1970s, the German band leader James Last developed a new technique for adding party ambience to his 'non-stop dancing' albums. These were collections of current pop hits and old standards, arranged for orchestra and edited so that they played in segue mode – without a gap between tracks. Last's innovation was to invite, after recording the music, 40 or so of his musicians and their friends to Deutsche Grammophon's Hamburg studio. Here they were plied with strong drink. At one session there were 40 bottles of champagne, 12 bottles of rye, 12 of gin and an unspecified amount of bourbon. Following a short but intensive drinking bout the company was led to an array of microphones and instructed to sing along and make appropriate party noises over tracks which had been laid down previously by the band (Willox 1976: 149). A photograph of one of these events shows Last with a beatific smile, hands blurred in mid-clap as he leads a throng of whooping and stomping accomplices through an uptempo number (96f).

We can compare this scene to the dingy back room of an English pub where, a few years later, Ian Curtis introduced a new kind of dancing to the stage act of post-punk band Joy Division. As his widow and biographer notes, in 'a distressing parody of his off-stage seizures ... [h]is arms would flail around, winding an invisible bobbin' while his legs jerked in an involuntary spasm (Curtis 1995: 74). According to several commentators Curtis's performance was almost unbearably intense (Middles 1996: 123, Savage 1996: 94). Blurring the line between rock act and real-life affliction he invested Joy Division's cold presence with a frightening ambivalence. It was never clear whether the singer was having an epileptic fit, or rather simulating an attack as a way of expressing some otherwise undisclosable inner tumult.

Now on the face of it these two music makers have little in common. Last, king of easy listening music, is not to be compared with Curtis, the epitome of the rock singer as suffering artist. Yet it seems to me that the similarities between them actually run quite deep. Both musicians go to extraordinary lengths to break through the boundaries of an existing style and both make a little headway. Last's construction of a new mode of hyper-conviviality for easy listening music is just as important as Curtis's pathological expressionism within post-punk. In each case the break with current practice depends on method much more than the stroke of genius. Attention to detail and the careful evaluation of change is all. Ian Curtis, for example, began by cutting himself with broken glass on stage before he developed his convulsive dance. Later he read Dostoevsky, Nietzsche and Sartre in order to acquire an appropriate set of references for song writing (Curtis 1995: 90). In a similar way, Last moved towards the 'party naturalism' of his work in the early 1970s through a combination of strategy and trial and error, as he adjusted repertoire, arrangements and production values over a long series of record releases (Willox 1976: 134–43).

We might then sum up the *modus operandi* of both these musicians as white-collar. That is certainly my starting point in this chapter, the idea that to produce popular music is not at all an intuitive act of expression, but rather something which depends on planning, research and the constant monitoring of the outcome of decisions. It is difficult to find a suitable name for this. Most terms used to describe art and music-making are tarnished by romanticism, and do not get across that aspect of knowledge production I have just been discussing. Given this difficulty perhaps the best way forwards is to take an existing title and then try to inflect it.

I want to suggest that people who make popular music are *creators*, that is agents who make musical differences in the form of texts, performances and sounds. Crucially, though, the musical creator is restricted in how much difference s/he can make at any given moment. In other words the unit of creativity is a small one. This is a key assumption in the discussion that follows because it will enable a wide range of musicians to be treated under the rubric creator. Just as importantly it means we can include all stages of music-making from 'writing' through 'performance' to 'production'. Lastly, a limited notion of creativity can be applied at different moments of popular music history, as well as across genres which make distinct, and often exclusive, aesthetic claims – rock, for instance, or jazz. Quite simply, the small creative act is a common denominator in pop.

Music-making and the radius of creativity

In the Introduction I argued that musicians are exemplary agents who through their creative practice demonstrate how one might act differently and in so doing rebut, at least to some extent, the exigencies of the capitalist system. The question is, though, how can this happen? In what sense might creativity emerge from the very social relations which perpetuate domination? The traditional Marxist response is to posit class antagonism as the source of artistic agency. Social classes are actors and their most progressive elements generate critical forms of art within dominant social relations (Goldmann 1977, Brecht 1980). The subcultural theory which emerged from the Centre for Contemporary Cultural Studies in Birmingham during the 1970s belongs to this tradition too, in that conflicted social relations are seen to produce subcultural resistance (Hall *et al.* 1976). Now the idea that music-making can represent social formations in struggle – not just class, but also, and particularly, ethnic formations – is central to the present study. It is a key aspect of the *popular* in popular music. We will return to it in Chapter 4. However in my view such an approach cannot on its own explain the complex, micrological nature of musical creativity, nor the way it is articulated with, rather than simply reflecting, social relations.

To fill the gap I want to call on the work of sociologist Pierre Bourdieu. His concepts of 'habitus' and 'field' provide for a fully social, yet highly articulated, account of cultural production, an account which shows how music-making is located both in its own particular domain and in larger social relations at one and the same time.

Let us look first at habitus. Bourdieu uses the word to describe the constellation of dispositions, acquired mostly in the early stages of life, which informs subjectivity and therefore action (Bourdieu 1984: 112–14, 171, Bourdieu 1990: 30–65, Bourdieu 1993d). In effect habitus is a mediator between social relations – class, race, gender, education and so on – and what people think and do – their 'practice'. Habitus should not be seen as a system of conditioning however. For one thing it can adapt, albeit in a limited way, to new situations. As Bourdieu puts it, 'habitus is a principle of invention produced by history' (1993e: 87). For the present argument the key aspect of habitus is the way it disposes musician-agents to play, write, record or perform in a particular way. Bourdieu calls such an orientation a strategy, meaning a semi-conscious but characteristic way of doing practice (1993b: 137) – for example James Last's laconic thoroughness or the sort of bohemian expression-by-design adopted by Ian Curtis.

Strategies are always deployed on a particular field. A field is a 'space of positions' governed by rules which are proper to it (1993d: 72). It is also a system of power relations in that agents struggle for dominant positions by mobilizing their accumulated 'capital', in other words quantities of power and prestige, be this cultural, economic, social or any other type current in the field (1993d: 73). For present purposes the most important field identified by Bourdieu is that of cultural production – actually literature and fine art – which he examines quite extensively (1993c, 1996). He suggests that since the mid-nineteenth century it has been marked by a struggle between on the one hand a dominant group, well endowed with economic and social capital, that represents established values, and on the other a dominated group, the avant-garde, which struggles to overturn the establishment

(1993g). At stake in this conflict is not only position in the hierarchy, but also the very nature of the field, in other words what aesthetic value consists in.

For Bourdieu, then, the field of cultural production has a strong individualistic and self-serving aspect. Artists strive to increase their own credit, and those who achieve success may then repudiate the very movements through which they have built their careers (1993g: 59–61). This emphasis on the self-interested nature of culture-making is important I think. It provides a useful counter to naive or ideological belief in the purity of art. None the less I would argue that cultural production may also be an altruistic affair. In popular music, perhaps more than any other cultural form, musicians claim to act on behalf of the community and for the collective good. Sometimes they seek to abolish the stratified field of popular music altogether with its division along lines of class, race and gender. At a less intense level it seems that most popular music makers have some notion of music as a common language capable of bringing people together.[1] In my view we should therefore see the field of popular music as the site both of a struggle for individual position and a utopian drive to make the world better through music. As I suggested in the last chapter, musicians (like all actors) tend to have a 'fuzzy' worldview which can encapsulate contradictions of this sort (see Chapter 1, Note 16).

In any event, the problem of interested action is complicated in pop by the fact that alternative or oppositional movements never have a straightforward antagonism to dominant forces. Pop mainstreams are not at all like art establishments in that they represent popular alliances rather than narrow middle-class interests, while alternative formations, particularly in the case of black musics, are more often 'parallels' in that they struggle for space beside dominant formations.[2] The field of popular music production is thus articulated in a different and more complex way than that of European art and literature.

With these caveats posted we can return to Bourdieu. For the present argument his most important point is that cultural production takes place at the intersection between habitus and field. Bourdieu explores this idea in his work on the literary and art worlds of nineteenth-century France (1993c, 1996). On the one hand, he suggests, the field of cultural production attracts and selects artists with appropriate properties and dispositions, on the other 'perception of the space of possible positions' within the field depends on the habitus of the artist (1993g: 65). What this means is that anyone trying to explain what artists have done ('the set of *social trajectories*' [original emphasis]) will need to establish:

> the configuration, at the moment, and at the various critical turning-points in each career, of the space of available possibilities (in particular, the economic and symbolic hierarchy of the genres, schools, styles, manners, subjects etc.), the social value attached to

each of them, and also the meaning and value they received for the different agents or classes of agents in terms of the socially constituted categories of perception and appreciation they applied to them.

(Bourdieu 1993g: 65)

Bourdieu thus imagines artists' careers in terms of a sequence of key moments in the complex interrelationship between field and habitus. Each moment produces possible constituents of the next one.

The space of possibilities (in translation the alternative term 'possibles' is sometimes used instead) is a crucial concept for the present argument and has important implications for the model of creativity I want to develop. We ought to examine it in detail. In the first place, as seen in the passage above, possibilities are a product of the relationship between the 'push' of subjective disposition and the 'pull' of objective positions. Although this relationship is marked by convergence, crucially it stops short of correspondence: possibilities emerge in the mismatch, or tension, between habitus and field. This is most evident in the case of the avant-garde where the field is characterized by 'a weak degree of codification', in other words its boundaries are not clearly defined. As a result people from quite diverse origins, including those without formal qualifications in art-making, can enter the field. Such variations in the disposition of agents who come to it then destabilize the field further (1996: 226).[3]

In fact this tendency is considerably more pronounced in popular music than in the avant-garde. As we saw in the last chapter it accounts for the teeming and anarchic nature of proto-markets where differences of class and ethnicity flourish (though not differences of gender to anything like the same extent). As a result there may be wide variations in the habitus of musicians working in the field of pop. What's more, in contrast to avant-garde arts, such differences are encountered in hegemonic mainstreams, as well as in alternative or counter-cultural movements. In both cases musicians enter the field from a range of social origins that spans suburbia and the ghetto. Sometimes these music makers are compartmentalized by race and genre, sometimes they are integrated, but always they generate possibilities which derive from differences in habitus and the way these inflect positions in the field.

The second site in which possibilities are produced is the field of works. Bourdieu uses this term to describe the historical accretion of cultural work done. He also includes established techniques and codes of production under the same head. As he puts it, 'the heritage accumulated by collective work presents itself to each agent [writer] as a space of possibles, that is as an ensemble of probable constraints which are the condition and the counterpart of a set of possible uses' (1996: 235).

In this context the work of the author consists in integrating perspectives – on forms and themes in the canon, but also, for the writer and painter, on the social world. Flaubert can apparently undertake this sort of integration extremely well. Bourdieu says of him, '[i]n situating himself, as it were, at the geometric intersection of all perspectives, which is also the point of greatest tension, he forces himself in some fashion to raise to their highest intensity the set of questions posed in the field ... an infinite universe of possible combinations locked in a potential state within the finite system of constraints' (1996: 100).

This is a very helpful way of thinking about creativity in popular music too, where 'the set of questions posed in the field' is enormous and has grown larger and larger throughout the century as recordings of stars, voices and styles have accumulated. Precisely because direct reference to the world is quite limited in music, though, the intra-musical nature of the field of work takes on an extra significance. We will come back to this issue shortly.

There is still a significant difficulty though. Bourdieu rightly emphasizes the point that there can be no possibility without constraint. However it seems to me these terms are spread too far apart to be of much use in explaining particular creative action, in other words why Flaubert (or James Last or Ian Curtis) made particular decisions at particular moments. When Bourdieu says that Flaubert '[situated] himself ... at the geometric intersection of all perspectives' we are offered little evidence to show how he did this (1996: 100). The danger is that in the absence of a local explanation which negotiates possibility and constraint, some notion of the ineffable power of the artist will drift back in.

To deal with this problem I want to add a third term: likelihood. Likelihood relates to the selection of possibles by the creator and the fact that some possibles are more likely to be selected than others. Thus, it is almost certain that the rock guitarist will play her electric guitar with a plectrum and it is very likely that she will use an electronically generated sustain in her playing. It is unlikely that she will hit a diminished thirteenth chord, play a solo with constant intonation, or indeed be a woman. This parameter of likelihood effectively divides constraint in two.

On the one hand, constraint can take the form of likeliness. The most repeated, most normalized tropes and figures (such as use of plectrum and sustain) are possibles in the sense that other possibilities could be selected (for instance finger picking and staccato). But a strong congruence between artist disposition ('I'm a rock guitarist') and position in the field of works ('rock guitar style') means that the first set of possibles are most likely to be selected.

On the other hand, *un*likeliness also represents a form of constraint. What tends to prevent the selection and combination of possibles is their distance from the dispositive centre of the musician's habitus. Instead of congruence the operative principle here is divergence which makes certain possibles in the field of works 'hard to hear'. One more point needs to be made in this connection. When they are made, unlikely selections of possibles will none the less be conventional. As Howard Becker (1982) suggests, 'the possibility of artistic experience arises from the existence of a body of conventions that artists and audiences can refer to in making sense of the work' (30). Thus part of the skill in selecting unlikely combinations of possibles is to demonstrate their possibility by providing some associative link back, as it were, to existing convention.[4]

We can usefully stop now and rehearse the argument of the section up to this moment. Bourdieu's theory of habitus and field, and his observations of cultural production provide a helpful way of understanding creativity in popular music. The key concept here is the space of possibles. Possibles arise, first, in the relationship between habitus (artists' dispositions) and field of musical production (the power relations among, and pattern of positions taken by, all artists); and, second, in that historical fund of practices, textual forms and codes called the field of works. Constraint and possibility are produced together in that while habitus and field are relatively stable the fit between them is never a tight one. We can augment Bourdieu's thinking here by adding a third consideration – the likelihood of the selection of possibles. With this set of terms and conditions in mind I want now to take a further step and assemble a general model – the radius of creativity – which can be applied to all sorts of popular music-making and perhaps the production of culture more generally (see Figure 2.1).

Creative space may be envisaged as circular. At the centre is the music maker, sometimes a single subject, sometimes a collective actor. The radius of creativity extends from the centre to an ill-defined circumference. Within the circumference are distributed creative possibles. The further along the radius one moves from the centre, the thinner the distribution of these possibles. Beyond the circumference is an area of impossibility, that is to say a domain where possibles cannot be heard.

The music maker identifies (hears) possibles according to a) the perceptual schema of her/his habitus and b) its point of intersection with the creative field.

The first factor explains why the density of possibles declines along the radius: the greater the distance from the centre the harder it is to hear. (The circumference represents a horizon of audition.) Just as possibles are more densely distributed towards the centre so too are customary patterns of selection and combination. The propensity to identify and select possibles within the ambit of 'strong' disposition near the centre represents one form of constraint on creativity. The difficulty of so doing further out along the radius, among the thinly distributed possibles where dispositivity is weakest, constitutes another.

The second factor, the point where habitus intersects with field, determines the particular universe of possibles traversed by the radius. Habitus, with its 'portfolio' of capitals (musical knowledge, economic wealth, general education etc.), will have an important impact here, affecting both the position and extent of the radius in the field. However because the field of popular music is lightly codified (people do not tend to need a specific portfolio of capitals in order to enter it) there is a relatively high degree of unpredictability about position and extent of radius, and therefore also about likelihood of the selection of possibles. This is one reason why popular music has changed so much and so fast in the late twentieth century.

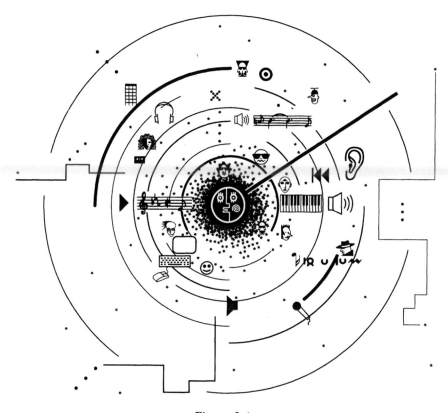

Figure 2.1

Although the radius has been presented as traversing a single, creative field this is better conceived as a composite, made up of two distinct but superimposed fields. These are the field of works (texts, sounds, genres, technologies and aesthetic strategies) and the field of musical production (a set of positions occupied by music makers according to scene, subculture, mainstream, alternative and parallel formations). There is a loose fit between the two; shifts in one radius will tend to impact on the other.

The economic field (consisting of economic positions organized according to the rules of the valorization of capital) needs to be considered together with the radius of creativity because a) its institutional framework in the form of 'the market' inflects the creative field and b) its inequitable distribution of economic wealth strongly shapes the habitus of music makers by class. However, as we saw in the first chapter, a field effect is also exerted in the opposite direction. In popular music a condition of accumulation is that radii may traverse the creative field with relatively little direction from the commissioning and distributing music industries.

The radius of creativity is a synchronic model for explaining creative action. To produce a historical view we need to generate a sequence of radii for any particular creator. This would plot shifting relations between disposition and position over time, and any consequent movement of the radius across the field. The sequence would also show expansion, contraction or (for most pop acts) the early disappearance of the radius. One rare but important pattern is for contraction to be followed by stability as in the case of superstars like the Rolling Stones who keep on selecting the same encrusted pattern of possibles over a long period. These stable trajectories tend to stabilize what is otherwise a highly unstable field.

Social authorship and voice

Possibility is the key term in this model. Represented by several sorts of icon on the diagram, there are in fact many different types and sizes of possibility. What they have in common, though, is the property of emerging at the junction between subjective experience and objective social relations. On the subjective side is the orientation of the music maker towards the future ('what will I do next?'), an orientation always informed by habitus and the weight of the past (for example: lower-middle class, art school educated, music lessons as a child). On the objective side are the positions in the field of musical production – cult retro for example, and in the field of works – surf music guitar with plenty of tremolo, perhaps. Possibility arises from the fact that these spaces and positions, though carried forward by the inertia of history, are constantly being transformed as possibles are actively perceived, selected and shaped to produce future music. Possibilities only become possibilities in the ear of the music maker.

In this section, then, we address the question of what kind of thing musical possibles might be. As we have just heard, that means examining how possibles are generated through creative action. Actually, creator seems rather too broad a term now. We need a more specific usage to get at the particular role in question. If it still has some legitimacy I would suggest 'author', in other words someone who authorizes possibilities.

Mikhail Bakhtin's work on heteroglossia in the novel comes in useful here. Bakhtin (1981) conceives the material of the novel as a 'multiplicity of languages and verbal–ideological belief systems'. They are socially located in class and profession, or by orientation and mood – 'the languages of rumour, of society chatter, servants' language and so forth' (311). Looked at in such a way the novel appears as a matrix of voices already spoken, with its dominant mode being the 'parodic stylization of incorporated languages' (312). What Bakhtin means is that the play of distinct language genres one against another 'unmasks' their limited and particular quality – idioms take on a piquancy and social significance by way of contrast and the dialogue between them.

Along with the emphasis on the social constitution of language used in the novel, Bakhtin proposes a new function for the author. S/he becomes a selector and combiner of voices. Sometimes this involves placing particular languages in the mouths of particular characters. But the author may also present them nondirectly, as when the narrative proper, that official voice of the novel, takes on a particular dialect or inflection (312). Thus, even when discourse is apparently neutral (not inside quotation marks), citation can occur. This suggests not so much Barthes' (1976a) frequently invoked 'death of the author' as a new role for her: editor and parodist replaces transcendental spirit (Bakhtin 1981: 314–15).

I think the notion of heteroglossia opens up productive ways of understanding authorship in popular music as well as in the novel. The multiple languages woven together by the author are analogous to the possibles selected and shaped by musicians. Above all, both kinds are historically given materials which are selected and combined to make the new. However we need to clarify some important differences between novelistic language and music before taking this route.

For Bakhtin the basic unit of heteroglossia is the utterance, a bounded piece of discourse from an identifiable language genre or particular speaker. There is no straightforward equivalent to this in music. In the first place, whereas utterances subsist outside the novel in everyday orality as well as in all kinds of written form (from memo to advertising slogan), musical statements belong mainly to one super-genre, 'music'; that is, an endogenous symbolic system produced and consumed in quite specific, socially and technologically prescribed settings. Music in modern societies is also an asymmetrical form of communication – many people listen, only a few produce. The effect of all this is that musical possibles belong to a well defined field of works (recordings, concerts, broadcasts and so on) rather than emerging from a diverse universe of widely used language types.[5]

A further class of difference between ordinary language and music that we need to examine relates to syntax. Perhaps the nearest analogue in music to the utterance is the phrase, in other words a significant sequence of notes, or fragment of melody. Yet, as Richard Middleton points out, music can hardly be reduced to syntagmatic segments of this sort.[6] Parameters such as timbre, tempo or metre which may persist over the length of a piece are also crucial in rendering musical character (1990: 177). Indeed, the parametric and the syntagmatic begin to lose their conceptual distinctiveness in popular music as repetition becomes more and more important. The riff, for example, is a syntagmatic unit with a clear developmental thrust, while at the same time its repetitive aspect makes it a metric and timbral 'anchor'.

One other important syntactic feature which distinguishes music from novelistic discourse has to do with the fact that in music many sound sources can be heard simultaneously. So, along with the successive play of utterances which Bakhtin describes (antiphony in musical terms), there is also a strong sense of parallel articulation (polyphony or harmonic development).

Given this multi-dimensionality it might be thought that the model of the discrete verbal utterance is simply not appropriate in the case of music. We listen in too many places and along too many planes to be able to pick out any such separable textual unit. Yet we do hear distinct *voices* in popular music. In fact voice seems to be a central term in the practical aesthetics of the form.

I want to suggest that musical voice has two dimensions. First, like Bakhtin's utterance it is socially and historically located. It may be a site of production, in other words a specific throat, instrument, recording studio, or city. But it can also be a text place, that is a particular phrase, beat, song, or even genre. Crucially, voice in this dimension may be mapped; we expect to know where and when it originates. The key coordinates are period, gender, class, ethnicity, sexuality and locale. 'Motown Girl Groups' is an example of quite a large-scale voice which encapsulates most of these factors. Others, pulled out of the air at random and with varying degrees of specificity, include the 'Smoke on the Water riff', 'house music "four-on-the-floor" beat' or 'the soprano saxophone'.

The second aspect of voice is really better described as voicing. By this I mean the textu(r)al properties which are initially attached to a vocal site by the author. A voicing may be syntactic (verse/chorus, for example), it may be parametric (rough/smooth, say) or it may combine both elements. Voicings call for an epithetic terminology.[7] We hear fast/slow, episodic/repetitive, funky/even-metred, melodic/dirgelike, diminuendo/crescendo and so on and so forth. It is useful to think of voicings in terms of binary oppositions like these just because they provide differential purchase on music as phenomenon, something which is notoriously difficult to analyse in everyday language. But however we describe it the point is that a voicing achieves particularity in pop through its relations with the time-place of voice. Site and sound form mutually constitute each other.

Paradoxically enough, this depends on disjunction as much as alignment. In fact I would suggest that the incredible specificity-without-reference that we find in pop depends on a poor fit between voice-place and voicing, a mis-alignment which sets off the voice, making it 'stick out'. This salience of voice can be heard most clearly when a single voice site is attributed with multiple voicings. One example would be Alicia Bridges' 1978 disco classic 'I Love the Nightlife' (1979). On the chorus Bridges sings in a tremulous vibrato. She switches to a cool mellifluous tone for the verse section and then, enouncing the word 'action' at the bottom of a long, descending vocal line 47 seconds into the song, interjects a guttural, third voice. This apparently small trope takes on huge significance. It becomes the 'hook' of the song, its affective fulcrum – even its political centre in that Bridges is advocating Action over and against Romance.

Perhaps this is too good an example. It shows such a strong articulation of site against sound that it can hardly be typical of the work-a-day voicing I am saying is inherent in pop. To illustrate this one might think about how music sounds when voice disappears. The most common experience of such a loss comes from listening to pop music which we know very well and that has been important in earlier life. Here site and sound are so strongly correlated with our own subjectivity that the actual voice (deriving from music's objective location in the field of the social) disappears. On the other hand in the case of the appropriation of old musical materials by musicians, voice can come back. What seems to be at work here is uneasy listening, the opening of a gap between site and sound through which voice jumps up.[8]

To return to Bakhtin, we might say that the way the sound of voice is articulated and rearticulated with its place-time in popular music is actually a form of citation. Strangely enough, Adorno (1990) proposes something similar when he talks about Tin Pan Alley pop being nothing but 'the schematic buildup' of 'pre-digested' parts (305). We are told that 'a musical detail which is not permitted to develop becomes a caricature of its own potentialities' (304). Up to a point. As usual Adorno homes in, and loads opprobrium on, a key aspect of the popular music aesthetic, namely the fact that parts (or 'voices' in the approach I am taking here) are always already used. But this means precisely that they have social value, that they are recognized by a community of producers and listeners (Hirschkop 1989: 297–9). 'Predigested' thus turns out to be an aesthetic good. What's more Adorno ignores the reflexivity and articulation at stake in caricature. In popular music hook lines, formulae, hack devices, colours are always being picked up, turned over and made to re-sound. So it goes when Alicia Bridges sings '. . . action'. Voice-sound grates against the place of voice and the banal tips over into the sublime.

How does all this affect our understanding of popular music authorship? I said at the beginning of the section that possibles in the field of musical works are analogous to the multiple languages deployed by the author of a novel. Both are historically given materials. Now we have a better idea of what this might mean, namely that *voice*, in its endemically dialogic state, is the building block of musical possibility. Once again Bakhtin's discussion of the novel provides an illuminating comparison. According to Bakhtin the novelist speaks 'through language, a language that has somehow more or less materialized, become objectified' (1981: 299). Using 'words that are already populated with the social intentions of others [the author] compels them to serve his [sic] own new intentions' (300). If we substitute the terms music for language and voice for word we have an extremely useful starting point from which to investigate authorship in popular music. On the one hand the argument that intention is socially circumscribed enables us to meet Barthes' (1976a) powerful criticism of expressivism. We can agree that the musical text is an amalgam of possibilities – possible voices, that it is, from the field of musical works. But on the other hand, we still have the social necessity of organization – the putting together of voices with aesthetic intent.

This formula represents what I am calling social authorship. The social author stands at the centre of a radius of creativity, but the range and scale of voices available to her/him/them will always be strongly determined by the compass and position of the radius on the musical field. Perhaps the biggest advantage of treating popular music authorship in such a way is that it enables one to be sceptical about grand claims to creative inspiration (sometimes made by musicians themselves) without discarding the notion of agency.

In the next section we will take up this approach in a case study of jazz composer, band leader and bass player Charles Mingus. Mingus is an emblematic figure in the genealogy of post-war popular music authorship. His case is ideal, if not typical, for two reasons. First, it involves a particularly thorough-going citation of voices. Authors in different popular genres and in other periods may cite less often, less reflexively and with a weaker sense of the possibilities of combination, but they all share that capacity to speak *through* musical voice which marks out the popular form and separates it from most forms of art music. In treating Mingus, then, the issues at stake in vocalization emerge in strong relief. The second reason for examining him is that despite being a neurotic and an often unhappy man he was able to successfully organize musicians and their voices in collective musical endeavour. Mingus is thus an excellent example of the social author who can put together possibilities even as he identifies them within the 'Mingus radius of creativity'.

Mingus Fingers

You, my audience, are all a bunch of poppaloppas. . . . All of you sit there digging yourselves and each other, looking around hoping to be seen and observed as hip. You become the object you came to see, and you think you're important and digging jazz when all the time all you're doing is digging a blind, deaf scene that has nothing to do with any kind of music at all. . . .
(Charles Mingus quoted by Dorr-Dorynek 1987: 16–17)

Running to more than two pages in its edited form this diatribe delivered to a noisy nightclub audience in 1959 has a curiously contemporary ring. It is the sound of the heroic gripe, the characteristic tone of the popular music *auteur* railing against a world which will not acknowledge him. Mingus chastises the audience for having misrecognized its own function, namely the appreciation of 'any kind of music at all'. Of course the inference is that his music is very much more, that it constitutes, as he says later, 'another language, so much more wide in range and vivid, and warm and full and expressive of thoughts you are seldom able to convey' (18). Now it seems to me that this judgement carries precisely the post-Romantic rhetoric of expression and genius which Barthes (1976a) finds so intolerable. The artist is a 'full' subject, endowed with an inner vitality which enables him to keep faith with what it is to be human when all around are philistines. Yet at the same time there is the kernel of something else. When Mingus says he deals in *'language ... wide in range and vivid'* (italics added) a weaker, more demotic author is suggested, an organizer of voices rather than an expressing machine.

From this point of audition perhaps Mingus's most animated voice is that of his own instrument, the double bass. In be-bop and after, the rhythmic function of the bass was a distillation of its role in swing. The walking, four to the bar figure which had first emerged during the early 1930s carried an even greater burden in the modern form as drummers now dropped snare and bass drum 'bombs' around the beat rather than playing on it. In this context groove depended very much on the disjunction between the four-beat pattern played on the ride cymbal and that of the string bass. Drummers might tap slightly ahead or slightly behind the pulsive walking bass in order to generate that inexorable forward motion which defines a swinging groove (Keil 1994a: 60–7). Dannie Richmond, Mingus's long-serving drummer, makes a similar point, but attributes the working-against-pulse to the bass player: 'I could see that he stayed completely on top of the beat, so much so that, in order for the tempos not to accelerate ... I had to lay back a bit, and at the same time, let my stroke be on the same downbeat as his, but just a fraction behind it' (quoted in Priestley 1985: 95).

Mingus's bass voice is doubly cited here: first through a misalignment between the place of bass (by convention this is restrained, set in the background) and the bluff and forceful voicing which emerges from it; second because that voice is produced in and against another voice, namely Dannie Richmond's cymbal play. We might say that the condition of possibility of Mingus's individualism as a player is dialogue.[9]

This use of dialogue can be heard in the voices of other jazz players to varying degrees. But what makes Mingus so significant as a social author is that from the mid-1950s he uses the bass as a *narrative* voice, making it unfurl each episode in the extended pieces which he now starts to write. During such announcing moments the bass often takes on the characteristics of other instruments. A good example of this can be heard on the first studio recording of 'Haitian Fight Song' from 1957 (Mingus 1957). The piece begins with a bass solo consisting of a string of 'blues guitar licks'. There are leaps into the upper register of the instrument and copious note bending before Mingus introduces, tentatively, a four-bar riff which builds in volume and sure-footedness over three cycles until trombone and alto sax present an answering riff with a skittering 12/4 feel. During the solos from the lead instruments which follow, Mingus keeps on interjecting one or other of these riffs into the standard walking bass line, alternately urging the soloists on or pulling them back. Finally in his own solo towards the end Mingus cites blues guitar again before introducing a climactic ensemble coda consisting of the two riffs heard in the introduction.

In effect, then, the role of narrator is enacted in the voices of others. Either the bass adopts an accent from outside the ensemble – that of blues guitar – or it anticipates and parodies the voicings of the band's own brass section by playing 'their' riffs. Yet all the while timbre and rhythmic attack carry the signature, *Mingus*.

If much of Mingus's own playing is concerned with citation the same principle seems to be at work in the selection and direction of instrumentalists. Above all, he wants to hear distinctive voices. Jackie McLean, alto saxophonist on the 1957 'Haitian Fight Song' sessions, explains how the band leader would constantly push him beyond the conventions of be-bop style: 'I hadn't been content with what I was doing with changes yet, and here comes Mingus telling me, "Forget changes and forget about what key you're in," and "all notes are right" and things like that, and it kind of threw me. . . . Mingus gave me my wings, more or less' (quoted in Rosenthal 1993: 122).

Interestingly, though, the kind of innovation Mingus wanted from his musicians had much less to do with formal avant-gardism than with their finding an idiom, that is to say a voice already heard. The sour tone of McLean, the acerbic and even more harmonically wayward style of Eric Dolphy, his preferred alto player in the early 1960s, or the smeary legato of trombonist Jimmy Knepper constituted quite particular, locatable voices. Like Duke Ellington, Mingus was always trying to construct a soundscape out of the characteristic dialects of his instrumentalists. Perhaps the major compositional method of both these jazz *auteurs* was the organization of a dialogical environment in which the musicians were obliged to speak as 'themselves'.

Dialogue, in the more literal sense of antiphonal exchanges on the model of everyday conversation, can be found in the Mingus oeuvre too. One of the most startling examples occurs in a studio recording of 'What Love' from 1960 (Mingus n/d), when after Eric Dolphy's solo an argument breaks out between his bass clarinet and the leader's bass. Over the next four minutes the pair exchange simulated curses, entreaties, outraged bellows and finally tender solicitations before the ensemble returns with a statement of the melody.[10]

I talked in the previous section about the placed aspect of voice, the attachment of voicing to person, region, period, mood etc. This aspect becomes very important in Mingus's work. Beginning with 'Haitian Fight Song' a group of tunes ('Better Git It In Your Soul' (1998/1959), 'Slop' (1998/1960), 'Wednesday Night Prayer Meeting' (1960), 'Eclusiastics' (1962)) summon up the sound of the Holiness churches which he had attended as a child (Mingus 1995). In these pieces the bass player calls out to the band or audience in the manner of a preacher: sometimes he shouts 'Jesus!' or 'I Know!' as though testifying to a strong and certain faith. Hand claps 'from the congregation' over stop time or as sole accompaniment to riffs and solos intensify the impression of church. On 'Folk Forms No. 1' (n/d) Dannie Richmond knocks out a snare drum figure modelled on a tambourine pattern used by gospel choirs. Taken together these tropes have a powerful effect. This is partly a matter of intertextuality – we hear snatches of sacred music – but it also has to do with the production of presence; not so much an 'authentic' realization of a church as a staged one, even, in Brecht's (1978) sense, a gested church.

Quite apart from these invocations of church, Mingus's compositions show an extraordinary breadth of reference to place and period. There are several more or less strict 12 bar blues among the sanctified series – 'Haitian Fight Song' for example – as well as other 'secular' blues. On 'Hog Callin' Blues' (1960) pig and whistle sound effects establish a Southern rustic milieu. Pieces which refer to early jazz include 'Jelly Rolls' (1998/1959), whose archaic melody is redolent of the work of Jelly Roll Morton, and 'Eat That Chicken' (1962) which picks up the jokey, hokey style of Fats Waller with vocal choruses and a fruity tenor sax solo from Roland Kirk. The theme of 'Fables of Faubus' (1998/1959) conjures up, in terms of line, harmony and metre, a Kurt Weill march in *The Threepenny Opera* (Weill 1966) – the 'Anstatt-dass-Song' perhaps. A later version, 'Original Faubus Fables' (Mingus n/d) has a lyric poking fun at a racist governor of Alabama and rendered in guttural half-song which brings it even closer to the Brecht–Weill model. Finally, on *[New] Tijuana Moods* (1987/1962) and *The Black Saint and the Sinner Lady* (1995/1963) Spanish, Latin-American and Caribbean musics are cited throughout: there are episodes of pasodoble, calypso, flamenco and mariachi music. On the latter there is some high romantic piano – shades of Rachmaninov perhaps.

It is clear, then, that dialogue and citation abound in the Mingus oeuvre. There is a constant sense of field beyond the text, of voice as place and as historical moment. The references are both musical – to genres, authors, instrumental voices – and extramusical – they gesture towards locale or to political events. The 'thickness' of the best of the work derives from this heteroglossia; precisely not a matter of eclecticism or the piling up of sources, but rather of what Bakhtin (1981) calls 'interanimation' – the sounding of one voice in and through another.

I suggested earlier that Mingus can be considered an ideal (if not typical) example of the social author. It seems to me that there are two aspects to this. First, he is engaged in a political project. By incorporating black genres from the past he helps to construct a history of African-American music-making which maps, at one and the same time, a black American 'structure of feeling' (Williams 1965). The cycle of church songs, for example, does not testify to the immanent presence of God so much as call on the audience to witness the social reality of black oppression on earth. And yet, at one and the same time, these numbers are joyous, affirmative, hard swinging. They propose a utopia beyond domination.

Writing in the early 1960s LeRoi Jones does something rather similar to Mingus. In *Blues People* (1995/1963) he identifies a strong continuity between musical form and the social history of African-Americans. Like the Mingus albums of the same period the book delineates a powerful cultural tradition which encompasses the vicissitudes of diaspora, from slavery to the struggle for civil rights. For both Mingus and Jones a key aspect of this journey is the way that musical diversity and hybridity are produced *through* the tradition. Actually, what Jones will later call 'the changing same' of black American music (Gilroy 1993: 101) is already being charted by Mingus in the mid-1950s, namely repetition and variation across black genres and musical voices. Yet in an important sense Mingus can reach further than Jones. As a musician, the techniques of musical dialogism which he develops enable him to produce a *pan*-diasporic utopian imaginary in which flamenco, European cabaret and Mexican table dancing are spoken through a black American voice. In effect, he listens out across a global field of musical works to construct a cosmopolitan network of possibility, and in so doing centres himself. That is one reason why Mingus is such an important author, an African-American who constructs a grand union of musical otherness in opposition to white and monoglot culture.

The second aspect of Mingus's social authorship has to do with forms of design and production in popular music. Crucially, Mingus arranges collective and individual voices in a new synthesis which anticipates the mid-1960s revolution in thinking about how music might be *put together*.[11]

Mingus began to write and arrange for his own bands under the shadow of be-bop in the mid-1950s. Be-bop was, of course, pre-eminently improvised music. But unlike early jazz in which improvisation was mainly collective, or swing where soloists were circumscribed by the constant intervention of the ensemble, in post-war jazz players are heroic individualists. In the work of musicians like Charlie Parker, Dizzy Gillespie or Bud Powell technical virtuosity and improvisatory stamina are elevated to a central position. Obliged to go on ringing the creative changes for chorus after chorus there's even a sense of desperation about bop soloists. They fly in the knowledge that they might fall back to earth at any moment. However the biggest danger is a pedestrian performance, the mere 'blowing session' which relies on stock phrases or 'licks', and follows the harmonic progression of the song – whether a blues or 32-bar standard – too obviously. We might say that for a modern jazz improviser the main constraint on creativity is the attraction of those regularly selected possibles which are located near the centre of the radius.

Mingus establishes himself as an *auteur* in opposition to such a tendency. The problem he faces is a double one – how to renew the ground of improvisation while moving beyond the now restrictive form of the standard or blues. Of course Mingus is not alone in dealing with these issues. Other pivotal jazz musicians respond by leaving behind what are taken to be the constraints of form *tout court*. Ornette Coleman abandons harmonic development, while John Coltrane turns to scales based on augmented harmonies, and then uses modal forms before ending up, like Coleman, in a 'free', unstructured environment.[12] What distinguishes Mingus is his social approach to the problem of innovation in mid-century jazz. As a composer/arranger his prime technique is to elicit a collective surplus from his musicians, in other words more than they could be expected to give within the terms of the solo-over-rhythm-section mode of bop. It is worth examining what this means because Mingus's working methods, to a greater extent than those of the more organic or univocal jazz *auteurs* just mentioned, pave the way for rock production, and therefore increasingly for popular music in general. He makes two related innovations here. He insists on working out quite complex arrangements orally, and he makes use of tape editing to overdub, lengthen and rearrange pieces in the post-production stage.[13]

Considering the first point first, Mingus generally rehearsed his musicians without using a score. The extent to which he initially wrote down compositions remains unclear, but in any case he would introduce them to the band by singing or playing the melody line for each instrument. Musicians had to learn their parts by ear without even a chord chart to refer to. On one tune where he contributed a solo the alto sax player, John Handy, claims not to have known the proper chord sequence at all (Sidran 1995/1971: 131). As for structure it seems that this emerged through a combination of oral instructions and collective decision-making. In the early days, for instance before the recording of *Pithecanthropus Erectus* (Mingus 1956), the band would spend a considerable time in rehearsal in order to work out arrangements (Priestley 1985: 76–7). But as Mingus built up a reservoir of musicians who had some experience of his methods progress became quicker. Of the *Blues and Roots* sessions in 1959, where nine players were involved, baritone saxophonist Pepper Adams said:

> If there was any music written down, I don't remember having seen any of it . . . I don't recall any rehearsal, there may have been one. But, with Charles, everything got changed up by the time you got to the record date, anyway. So having a rehearsal was really not of much benefit for the most part.
>
> (Quoted by Priestley 1985: 109)

In fact this 'changing up' continued right through to the moment of performance. Many of the gospel-style shouts in both live and studio performances were instructions to the band. For example on 'Cryin' Blues' (1960) Mingus brings the ensemble back at the end of the piece by repeatedly yelling, 'Going home'. Again the double voice: this time Mingus is both intervening in the production process in the studio and gesturing towards another genre within the text itself.

In an important sense composition, improvisation and recording are elided in the Mingus method. Not only does the process of writing go on during performance, but it also continues at the recording stage. Mingus is unusual among jazz *auteurs* in his free use of tape editing, a technique realized most completely on *The Black Saint and the Sinner Lady* (1963). Brian Priestley has documented the extent not only of splicing – which enabled the repetition or extension of certain passages – but of overdubs too: Charlie Mariano's alto sax breaks were added a week after the ensemble had first performed (1985: 154–5). Yet what is interesting is that the editing aesthetic is already implicit in Mingus's earlier work. As Gunther Schuller (1986) points out, so-called 'extended form' on the *Pithecanthropus Erectus* and *Clown* albums depends on the repetition of one part of a chord pattern until 'the soloist or the "composer" feels that the development of the piece requires moving on to another idea' (21). An associated trope, the introduction of riffs during a solo to produce a drawn-out, antiphonal tension, also has this aspect of improvised composition. As a composer, then, Mingus improvises dynamics and plays with time, stretching the faculties of his players as much as the form of a piece. Musical dialogue between voices is in quite a crude sense a correlate of the social dialogue which Mingus supervises during production.

What conclusions can we reach about Mingus as a social author? Most importantly, I think we need to abandon the idea of expression from within, which has become a commonplace amongst popular musicians, fans and critics – especially in jazz and rock. Mingus, putatively a self-sufficient creator, in fact works with colloquial voices. Even the voice of his own instrument is employed as part of a dialogue, or spoken through. We might say, then, that authorship consists in the selection and combination of what is 'out there', that is possible voices, more or less difficult to hear, in the field of works. Conceived in this way authorial intention certainly persists. In part it is an effect of the Mingus habitus, partly it derives from the exigencies of the jazz scene. Most of all we can hear it pushing forwards in the gap between these two. But whatever its source the crucial point is that intention will now be refracted as it jostles its way through the social data of voices, players and techniques *en route* to the realization of the work. As Bourdieu says, talking about literary authorship, 'these freedoms [to select possibles] augment each other in the billiard game of structured interactions, thus opening a place ... for strategies capable of subverting the established distribution of chances and profits in favour of the available margin of manoeuvre' (1996: 239).

This makes social authorship much more complex than expression. Charles Mingus not only has to select voices but also to *integrate* them, even as they are reverberating one against another. At times such integration appears spontaneous; it is done quickly and without much time for reflection. At other moments it is a more studied process. But in either case what counts is the ability to collate voices in a chorus which is redolent with utopian possibility. Above all the method is historical. Hearing backwards, the Mingus oeuvre affirms both continuity and variation, suffering and the transcendence of suffering, in the African-American musical tradition. Blowing forwards, it projects a cosmopolitan alliance of Other voices into the future.

It would be wrong to consider the organization of heteroglossia as a seamless process though. On 10 October 1962, two days before a specially commissioned concert in New York for large band, Mingus punched Jimmy Knepper in the mouth, breaking a tooth and destroying the trombonist's embouchure. Knepper's offence was to suggest, having already copied many parts for the concert and now faced with a demand to write new material, that the composer should be responsible for scoring his own work (Priestley 1985: 147). Earlier I pointed to a split within Mingus the author-subject. On one side a self-mythologizing, embattled hero, on the other a social organizer of musical voices. The Knepper incident suggests that this schism was not just a matter of the troubled Mingus psyche (important though that was), but also had to do with contradictions which are deeply inscribed in the practice of popular music authorship as it emerged in this period. As well as being an outrageous act of violence, the assault on Jimmy Knepper was an enactment of these tensions.

Performance – theatre and process

So far in the chapter I have not made a distinction between authorship and performance. For in an important sense it is the elision of these moments which distinguishes popular music's mode of production. Mingus makes such a good example of the popular creator for that reason. It is difficult to separate thinking-up from sounding-out in his practice – they run together. Still, even though it is often difficult to separate it as a practical activity we ought to examine performance as an orientation, a way of going about music-making.[14] In fact I would argue that considered in this way performance is central to the aesthetics of pop. There are two aspects to it. First, the term can refer to process, the ongoing nature of musical production which we have already noticed in Mingus's work. From this perspective performance hints at the uncompleted nature of pop – the fact that there tend not to be great works so much as versions, mixes and shifting genres. In short, performance refers to creation-in-*progress*. Second, popular music-making has a theatricality about it. There is a self-conscious awareness on the part of musicians and audience of the gap between them, a gap which even the most naturalistic of performers in the most intimate of environments (a pub back room, say) have to confront. From this perspective creation includes the struggle by musicians to *get across* to an audience.

So, performance mediates creativity and pushes authors into taking account of it. The stark contrast here is with classical music where performance is not only a separate activity from composition but also cast in a subservient role to it. Actually, this difference in the relationship of performance and authorship between classical music and pop opens up some useful lines of inquiry. We ought to begin by examining them.

The most important element in classical music is the *musical work* written by a composer who is only incidentally a performer. Historically, the institutions of the work and the great composer emerged during the romantic movement, gathering strength over the course of the nineteenth century. As embodied in the score, the work represents an ideal form of music because it is supposed to show the pure intention of the composer expressed at the level of the musical idea. This is the cult of the author in its strongest form with performance cast as a supplicant activity, an attempt to realize the truth of the work, and behind it the composer's intention, in sound. However such an attempt can never fully succeed because it is precisely its ideational, unrealized state which encapsulates the purity of the work (Goehr 1992).

Christopher Small sketches out some implications for performance of this elevation of the work. To begin with he notes that there has been a 'virtual freezing of the repertory' (1987a: 7). As audiences have become less and less responsive to contemporary music during the twentieth century so a static canon of works, mainly from the nineteenth, has been constructed. This canon is ritually confirmed and passed on through the medium of the concert and, in particular, through the spatial organization of the concert hall. Small points to the way that performers and audience are seated in opposing arcs with 'the conductor's podium . . . at the point of intersection of the two foci of attention, the power centre of the entire proceedings' (9). In effect the (long dead) composer's intention is re-enacted by a series of performance units: first the score – the mark of the composer's presence; then the conductor – a manager-priest who administers that presence; next the musicians – servile operatives who follow the score as it is interpreted for them; and finally the audience – passive receivers of this doubly re-inforced re-presentation.

Significantly, the big disputes in classical music performance have not been about challenging this system so much as trying to make it work, even to enforce it. Clearly the institution of the conductor in the mid-nineteenth century as a mediator on behalf of the composer was crucial here. In the 1850s Berlioz specified that he must be entirely visible to the whole orchestra, and stressed the importance of facial expression as a means of command (Attali 1985: 66–7). By the 1930s the conductor Wilhelm Furtwängler was arguing that his rival Arturo Toscanini's 'literal render-ings' of the score were platitudinous. 'Anyone satisfied with the "notes" knows nothing of the secret of the great works.' Beyond mere submission to the score Furtwängler offered to capture 'the sense and spirit of the music'

(Furtwängler 1989: 68), a sense which depended on 'living reality, i.e. . . . the great man' (71). In other words the conductor intercedes for the composer, striving to maintain his presence.

How is this composition–performance system different from the arrangement in popular music? The most obvious distinction has to do with the status of the work. Over the course of pop's short twentieth century there has been a progressive shift in emphasis away from the scored song-work towards the song-performance realized on record and broadcast. We can map this shift in terms of changing music industry structure, especially the decline of publishing and the concomitant rise of record companies and other music-using media (Sanjek 1988).

In a discussion of the aesthetics of rock music Theodore Gracyk (1996) offers one way of understanding such a development. He argues that in rock the work now consists primarily in the recording. It is an 'autographic' work because *'the history of production rather than notational determination is the key to individuating the work'* (1996: 32, original emphasis). Directly controlled by musicians, recording represents a single stage of writing down in sound. The other side of the coin for Gracyk is that performance withers away. As he puts it, '[t]hese musical works are *played* on appropriate machines, not performed' (18). In other words we get to hear identical versions of the recording-work through the medium of phonographic reproduction, not discrete renditions of a piece in performance as in classical music.

I think Gracyk is right to highlight the central significance of the record, and to suggest that 'live' is the exception rather than the rule in rock (see also Frith 1983, 1988a, Mowett 1989, Chanan 1994, Thornton 1995, Auslander 1996). But he is wrong to try to hold on to a notion of the authentic and original work, even when it is identified with the recording. Quite simply, a strong performative element inheres in recording and other kinds of mediation which makes Gracyk's notion of the work as a singular and authentic expression of artist intention rather beside the point.

Above all, modern popular music, including rock, is *processive* music. It is constructed in a sequence of multiple takes, overdubs and editing, and is then distributed across different kinds of media. Actually this process varies considerably as stages are compressed or articulated in different ways (see Wurtzler 1992). The result is that there tend to be many manifestations of a song-performance. We noted the emergence of some of them in the discussion of the cross-media star in Chapter 1. Here is a longer, although by no means exhaustive, list of types. Some involve recombination with other types:

- recording played at home (including album, various single versions and re-mixes),
- radio broadcast of recordings,
- radio broadcast of specially recorded session,
- music video,

- live concert,
- live concert recording,
- live concert broadcast,
- club record play by DJ as part of long mix.

Gracyk would have it that these are all 'instantiations' of a primary recorded work (25). However there are at least two problems with this. First, we do not generally hold the evidence needed to show which is the true work – that is, according to Gracyk, the version intended as authoritative by its author(s) (51–3). In fact it is unlikely that most popular musicians, even album-oriented rock bands, consider their work in this way.

Second, Gracyk does not properly deal with the problem of music as mental construct. The blues in E, 'Love Train', the breakbeat, a really dirty overdriven valve amp guitar sound: these will be manifested in sound form on a recording, but they can also take the shape of musical *ideas* capable of being realized by music makers in different versions, times and places. The big difference with classical music is that such mental constructs do not have priority, that is they are not created before performance, but in and through it. As a result musical ideas have a temporary and fluid existence in pop.[15] They are always being abstracted from a concrete sounding only to be sounded again in different but connected ways in the next recording, re-mix or other performance context.

This links back to voice. I said earlier that voice has two aspects: site and sound. Now I want to add a third. For popular music makers voice is also the voiced idea or imagined sounding. Its temporary and fluid existence is a product of the fact that, as Gracyk points out, it is extremely difficult to keep in mind particular sounds (1996: 58–61). Again the contrast is with classical music where composers and players not only use kinaesthetic schemata and readings of the score, but are also able to make normative assumptions about the timbre of particular instruments in order to imagine musical sounds in quite a precise fashion (Cook 1990: 71–121). For popular musicians on the other hand a voicing, in whatever combination of parameters and at whatever unit length, is much more effervescent and contingent. In order for it to be sustained and developed it needs to be constantly 'played back'.

All this is by way of suggesting that Gracyk both under-estimates and over-estimates recording. He under-estimates it because he fails to hear recording, or more generally the mediation of music, as part of a continuous process of performance and creation. We will return to this point in a moment. Gracyk then over-estimates the importance of recording in that he treats individual records as though they were the great works of great authors. Much of this chapter has been concerned with showing the weakness of such a view.

We have just been examining the processive side of performance. I want to turn now to its other aspect, the *theatrical*, with which it is intimately linked. Indeed, I would argue that the relationship between them is central to popular music aesthetics. By the theatrical I mean the way that music-making is staged as something performed *by* musicians *for* an audience. What counts here is the knowledge that music is not only being made, but being made to be heard, and sometimes to be seen too. To put it another way, the theatricality of popular music performance derives from performers conceiving themselves as performers and audience members thinking that they are members of an audience. Richard Schechner describes performance as 'behaviour heightened, if ever so slightly, and publicly displayed; twice behaved behaviour' (quoted by Abercrombie and Longhurst 1998: 40). I think this broad definition gets at popular music's theatricality quite well; it can be applied to all kinds of performance, from camp to naturalistic.

Now in one sense there is a tension between the theatrical and the processive. Theatrical performance represents a punctuation in the continuum of production-mediation-distribution we have been examining. There is an implicit injunction which runs, 'Stop, and listen to us making these sounds!' This is clearly true of live performance, but it also applies to recordings which should, ideally, *arrest* the listener and impose a theatrical relation of audiencehood even in the banal and comfortable setting of the home. We might say (*pace* Marx) that the record is congealed performance.

However on another plane, inside the radius of creativity, the two aspects of performance converge. For here, even as the music maker begins to identify and select possible voices, s/he is anticipating how they will sound. In other words social authorship of the kind I described earlier in the chapter also includes an element of performance to the self (as other). Howard Becker's concept of the 'editorial moment' offers a useful way of understanding this phenomenon (1982: 198–212). For Becker the key juncture in art-making is the moment of choice before a creative action. As he suggests, 'developments [during the origination of a piece] contain an infinity of choices we might investigate; the sum of those choices is the work' (199). So far we are quite close to Bourdieu's position. Choices are like possibles which may be selected and combined to produce a piece. But Becker goes further by pointing to the way that choices are not usually made by reference to a set of rules of artistic production. Nor does there tend to be a well developed language with which to reflect on choices. As he points out:

> Jazz musicians say that something does or does not 'swing'; theater people say that a scene 'works' or does not 'work'. In neither case can even the most knowledgeable participant explain to someone not familiar with the terms' uses what they mean.
>
> (1982: 199)

What does give these terms meaning, however, is a practical understanding of common standards, an understanding derived from orienting oneself towards the likely reaction of the audience. Becker shows the importance of this in a discussion of photography. Here practitioners have to learn 'to recognize consciously what others will respond to more or less unwittingly' (201). Antoine Hennion (1990/1983) notices a similar phenomenon at work in a popular music recording session where, as he puts it, 'the aim of the entire organization of production is *to introduce the public into the studio*'. Members of the production team, from engineers to singers, act as audience for one another. They also engage in what Hennion calls '*collective anticipation* (the dynamics of the group constitute a first production–consumption which one hopes will repeat itself first through the media and later among the public)' (203, original emphasis).

What writers like Becker and Hennion are suggesting, then, is that creative action has a performative dimension right from the start. There must always be a notion of the audience, in other words a consciousness of another who will attend to the music one is making. This is a key point for the present argument. It represents another nail banged into the coffin of expressionism. For not only are voice-ingredients located in the social world, so too is the creative act. Never a pure enactment of subjective intention, it must, as a condition of its possibility, have an awareness of itself as a performed act in a social milieu, at a particular time and place.

Performance – loud, clear and interrupted

Performers in popular music may or may not see it like this though. Sometimes artists reflect on their own performativity, but in other cases what counts is 'just doing it'. In fact what makes the short twentieth century of popular music so interesting is the sheer diversity of performance strategies that have emerged. Each has handled the question of the nature of performance and the extent to which this should be foregrounded in quite a different way. These strategies range from the mediated sincerity of the radio crooner in the 1920s, 1930s and 1940s (Scannell 1996) through the virtuosic showmanship of the heavy metal guitarist (Walser 1993) to the reserved shamanism of the contemporary club DJ (Chapter 5). Now at one level such diverse approaches to performance represent adaption to new music media. However this is never a matter of simple response to changing technology. Different performance aesthetics are also strongly axiological. Each makes exclusive claims to performative validity, each criticizes other modes of performance. And usually, because practical questions of performance arise in relation to mediation, arguments return to the uses and abuses of technology.

By way of opening up some of these issues I want to examine one particular performance aesthetic, 'rock authenticity', and the critique that has been made of it in popular music studies (Frith 1983, 1986, but see also Goodwin 1992, Thornton 1995, Auslander 1996). A good place to start might be Simon Frith's essay, 'Art versus technology', where he makes the following observation.

> The continuing core of rock ideology is that raw sounds are more authentic than cooked sounds. This is a paradoxical belief for a technologically sophisticated medium and rests on an old-fashioned model of communication – A plays to B and the less technology lies between them the closer they are.
>
> (1986: 266–7)

I think this deconstructs very effectively a strong naturalistic discourse where, for instance, Humbucker pickups and Marshall valve amplifiers are treated as though they were timeless craftsman's tools, while the use of sampling or sequencing technologies is considered to be a form of trickery. Of course Frith's point is that such a distinction is ideological. In other words it is not just a false way of thinking, but also implicated in relations of power. Hard-rocking guys consider their authentic mode of performance to be *superior* to manufactured forms of pop. As Frith suggests, what is at stake here is 'the slide from "fakery" in terms of technology to "fakery" in terms of commercial manipulation' (267) – an ideological move if ever there was one.

Now on the one hand this line of argument has been very effective in deflating rock elitism and the uncritical celebration of 'real' music. But on the other hand it has led to a rather repetitive deconstruction of authenticity in popular music. Here are two quite recent examples. In her book on dance music culture Sarah Thornton (1995) devotes a chapter to deconstructing the enculturation of technology in post-war pop. She shows, in an illuminating historical account, how successive generations of musicians and fans have struggled to 'authenticate' their own appropriation of technology (26–86). Invoking Baudrillard, Phillip Auslander suggests that authentication has actually unravelled in recent years.

> In the case of live and mediatized performance, the result of implosion [a term used by Baudrillard to suggest that representation and reality have merged in the contemporary era] is that a seemingly secure opposition is now a site of anxiety, an anxiety that infects all who have an interest in maintaining the distinction between the live and the mediatized.
>
> (1996: 203)

The central assumption of both these discussions is the notion that media technologies have fomented crises of authentic communication amongst a silent majority of 'sonic conservatives'. People are constantly being thrown into doubt about the ground of performance. However I want to argue that the aesthetics of pop performance cannot be reduced to this issue. It is not that technology and mediatization are unimportant as we will see in the next chapter, just that they are implicated in a larger question concerning the *possibility* of performance *qua* performance. The banal but vitally important point to keep hold of is that musicians continue to believe in the possibility of getting across to an audience in the postmodern era. Audiences continue to believe in the possibility of being touched. Yet both have reason to doubt how far this authentic relation (in which real communication takes place) can be completely realized in performance – whether live or mediated, naturalistic or camp as anything. This is partly a matter of competence. Performances may simply not be good enough in the sense of reaching a notional threshold of accomplishment. As Simon Frith suggests, '[p]erformers always face the threat of the ultimate embarrassment: *the performance that doesn't work*' (1996: 214, original emphasis).

But why such a breakdown might occur is not necessarily clear. Performance criteria often remain unenumerated (nobody can say what they are, as Becker observes) or their relative weighting may be disputed even within a small taste community. Moreover, well established music makers with excellent track records can, and often do, generate bad performances, while if a performance is great the reason is generally more opaque than in the case of a bad one. The point is that there seems to be something about the performance relationship which is fundamentally volatile, given to interruption and undecideability.

In order to investigate this problem I want to refer to Jacques Derrida's essay, 'Signature Event Context' (1991). Here Derrida deconstructs the common-sense view of writing as communication, that is a system for transporting ideas. His initial move is to emphasize the central importance of absence for writing. One writes because one is absent from the addressee. Of course, as Derrida points out, all signs suppose absence (they stand in for presence). But because writing consists pre-eminently in the negotiation of absence, then it should be considered a *primary* sign system, and the model for all forms of communication (84–90).

What kind of absence is at stake here? As conventionally understood, writing mitigates absence by maintaining an approximation of presence, an approximation which is represented by the mark of the written word. Against this notion Derrida argues that writing actually supposes a *radical* form of absence. This is because writing is premised on iterability, in other words the fact that someone other than the addressee can read the writing: an absent other. The same factor applies in respect of the sender. If the author changes her mind about a message or dies, the writing continues to act. Derrida argues that such complete absence of original intention and context is a pre-condition of writing as a system (90–4).

Deconstruction of the concept of communication along these lines has become quite a well known critical approach by now. It informs large areas of cultural studies, including the authenticity critique in work on popular music. But, and this is the crucial point, there is a postscript to Derrida's essay, and to deconstruction more generally, which is not often acknowledged by communication sceptics.

People sign letters or mark their names on books and articles. By extension they have an 'oral "signature" that is, or allegedly is, the presence of the "author" as the "person who does the uttering"' (Derrida 1991: 107). Signatures are thus a mark of absolute hereness and nowness. Each signature invokes the singular presence of the addressor. Yet, as Derrida has already argued, this is an impossibility because writing, of which the signature is an instance, supposes iterability and absence. Still, people do sign their names, they do speak as though they were present. Derrida's conclusion is therefore not that signature effects are impossible, but that '[t]he condition of possibility for these effects is *simultaneously*, once again, the condition of their impossibility, of the impossibility of their rigorous purity' (107, my emphasis).

For present purposes the big advantage of Derrida's approach to writing is that it can be directly applied to musical performance. Music has all those attributes of (or pretensions to) communicative facility which Derrida discusses in relation to writing. Its 'alogenic' nature and weakness as a denotative system (Born 1987) which would distinguish it from ordinary language in a semiotic approach are simply not relevant here. What does count is music's iterability and therefore the fact that, while it is premised on absence and a profound gap between performer and audience, musical performances none the less persist.[16] Crucially, these conditions apply in every form of mediation: to live music as much as recorded, to broadcasting as much as to the music score.

The question is, how do performers cope with all this? The short answer is through a range of different strategies, several of which we have encountered already. To understand their rationale and the relations between them I want to set up a model of popular music performance types (Figure 2.2). If one imagines a communication model such as Laswell's (McQuail 1994: 50) which shows a continuous axis or channel of communication running left to right, from sender to receiver, then in Figure 2.2 the axis has fractured in the middle. (The diagram is really an attempt to demonstrate graphically the Derridean notion of communication interrupted.) As in a splintered branch there are now *two* axes which intersect at an oblique angle, but also overshoot one another.

The diagonal axis represents performance considered in relation to origination. It extends from the moment of emergence of the performative act in the subject at the bottom left of the axis (marked 'Origin/the Subject') into the process of performance where intention is mediated and transformed towards the top right of the axis.

Located around Origin is what might be called the *expressionist* mode of performance. It is concerned with truth to the subject, a full issuing out of music from the inner being. Expressionists believe, above all, in asserting presence, a goal which as we have just heard is contradicted by iteration, the

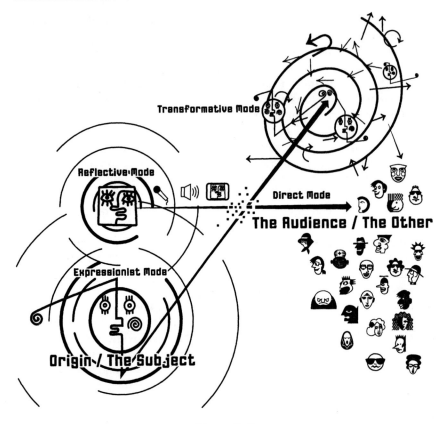

Figure 2.2

fact that music is always 'music', vocalized and external to the subject. To put it more concretely, rather than expressing himself,[17] the singer can only sing in an expressionist style. None the less this does not prevent performers from trying to transcend the rhetorical dimension of music and to *truly* express themselves. Indeed, the desperation of this attempt defines expressionist practice. As Hal Foster puts it, '[s]uch is the pathos of the expressionist self: alienated, it would be made whole through expression, only to find there another sign of its alienation' (1985: 62).

Peter Wollen (1993: 113) suggests that expressionism was imported into be-bop at mid-century via the abstract expressionist art scene in America. However it is only with the advent of rock that it gets taken up in mass mediated music. This comes partly as a diffuse legacy of romanticism, but also in Britain through the art school education of musicians (Frith and Horne 1987). The interesting point, though, is how quickly it becomes conventionalized. Here is John Lennon expounding expressionist doctrine some time in the late 1960s – already with a weary sense of its hopelessness.

I resent being an artist, in that respect, I resent performing for fucking idiots who don't know anything. They can't feel; I'm the one that's feeling, because I'm the one expressing. They live vicariously through me and other artists.

(Lennon in interview with Wenner 1972: 11)

Just as with German expressionist painting of the early twentieth century rock had a primitivist aspect too, in this case the notion that the blues might provide young white men with something that old black men were thought to possess – the secret of presenting oneself truly, directly, intensely. For, with almost the sole exception of Jimi Hendrix, this was a white mode. Notable rock expressionists include the Doors ('Break On Through' constitutes a slogan and manifesto), Bob Dylan in his electric period and Led Zeppelin. The tendency crops up again in punk and after – for example Joy Division, hardcore (see Chapter 4) and grunge all have a strong expressionist bent. Going back before rock, Johnnie Ray represents a sort of naive proto-expressionism.

As I have implied, expressionism is a self-deluding and ultimately reactionary performance strategy. Actually, it would deny that it *is* a strategy, since 'strategy' suggests there are alternative strategies rather than expression itself. Most importantly for the present argument, expressionism represents an attempt to suppress citation and present pure emotion. In this sense it is a profoundly anti-creative doctrine because it denies that creativity consists in an *encounter* between the musician-subject and objects in the field of works, or social relations more generally. Instead it proposes a kind of subjective supremacism – everything comes from within. Yet expressionism cannot be discounted because it encapsulates, albeit in an excessive and fetishized form, a necessary urge in any act of performance, that is to give voice with present intent. Besides, as we will hear shortly, it is often redeemed through being corrupted by other performance modes.

At the other end of the diagonal axis (Figure 2.2) lies the *transformative* mode of performance. Performance here is concerned not with truth to source so much as variation of that which has already been played and sung. Actually we considered it earlier under another name: social authorship. Social authors like Charles Mingus inflect a tradition, nudging it and turning it a few degrees. All I would want to add here are some reflections on the relation between Origin, tradition and its ongoing transformation.

The transformative mode of performance always includes a 'listening backwards' in the direction of Origin. The key point is that Origin will, in almost every case, be a collectivity, a historical moment or geographical place rather than an individual subject. The transformative then involves mediation between this source and the ongoing now of performance. Because it is premised on vicissitude, the transformative constitutes the performance mode *par excellence* of diasporic music cultures. This is the theme Paul Gilroy (1993) develops in *The Black Atlantic*. Gilroy recounts how an African diasporic tradition of music and culture has been able, through the memorial experience of slavery and racial terror, not only to negotiate historical change and geographical displacement yet also to produce music which maintains a vision of a better world.

It seems to me that the transformative represents the utopian imperative of pop in its most developed form. Those features which mark it – versioning, bifurcation, repetition/variation – testify to solidarity and the redemption of human agency, but also to a notion of the past which teaches change. For these reasons the transformative can (and should) be borrowed by all sorts of music cultures.

So far we have been examining that axis of performance which extends diagonally out and away from Origin. However, as we have seen, performative acts always include an audience, that is an Other subject with whom the performer would communicate. The horizontal axis represents the dimension of performing to or for the Other. To repeat what I said earlier, in this scheme the straight, uninterrupted channel which leads from sender to receiver in the classical model of communication has split in the middle (Figure 2.2). The two halves are still attached and it is possible for something to get across from one side to the other. However, because of the break each tends to be oriented in respect of one pole, rather than providing a continuum between the two. In the case of the horizontal axis this orientation is toward-the-Other.

At the far right of that axis we have the *direct* mode. This was the dominant mode of popular music performance before rock and roll; its key value – sincerity (Scannell 1996). Sincere address involved the performer giving her/himself over to the audience with both charm and conviction. It emerged partly as a way of compensating for the loss of signs of presence brought about by the advent of mass communication. Music makers developed new tropes of hyper-intimacy which involved using technologies of spatial extension (microphone-speaker and camera-screen) to pull the audience in 'close'. Soft crooning and constant smiling are two examples. Another is the deployment in Hollywood musicals of 'internal audiences' shown sitting in theatres or gathered round a singer in the more organic setting of café or hay barn (Feuer 1993: 26–30). Such techniques were all intended to heighten the sense of complicity with performers on the part of the real, external audience. Hence too James Last's dubbed-on party ambience: a last-ditch attempt to intensify pop intimacy in the age of rock.

In rock, though, this kind of mediated sincerity, or being on the side of the audience, became highly suspect. What Barry Shank calls the 'purification of the expressive impulse' (1994: 147) in punk was actually a central plank in the aesthetics of rock ten years earlier. In fact it seems that successive movements to renew rock, including various neo-punk tendencies (see Marcus 1993), have all tried to get rid of signs of deference to the audience. One way has been through facial expression. The range of looks used by rock musicians in videos, publicity shots or live performance typically extends from the sneer to the emphatically blank. It as though rebuffing the audience with an angry and aggressive posture provides the only guarantee of being true to it.

Outside of rock, and indeed in parts of what remains of it, the direct mode of performance has been supplanted more and more by the *reflexive*. Situated to the left on the horizontal axis (Figure 2.2), performance here is still oriented towards the audience, but includes a strong awareness of its own, iterative nature. Here, we encounter voice – the already sounded – again. In earlier discussions the emphasis was on voice as a raw material which might be identified, selected and combined by the musician-creator to produce new music. However the key aspect of reflexive performance is the *display* of voice by means of an (unspoken) announcement which accompanies it like, 'that's the sound of it' or 'now we're doing it like this'.

Reflexivity has become increasingly important in popular music and has encroached more and more on the other modes of performance. It is perhaps tempting to read this as a symptom of postmodernism: voice reduced to sound-spectacle or simulation with no real purchase on the world (Jameson 1991: 16–25). However I would argue to the contrary that reflexive performance is the continuation of agency in a period when other modes of performance have been exhausted. Furthermore, reflexivity has enabled the *recovery* of other modes of performance.

I want to finish the discussion of performance by examining one such case, that of the Velvet Underground. On first listening, the Velvet Underground seem to encapsulate rock expressionism in full scream. We hear this in a cycle of songs ('I'm Waiting for the Man' (1967); 'White Light/White Heat', 'Sister Ray' (1969)) where the dominant motif is the enormous quaver (eighth note) pulse built around Maureen Tucker's drums. Against this unrelenting throb individual instruments grate in cacophonous protest. Periodically, bass, organ or guitar lurch arhythmically to the front of the mix. This is collective expression, the sound of primordial emotion or pure presence.

Some elements are missing though. On this reading we lose any sense of the Velvet Underground's piquant style, and in particular the fact that, rather bizarrely, these songs are high camp. On 'White Light/White Heat' Lou Reed sings with an ebulliently queer lilt: 'White heat, it tickle me down to my toes / Oo oo have mercy white light – goodness knows!' The phrases might be out of the mouth of one of the 'A men', the gay amphetamine freaks who hung out at Andy Warhol's Factory studio (Warhol and Hackett 1990). As for the rhythm, if it is primitive it is also crassly popular. A stripped-down version of a generic pattern (lineage: 'Lucille', 'The Twist', 'Woolly Bully'), the pulse caricatures the vulgarity and brashness of rock'n'roll by abandoning the customary accent on the third beat. In this guise the monadic rhythm comes across more like a pop music joke than the sound of savagery.

Now if we map this textual analysis on to the performance schema in

Figure 2.2 what's interesting is that the Velvets seem be located in *two* modes, two modes, moreover, which one would imagine to be mutually exclusive. First they are expressionists. This is intensely subjective music, a direct manifestation of tumultuous psychic energy. Yet at the same time the camp distantiation from the material, the invitation to 'look at us doing this faggy, junky stuff', places the group firmly in the reflexive mode. They want to make sure the audience can hear them doing the thing they do. This aspect redeems the outflow of angst, and helps to convert rage into a demotic affirmation of life, albeit in a (reflexively) strange and Other form.

In fact this example of musical performance being located in more than one mode is not so rare. Almost all expressive or direct performances have an aspect of the reflexive or transformative about them. For without such an inflection, monstrous pomposity and self-indulgence (in the case of expression), or grotesque sentimentality (in the case of the direct mode) become all too palpable. By the same token the reflexive and transformative need some sense of ground or communicative possibility which can only be obtained from one of the other modes. Performance, to return to Derrida's formulation, can neither be wholly pure nor wholly impure.

Summing the chapter up

In this chapter I hope to have shown how making popular music involves agency, or what I have reluctantly called creativity. The argument has been that creation occurs on a small scale. It involves an accumulation of many little acts rather than any grandiose gesture. What's more the radius of creativity of musician-subjects is circumscribed. The minimal room for manoeuvre which they have emerges in the lack of fit between the two powerful structuring apparatuses of habitus and field.

Musicians then work with possibilities that are given, rather than summoned up freely by the imagination. In this context it is difficult to make new or different music because possibility is so constrained – by the magnetic attraction of conventional patterns and choices near the centre of the radius, but also by the difficulty of hearing possibilities near the outside.

What is then surprising is the extent to which extraordinary music can be made given the low availability of creative choice. The concept which might explain this is social authorship. The social author, such as Charles Mingus, cites and inflects *voices*, that is musical sounds and forms which have already been produced, musical possibles in other words. Crucially, voices are attached to site, for example class, gender, race, region, text place. What counts is how the social author selects and combines voices, and the way in which voice-sites are, as a result, thrown into relief or given another perspective. Effective social authorship produces thick texts which speak of the social lives of people, particularly oppressed people, but which also promise the possibility of change.

The chapter began with the assertion that popular musicians were 'white-collar'. The point of using this description was to emphasize, contrary to the mythology constructed in interviews and pop biographies, how far musicians are engaged in banal and careful clerical work. Yet musicians perform too. First there is performance in the sense of carrying on production, doing it again in different media and in different versions. The processive, unfinished aspect of popular music is central to the form. Second, musicians perform before an audience; they not only show off but also try to *reach* the audience.

This is complicated by an inevitable split in the axis of communication from subject to other. Precisely because music has to have a voice of one kind or another, the fact that like all 'writing' (Derrida 1991) it repeats what has already been played and sung, the performer cannot get across her/his original and true intent. Considered in this way – as an interrupted act – performance now appears in four fragmented modes: expressionist, direct, transformative, reflexive. These represent performance *positions* which may be adopted and even combined by musicians. They have distinct political and aesthetic implications which arise from the way that each denies or accommodates the impossibility of performance.

How do performance and creativity relate to one another then? The key point here is that while creative acts can be considered in isolation for analytical purposes, this only defers the issue of performance. For it is in performance that acts of creation are realized. This has nothing to do with stages – first creation and then performance. For as we have heard the problem of performance arises even as the musical idea coalesces or a particular voice is selected. Rather the issue is that performance complicates creative agency, making it difficult to understand simply as a product of rational choice, or the straightforward selection of possibles. Above all performance introduces ambivalence and incongruity and, in so doing, ups the stakes in creativity. In the next chapter we investigate some ways in which this happens by examining how musicians have used technology to throw voices across time and space.

|3|

Technology: the instrumental instrument

> When first consciously produced, [the musical note] was wholly
> attached to its instrument and had no other association. Thus the
> original rattle rattled as the thing it was; the rattling sound is merely
> its verb, as it were. The thunder stick whirred and the drum beat itself:
> that was the main thing.
>
> (Bloch 1985: 140)

In an essay called 'Magic rattle, human harp' Ernst Bloch (1985) traces a
long historical cycle in the conception and use of musical instruments in the
West. In the primordial phase, Bloch suggests, there was a definite connection between instruments and their sounds ensured by music's function in
ritual. He explains this in the passage shown above. However, a barren
period of metaphysical speculation about musical form and meaning then
followed. In the Classical age and after, rather than sounds belonging to
instruments, they were heard as part of an abstracted realm of 'the spheres',
located in the ether above the material world of lived and heard experience.
During the eighteenth and nineteenth centuries, though, Bloch detects a
return to the archaic conception of music as sound-making with the arrival
of the opera singer, or what he calls the 'human harp'. Here 'the musical
note has a definite site, namely a body that sings in the process of acting'
(143). What Bloch likes about opera is its localization of music in the body,
so that the body takes on the character of an instrument which is also a
human subject.

What seems striking about this exposition is how prescient it is about
popular music-making and its connection with technology. Bloch touches
on what will be central issues in the aesthetics of production and reception
in pop: relations between the performer's body and instrument, how sounds
are attached to instruments and the way musical sounds are imagined in the

abstract, 'away' from their source. In effect, Bloch's essay suggests a strong continuity between music-making apparatus in the past and the contemporary, popular mode of production.

This runs counter to the approach of an important research strand in popular music studies which posits a radical break in methods of making music with the coming of phonography. Actually, there are two camps here. One characterizes the development of recording as the progressive loss of authentic musical interaction. For example, Charles Keil (1994b) suggests that, in the case of blues and polka, recording encapsulates 'a perfectible Apollonian dream life' and the decline of communal music-making (216). He pines for the messy interactivity of live performance. Paul Théberge (1989) sees the advent of multitracking as driven by a Weberian imperative towards technological rationalization. In rock music this results in an ideological effect of organic community, at odds with the reality of a routinized production process.

Meanwhile, the other camp agrees that recording has destroyed the primacy of 'live', organic performance. But instead of offering a critique of the conditions of musical production, it calls for recognition that in the contemporary period making music is inherently artificial and dependent on technology. Musicians and fans should acknowledge this, and understand that the aesthetics of artifice are both necessary and desirable (Frith 1986, Goodwin 1992, Harley 1993, Thornton 1995).

These debates have greatly helped analysis of the processes of musical mediation and reproduction. However I want to suggest in this chapter that the idea of a binary opposition between live and recorded music, one related to contested notions of authenticity and artifice, also obscures our understanding of the meaning of music technologies. Broadly, what is missing in both approaches is a sense of how popular musicians have responded to the progressive mediation of music-making over the course of the twentieth century by carrying on performing – in whatever milieu is available. At stake here is not so much an opposition as a continuum between musician–audience co-presence on the one hand and various kinds of distantiation and manipulation of sound on the other.

This continuum represents a technosphere, that is a domain of imaginary possibilities and constraints which lies between performance on one side and the more or less remote reception of sound on the other. The technosphere is thus premised on the idea of a performative gap or dislocation, but also a belief on the part of musicians that this might be bridged. In this sense it is hardly a new phenomenon. As we saw in the last chapter, to perform music always means coping with a broken channel of communication, or what Derrida (1991) calls 'impurity'. None the less something does change with the advent of mass communication. To use Derrida's terms again we might say that with sound recording the *writing* of music takes on a different form. This calls for new kinds of signature and new ways of delimiting context.

What has that meant in concrete terms? We can identify at least three tendencies at work. The first might be described as documentary, its goal being to carry the truth of an original, *un*mediated performance event across the air to listeners. It is conservative in that it wants to repress all that the technosphere implies (new opportunities for framing performance) by going back to the ideal context of concert hall or bar where musical interaction with the audience is, purportedly, immediate. The documentary approach is dominant in the earliest period of the technosphere – the 1920s to the 1950s. However even in the period afterwards it persists as a kind of constant, low-level anxiety about technical possibility and the truth of music.

A second approach has been important continuously, throughout pop's short twentieth century. Closest to Bloch's conception of the human harp, this tendency focuses on body–instrument relations. We can call it ventriloquism. The uncanny aspect of the instrument as an extension of the body (or indeed the body as a form of instrument) comes to the fore here. But now, instruments occupy a liminal zone, acting as a conduit between the musician's body and the technosphere itself. In this sense the singer-with-microphone as much as the guitarist or saxophonist is a ventriloquist. Each of them is involved in configuring their bodies for voice-making and throwing. Strong examples of ventriloquism include scat singing, the playing of electric guitar, amplifier and effects, or scratching and editing tropes performed by the DJ.

A third approach is oriented towards the far side of the technosphere. The aim here is to construct a sonic environment, a virtual dimensionality which never existed 'originally'. In historical terms this is the last strategy to develop. It can be first discerned at the beginning of the 1950s with the advent of techniques such as tape echo. It reaches an advanced stage with Phil Spector's Wall of Sound in the early 1960s. Today it is the dominant approach. All popular music now takes on the aspect of a virtual sonic environment – although it can perhaps be heard to most extravagant effect in dance music.

In what follows we will trace these developments from the beginning of pop's short twentieth century to recent developments in digital technology. The goal here is not a comprehensive history (there is not nearly enough time for this anyway), but rather the identification of key conjunctures when the rules of the game change and, as a result, the new technical possibilities become available.

Audio recording – a case of late development

In considering music technology historically, the first question that arises is why techniques of sound manipulation in recording were so slow to develop, comparatively speaking. Edison first demonstrated the cylinder phonograph in 1879. Recorded music became available on the market in the 1890s. But it was not until the mid-1960s that regular multitrack recording with asynchronous performance by musicians was instituted. The striking contrast here is with developments in the cinema. Nöel Burch (1981) describes the early history of film from the 1890s to the 1920s 'as one vast inward penetration, as one long "forward tracking", involving "pans" right and left of increasing amplititude' (28). In effect there is a shift from a frontal mode where a whole stage-tableau is presented as though from the back of the theatre stalls – c.1906, to a position in which filming is done from deep within the space of the action – c.1920. Crucially, there was no equivalent to this in the case of sound recording. Nothing in the recording studio compared with the penetration and fragmentation of space produced by multiple camera angles, or the recomposition achieved through continuity editing. Certainly no attempt was made to emulate the language of camera–object relations as it developed in Hollywood.[1] Instead, during the long, documentary period before multitracking, the microphone stayed resolutely outside the ensemble, and the performing system – small group, orchestra, solo performer – was consolidated as a hermetic unit.

Now a technological determinist explanation, in other words one in which technology is seen as a primary and self-sufficient phenomenon (see Winston 1995), would stress the absence of magnetic tape, and consequently the lack of an editing or sound-on-sound facility, until the post-war period; but this is unsatisfactory. Optical sound recording on film, and hence opportunities for splicing, had been in existence since 1926, and Les Paul was recording multi-part guitar pieces using two separate disc recorders as early as 1930 (Cunningham 1996: 21). The problem, then, is not really one of technical possibility. It seems to me, rather, that conservatism in the musical apparatus had more to do with the absence of an *imagined* world of manipulated sound. This bears, in part, on the fundamentally different relationship between space and time in narrative forms and in music.

In a film the assembly of shots according to the conventions of film language works not only to organize the space of the story as Burch emphasizes, but also to structure the passage of time. Generally, cuts from shot to shot involve lapses of time, and sometimes even a backward movement, the flashback. Pauses and 'timestretch' may also occur. The point is that film narrative depends on a double temporal system consisting of story time – the inferred time of the events portrayed, and discourse time – the time it takes to tell the story, often called 'running time' (Chatman 1979: 70–2). Simon Frith argues that a similar splitting takes place in the case of music: 'our inner experience of time is not the same as the experience of real time' (Frith 1996: 146); or, as John Blacking puts it, the 'essential quality of music is its power to create another world of virtual time' (quoted in Frith 1996: 149). However what is significant for the present argument is that this construction of fictive time is not confined to music which has been produced using sound-on-sound techniques. Rather it is an aspect of music *tout court*. Metre, melody, tempo and harmonic development (timbre should be included here too) constitute a complex field of temporal indicators, while phrasing can be considered a sort of time sculpture. The control of such elements in 'real time' performance is a key aspect of musicianship, often strongly associated with notions of instrumental virtuosity.

In an important sense, then, conventional composition and performance techniques already embodied a plenitude of temporal articulation in the era of documentary phonography. So, whereas in film the urge to tell a story drove the development of a film language based on the fragmentation and recomposition of time, in music the temporal manipulation of sound in the studio was redundant; there was no narrative dividend to be earned by it.

If the *adequacy* of real-time performance was crucial in keeping the ensemble intact in front of the microphone, just as important was the radical sense of *loss* which came with phonography. John Corbett (1994a) has discussed the implications of a technology which provides music without the sight of its performance. He argues that the disembodied sounds emerging from playback systems promote a fetishistic cult of fidelity. Surface noise and other blemishes in reproduction take on a special significance here, 'threaten[ing] to expose the visual lack – and potentially the industrial construction of musical autonomy – produced by recorded music' (41–2).

But there is more at stake here than the loss of the image of production. The experience of sound itself is also impoverished in radio and phonographic reception. On its own, sound provides little evidence about range and direction. Binaurality yields some directional cues: one infers the position of a source partly by appreciating the difference between sounds picked up by each ear. Degrees of loudness and reverberation also help to indicate depth of field. But consisting as it does in changes of pressure in a body of air all sound tends to take on the characteristics of an environment – it surrounds us. Thus our ability to locate its point(s) of production usually depends on a visual complement. We need to confirm auditory position with a sighting. In the case of sound emitted from a loudspeaker, though, both binaural and visual cues are eliminated. As Rick Altman (1992) puts it, '[w]hereas live sound provides an extraordinary number of variables, each permitting and promoting selective attention, recorded sound folds most of these variables into a single undifferentiated source' (29).

I want to suggest that this homogenization of multi-aspected sound emanating from the loudspeaker played an important part in reinforcing a conservative, documentary approach to the process of recording music. Once again a comparison with the cinema is useful. There the cartographic certainties of the visual image on screen underwrote the fragmentation of filmic space. Ultimately the audience knew where it stood in relation to the action because the emerging conventions of the 180° rule, eye line match and so on were built on notions of perspective already prevalent in western culture. In recorded music, though, there was no aural equivalent of the powerful code of perspective. Microphone–loudspeaker monophony and the inability to project a visual image of performance thus left music makers and audience bereft of a sense of their mutual disposition.

It is difficult to evaluate the psychic impact of this deprivation on listeners. Dave Laing (1991) speculates that with the advent of phonography at the end of the nineteenth century 'the scopic drive was displaced from the body of the singer, the musician and the instrument onto a new physical object, the phonograph or gramophone itself' (8). He points out that pictures from the period show listeners gazing raptly at the acoustic horn as though searching for the origin of the disembodied sounds emanating from it. What is certain is that from the earliest days of recording the music and media industries were engaged in an incessant pursuit of 'fidelity' at the playback stage. This quest became particularly intense during the inter-war period. In 1922 Columbia introduced 'a silent record surface' (Sanjek 1988: 63). Two years later, just as electrical recording was being developed, the Victor company brought out an acoustic phonograph, the Orthophonic Victrola, capable of delivering a much wider frequency response than previous equipment (Gelatt 1977: 222). Then, during the 1930s the response range of records was continually uprated, even outpacing the capabilities of most home phonographs (270). Meanwhile the radio industry had adopted its own disc transcription system at the beginning of the decade with a still wider frequency range (Sanjek 1988: 131–2), and in 1934 Station W2XR in New York began direct '"high fidelity broadcasting"' (Gelatt 1977: 270).

This, then, was where the technological imperative lay during the documentary period – in the pursuit of sonic fidelity, the obsessive search for the wholeness of a performance none the less constituted in lack. It is as though by ensuring the fullest accuracy in the auditory channel recompense might be made for the absence of the visual and of localized sound. In much the same way that the integration of temporal control in real-time musical performance worked to keep the microphone outside the ensemble so too did the pursuit of fidelity. It emphasized the separateness of the musical event, the fact that performance was pro-phonographic and therefore real.[2]

Dissemination and crystallization

Recording technology was thus conservative in character during the long, documentary period. That is to say the effect of marketing discourse and technical development in the record industry was to close off the creative and performative potential of the new apparatus. As we have seen this was very much an official approach, championed by the music industries on commercial grounds. The waning hegemony of the publishing industry and its commodity, the song, was another significant factor here. For while the song remained the pre-eminent musical artifact then the emphasis in the recording and broadcasting apparatus would always be towards *rendition*, that is to say the execution of an existing text, rather than the production of a new one.

Despite this conservative regime, early recording did have democratic implications for music-making. Popular musicians were able to make use of the new apparatus creatively and with an emerging sense of purpose. There were two ways this happened in the documentary period. The most radical form of intervention by musicians in the technical system might be described as ventriloquism. It did, in significant respects, challenge the norms of documentation. We will come back to it shortly. The other way musicians made their own, autonomous, use of recording was in the dissemination and crystallization of musical styles and idioms. This did not really contravene the documentary mode since it was based on the reception of records, that is to say on listening. The key factor here was the breakthrough of phonography as a mass medium.

US record sales climbed from 25 million in 1914 to 100 million in 1921 to reach a pre-Depression peak of 104 million in 1927 (Gelatt 1977: 212, 246). Within that mass market independent companies like OKeh and Gennett then produced 'race records' by black artists for black audiences (Kennedy 1994). Race records were bought in large numbers. Mamie Smith's 'Crazy Blues', the first race music hit, sold 75000 copies in Harlem in its first week of release in 1920 (Carr *et al.* 1987: 463). While, according to Todd Titon, among rural black Americans, 'between 10 and 20 per cent had phonographs and a larger proportion had records' in the 1920s (quoted by Small 1987b: 401). Altogether, by 1925 black consumers were buying an estimated five or six million records a year (Ogren 1989: 91). This new record culture was also a diverse one. Paul Oliver (1968) cites discographical research by Dan Mahony suggesting that race records covered country and city blues, vaudeville and instrumental music, as well as religious music (7).[3]

Crucially, the take-off of African-American music as a recorded medium should not be seen simply in terms of market. As several writers have suggested race records were an important means by which idioms spread and styles coalesced (Small 1987b: 401, Chanan 1995: 56–7). Crucially, the mass circulation of records led to a new kind of mediated orality, whereby young musicians learnt their craft listening to the phonograph as much as by reading music or watching performances (Oliver 1968: 9–10, Eisenburg 1987: 115–16). This enormously extended the possibility of participation in music-making. Significantly, it enabled white musicians to copy black styles as well.

We get a strong sense of this process of the phonographic dissemination of style in an account by the trumpet player, Jimmy McPartland. McPartland describes the way the 'Austin High School Gang' of friends learnt to play recordings by the New Orleans Rhythm Kings (itself a white band) in the early 1920s:

What we used to do was put the record on ... play a few bars, and then get all our notes. We'd have to tune our instruments up to the record machine, to the pitch, and go ahead with a few notes. Then stop! A few more bars of the record, each guy would pick out his notes and boom! We would go on and play it. Two bars, or four bars, or eight – we would get in on each phrase and then play it. But you can imagine it was hard at first. Just starting, as most of us were, we'd make so many mistakes that it was horrible on people's ears.

(McPartland, in Shapiro and Hentoff 1962: 123)

The scene McPartland describes here, by now long familiar. to popular musicians, represented a paradigm shift in the 1920s. It represents the *dissemination* of music through recordings.

But there is something else at stake here, beyond the diffusion of repertoire and idiom. We might call this the *crystallization* of style. The time constraints of the 10 inch, 78 r.p.m. disc played a part in this. For example, it is likely that the typical four-stanza structure of classic blues emerged as a norm because of the exigencies of recording (Eisenburg 1987: 116). More than this, LeRoi Jones (1995/1963) suggests that imitation of records 'actually *created* whole styles of blues' (102, original emphasis). The nasal style of singer Ida Cox, for example, was spread initially by her live performances on the vaudeville circuit. Then from 1923, when she made her first recordings, other artists outside her home territory of St Louis, Missouri heard the records, picked up the inflection and developed it (102). What seems to be at stake in this process is a form of close listening which, paradoxically, is not followed by replication on the part of the performer, but rather the intensification of idiom. As Michael Chanan (1995) notes, with the advent of styles based on recording, nuanced *sound* became the most salient feature, rather than a prior song structure (19). Lacking any registration in the form of a written score, music thus turned into something mutable, given to being sounded again in a similar, but significantly different way by the next musician in the performance continuum.[4]

Ventriloquism

In an important sense dissemination and crystallization were by-products of recording. Musicians used records, by listening and re-playing, as an aid to copying and composing new material. But this could take place anywhere there was space to set up a phonograph and get out instruments. The studio was not part of the process.

However another, and in many ways more radical, appropriation of the recording medium was forged by musicians in the practice of recording itself. The word ventriloquism seems to signify this practice quite well. In conventional usage ventriloquism means 'the art of producing the voice in such a manner that it shall appear to proceed from some place altogether distant from the speaker'.[5] The term is derived from the Latin – *venter*, meaning belly and *loquor*, to speak. Amongst the Romans it was supposed that voice throwing depended on the use of the stomach. This emphasis on the embodied production of sound is crucial for the present argument. And there is a link to Bloch's human harp too. What is at stake seems to be the voice emerging from the body. However in the case of ventriloquism in popular music we can add two extra factors. First, voice not only means those sounds produced by the human thorax and larynx, it also includes the production of sound by instruments. Second, there is a further stage: the transmission of voice into the technosphere through some form of interface such as recording horn, microphone, guitar pick-up or record deck.

If ventriloquism belongs properly to popular music we can nevertheless trace its early development in the recording of classical music. We get a sense of this from a vivid description by the pianist and accompanist Gerald Moore of recording at H.M.V.'s Hayes studio in 1921 (1966: 52–4). What stands out is the physical difficulty of transcribing music to disc using the early, acoustic method. To maximise resonance in the studio the walls and floor were made of unpolished wood, but this meant that voices boomed and footsteps thundered. And even though a piano tuner had filed down the felts on the piano hammers for greater percussive effect Moore was still forced to play *forte* the whole time to produce enough volume for adequate recording.

These conditions made balancing the piano against other instruments and voices particularly problematic. The enormous acoustic horn which jutted into the studio in order to pick up sound for transcription was too big to be shifted. So instead the piano itself became the moveable object. At the start of a session test cuts were made, and the instrument trundled up or down the studio until the balance was considered satisfactory. This could be a long process. When the recording of a master finally got under way duetting singers would jostle and push in an attempt to climb right into the trumpet, and so ensure a good take at the expense of their colleagues. From Moore's vantage point it was the singers' buttocks, not their voices, which made the greatest impression (53).

This cheerfully downbeat description is illuminating in a number of respects. Most tellingly, Moore reveals the extent to which acoustic recording was concerned with the throwing of voices. It would perhaps be simplest to see this as a matter of technical constraint. Indeed, when electrical recording was introduced in 1925 microphones and amplifiers removed the need for studio gymnastics. As Read and Welch point out the power of the microphone to pick up more distant sound sources 'would permit more natural positions for singers and instrumentalists' (1976: 247). In other words musicians were able to set themselves up in a configuration which approximated live performance. Furthermore large orchestras, previously unrecordable, could now be arrayed before a frontal microphone (1976:

127–32). A major impact of electrical recording was, then, that it restored an element of concert staging to performance in the studio, so reinforcing the documentary mode.

But the microphone also facilitated a strikingly artificial technique, namely crooning. Singers could now declaim *softly* into the microphone over the sound of a big band (Whitcomb 1973: 100, Lees 1987: 105). Read and Welch (1976) observe (with distaste) that this studio practice quickly spread to the stage – in effect recording established norms which live performance then emulated (239). I want to make a rather different point though: for all its apparent restraint crooning is a projective technique. The intimacy conjured by the crooner depended on her or his ability to reach forward by means of the technical apparatus to the individuated ear lobes of a mass audience listening at home on radio or phonograph. There is, in this sense, a strong continuity between Gerald Moore's percussive piano playing to the acoustic horn, and the murmuring of a crooner before the microphone. Both are forms of ventriloquism, both are concerned with a distinctly phonographic imperative to *transmit* sound across the technosphere which performer and audience share, yet which also separates them in time and space.

The difference then arises in respect of aesthetic intention and effect. Whereas acoustic recording of classical music involved the unwanted imposition of ventriloquial methods, crooning represented a reflexive technique. This was precisely why it was considered so scandalous. Crooning was an affront to the documentary regime.

Another kind of voice-throwing trope, scat, constitutes a different case again. Louis Armstrong claims to have 'invented' scat singing in 1925 when he dropped the lyric sheet for 'Heebie Jeebies' at a recording session. As he recalls it, 'there wasn't any use in spoilin' this master, so I just went in there and started scattin' and they kep' it' (Armstrong, quoted in Ogren 1989: 97). Now in the first place, scat provides a strong example of the diffusion and reinforcement effect of recording. Within a few years it had become part of the evolving generic toolkit of jazz. For some musicians, like Cab Calloway, it became a major performance technique. Beyond its repertory function, though, we can hear something else.

In scat the singing voice becomes an almost pathological destroyer of meaning. Through the articulation of syllables (sometimes pseudo-words too), and a strong sense of phonetic idiom scat takes on the character of a *faux* language. Critically, though, it is a meaningless language; its lexis is entirely fantastic, its syntax a strange parody of speech rhythms. Whereas the singer of a song with lyrics is engaged to a greater or lesser extent with reference to the world, the scat singer abandons representation altogether. Instead her voice becomes an uncanny index of the body. Gary Giddins (1985) argues that exponents such as Leo Watson and Slim Gaillard 'used scat to underscore the irrepressible, childlike quality that had circled the outskirts of jazz' since the early 1930s (162). My point would be that the innocence of scat is contrived, masking as it does a certain scandal. For when the voice becomes a wordless instrument it abandons its normative function of enunciating discourse, and instead enunciates the body: chest, throat, but chiefly tongue. Meanwhile in its articulation – Gary Giddins puts it nicely, 'from Armstrong's biting consonants (bop-ba-du-ZET) to Sinatra's wan shoobie-doobie-do' (1985: 162) – scat *sounds* like language.

It is the contrast, then, between sounds which ought to mean, and a body which ought to keep silent that offers the pleasure of scat, and also its politics. Scat undermines lyricism, the sentimental assumption that music can yield up the being of its creator to her audience. It is no coincidence, then, that wordless singing is first used in recording. Hidden by the walls of the studio, and the asynchrony between performance and reception the scat singer exploits the artifice of the phonographic apparatus to produce embodied sounds without a face.

From around the same time, the mid-1920s, the ventriloquism of the human voice which we can hear in crooning and scat is matched by a vocalization of instruments. Jazz musicians develop styles whose sound is intensely idiomatic rather than proper to the instrument. By the late 1930s tone and timbre have become the defining characteristic of a new dual entity, the player-instrument. Names like Coleman Hawkins, Ben Webster and Lester Young come to denote not just consecrated virtuosi, but particular tenor saxophone sound types. Now according to Doug Miller (1995) the sax is especially susceptible to sonic articulation because it 'is an imperfect piece of engineering, and this gives it considerable scope for variations in timbre' (157). Miller argues that the potential of the instrument is in fact most fully developed not in jazz, but in rhythm and blues where, during the 1940s, sax players produce a panoply of new sounds from the honk to the scream.

For Miller rhythm and blues sax is a translation of African-American field hollers and gospel shouts into an urban–commercial milieu. LeRoi Jones (1995/1963) also links post-war rhythm and blues to the black vocal tradition, but points up a more contemporary cultural agenda. Musicians wanted 'to make the instruments sound as unmusical, or as *non-western* as possible'. This was a reaction, Jones claims, to 'the softness and "legitimacy" that had crept into black instrumental music with the advent of swing' (172), a reaction made more intense because swing had been adopted as a hegemonic pop style by the culture industry and white mainstream audience (174). Jones is surely right to emphasize the countercultural agenda here. But rhythm and blues's difference from swing is constructed not just through an appeal to black cultural roots; it also represents a vernacular form of research and development in music technology. In effect the saxophone is removed from its embedded role in the big band and rigorously tested as a sound-making device in the stripped-down, open context of the small 'jump' combo. Here, working at the extremes of the instrument's timbric and tonal range, players develop a set of new techniques such as flutter tonguing, false fingering and overblowing in order to reconfigure its sonic architecture (Miller 1995). Beyond a harking back to folk roots, then, we can hear in this a thoroughly modernist urge to upset traditional correspondences between instrument and voice. Honks, screams, smears and 'melismatic' figures replace the stable legato of the officially configured instrument.

Along with scat singing, sax neophonics in rhythm and blues constitutes perhaps the most fully developed manifestation of an aesthetics of ventriloquism in the pre-tape era of mediated music. An important plank of my argument so far has been that such a projective mode can be seen as the obverse of documentary recording – that is it encapsulates an urge by musicians to push forward through the technosphere. On the one hand we have enclosure and separation from the audience in the studio, on the other the ubiquity and intimacy of mediated sounds heard on record or radio. Musicians then find new ways to negotiate this opposition between mediated remoteness and media power. Ventriloquism in this sense represents an aesthetic proper to the phonographic apparatus.

What does that mean, though? One way of understanding the impact of recording, as we saw at the beginning of the chapter, is to compare it with live performance so as to establish the difference in values between the two modes. Charles Keil (1994b and Keil and Feld 1994) does this in a discussion of blues and polka in America. Noticing a strange shortage of live recordings in these genres, he suggests it is '[b]ecause early on ... all participants in the rites of blues and polkas heard the recordings not as mere echoes but as perfected echoes of their live experience' (1994b: 214). Live music represented untidiness, participation and feedback which would, if heard on record, bring the wrong sort of expectations. Elsewhere he says that 'recording is not an intensification so much as a distillation, a clarification maybe, the cleanest version you can do' (Keil and Feld 1994: 296).

This is a highly suggestive argument. Live and recorded do indeed carry distinct values, which imply a certain segregation between them.[6] But I think Keil is wrong to hear the two modes as being in *opposition*: clear versus messy, solipsistic as opposed to interactive. The key point is that even before the advent of tape, with all its opportunities for phonic manipulation, recording was implicated in much more than 'clarification'. As we have heard the ventriloquial techniques of crooning, scat and the honking saxophone were both embodied and artificial at one and the same time. Each depended on a subversion of phonic norms, and the interpolation of the body into sound-making. Each could be recorded, or performed live. Certainly scat had emerged first in the studio, while the honking sax style was preeminently a theatrical, live mode; and crooners had begun with megaphones in dance halls, but found their métier with the microphone (Chanan 1995: 70).

What is important, though, is that all of these techniques were products of a new music-making culture in which the mass media had upset received ideas about performance, disclosure and musician–audience relations. In effect radio and phonography set new aesthetic problems which called for reflexive, creative solutions. Significantly, the music industries did not see it this way at all during the long documentary period. Even after the advent of tape recording with its facility for complex manipulation of sound, technological development was 'led from below' by the vernacular research of musicians and engineers at the margins of the major record companies.

Tape delay (1) – on the cusp of the big sound

Magnetic tape was first used in studios early in 1949. By the following year it had almost completely superseded direct-to-disc recording in America (Gelatt 1977: 298–9). One key effect was a sharp drop in the cost of recording, up until then an extremely centralized and expensive process. By the mid-1950s relatively low-cost studios equipped with tape decks offered a dependable service in every big city, as well as many smaller towns. As the literature has it (Chapple and Garofalo 1977, Frith 1983, Gillett 1983/1970, Chambers 1985, Cohn 1989/1969) the small independent record companies which introduced rock'n'roll were predicated on the existence of such cheap recording facilities. Tape became the harbinger of a revolution in popular culture that brought the means of production within the ambit of a political economy of local entrepreneurs, so opening up access and allowing a more decentralized music-making culture.[7]

In an important sense, then, the advent of tape paralleled the emergence of a mass market for records in the 1920s. Both played a key part in the dissemination of music and the crystallization of styles. However if tape helped to revolutionize the social basis of popular music-making, then a significant part of its potential as a means of production remained unexplored, even repressed. For it was not until the mid-1960s with the advent of rock that tape's facility to manipulate the *time* of musical performance was widely appreciated. Certainly, tape was used in the construction of new kinds of virtual sonic *space* (we will come back to this important issue in the next section), but the fact remains that as far as the temporal dimension of performance was concerned a profound conservatism reigned in the 1950s, just as it had in the 1920s.

Some sense of this can be extracted from the story of guitarist and technical innovator, Les Paul. We have already noted the disc-to-disc recording experiments Paul undertook in the 1930s. By 1950 Paul was successfully using two Ampex tape machines to produce multi-part recording. His technique, now known as 'bouncing', consisted in recording a musical part on to the first machine, then playing it back for recording on to the second machine while a second part was simultaneously performed live. The resulting, two-part recording was next bounced back on to machine one, while a third, live part was laid down at the same time. In principle this process could be repeated again and again in order to build a many-part recording. The only limiting factor was a deterioration in sound quality caused by the accumulation of extraneous tape hiss at each overdub stage (Théberge 1989: 105, Cunningham 1996: 24–9).

Les Paul used this technique to produce a series of highly successful records performed with singer Mary Ford at the beginning of the 1950s. Yet despite Paul's breakthrough into sequential recording and the popularity of the results, these methods were not widely taken up. What makes this seem even more surprising (and more galling for Les Paul) was the fact that full multitrack recording machines had been developed by the mid-1950s. In this connection Paul describes walking down the hall of a studio with an engineer and coming across an eight-track recorder under a plastic bag.

> He said, 'Look what you started, Les'. And I saw this machine and said, 'What's it doing in the hallway?' He said ... 'What are you going to do with it?'
>
> (Paul, quoted in Cunningham 1996: 27)

Paul's astonishment at finding a powerful multitrack machine lying unused on the floor begs an important question: how can we account for such phonographic conservatism?

It is not easy to find a definite answer, but likely factors are the sheer inertia of the documentary mode and the persistence of anxiety about the authenticity of (hidden) musical performance. I want to turn now to another, rare, example of sound-on-sound production from the period to explore this hypothesis. It is the 1957 album *Zoot Sims Plays Alto, Tenor and Baritone* where the eponymous sax player accompanies himself in *faux*, three-part harmony.

Sims was a tenor saxophonist who had risen to prominence with the Woody Herman Herd of the late 1940s. A white swing band, the Herd had become increasingly influenced by the innovations of be-bop, and did much to popularize the new style. In particular Herman's tenor sax section, including Sims and known collectively as the 'Four Brothers', developed a technique where fluid, contrapuntal lines were combined with a clear, uninflected saxophone sound in the manner of Lester Young. On *Zoot Sims Plays ...* this approach is then developed 'virtually', by means of over-dubbing.

The sleeve notes do not explain precise recording methods, but it is probable that two twin-track, stereo recorders were used (stereo recording had been introduced in 1954). Once a take of the ensemble, consisting of piano, bass, drums and a single horn, had been made the extra horn parts would have been dubbed on by bouncing from machine to machine. The results are stunning, with an extraordinary separation between saxophone voices, and a sense of precision and restraint which sounds utterly inorganic. The ensemble parts could never be mistaken for the work of a real saxophone section. This has partly to do with the arrangements which tend to delineate contrapuntal lines rather than the homogeneous 'head' themes of conventional, post-swing jazz.

'Blinuet', for example, begins with an emphatically baroque descending figure carried by piano and bass before a two altos and tenor 'section' introduces the theme. This is a repeated and varied riff played over a twelve-bar blues, chord progression. On the third chorus the tenor leaves the saxophone ensemble to weave a contrapuntal line in and out of the riffs, now carried by the pair of altos. Then, on a bridging passage in the middle of the piece, this formation is inverted with an alto improvisation over a two-tenor, riffing ground. In each case the parts seem to have been written precisely for overdubbing. It is as though the composer, George Handy, has in mind the temporal–spatial distantiation of the sound-on-sound technique as he writes the score.

Zoot Sims Plays . . . encapsulates all the contradictions of an emerging aesthetic of phonographic artifice. On the one hand it cleaves to existing form. The virtual saxophone ensemble could quite easily have been made up of three individual players in real time. There is nothing here of the psyche-delic embrace of fantastic sound which marked multitrack production in rock ten years later. Sims and Handy are true, on a formal basis, to the jazz tradition. On the other hand the album does gesture towards something unreal, as I have been arguing: the artificial separation of saxophone parts and the virtual multiplication of Sims. In an important sense the documen-tary mode is being tested here – limits are being sought.

We find this aesthetic ambivalence in hi-fi subculture more generally. In 1949 hi-fi mania swept affluent America inaugurating a new approach to listening. Claims for the faithfulness of reproduction by manufacturers now reached an unprecedented level of fervour (Gelatt 1977: 297–98). But as Keir Keightley has shown, hi-fi discourse in the 1950s was not only concerned with truth to an original performance. Just as important was a quite contradictory proposal that the listener should be immersed in sound, and even mentally transported away from domestic realities to an 'else-where' (Keightley 1996: 169). Sims's audience – self-consciously sophisti-cated, white, middle class and male – would certainly have included hi-fi aficionados. Significantly, the same ambivalence concerning the real and the artificial which we encounter on his album can heard in hi-fi discourse more generally.

Emerging contradictions in the hi-fi project were actually prefigured by developments in sound engineering before the Second World War. I suggested in the last section that the documentary mode of recording was officially sanctioned by the music industries. This was certainly true for record companies. Here the dominant approach had been laid down by Western Electric's J. P. Maxfield, the engineer chiefly responsible for the electrical recording system introduced in 1925. Maxfield favoured the auditorium concept whereby the goal of recording was to reproduce the ambience of the concert hall with all its 'natural' resonance. A single microphone represented the ear of the ideal listener set at a distance from the ensemble (Read and Welch 1976: 245–7). However in the film industry a quite different approach developed. From the early 1930s boom microphones were used to collect both ambient and localized sounds. In the latter case mikes were placed close to individual sound sources. The multiple inputs were then mixed down on to the film soundtrack (Williams 1980, Wood 1984, Altman 1992, Chanan 1995: 59–60). Significantly, both positions were realist: the former claiming to minimize mediation by reproducing the environment of a live performance, the latter aiming to compensate for the inadequacy of the single mike-as-ear by correcting the audio signal at a second, post-production stage.

This dichotomy came increasingly to the fore after the war. Representing the first position was George Martin who recorded the London Baroque Ensemble at EMI's Abbey Road studios in 1950. Martin, of course, became an arch-manipulator of sound in his role as producer of the Beatles. In 1950 he took a quite different position. As he puts it:

> I ... gained from these sessions an early lesson in recording. By careful placement of the microphone it was possible to record using only one microphone. The natural acoustics of the studio gave the recordings their fine sound, and I learned that to obtain a natural sound one should use as few microphones as possible.
>
> (Martin 1979: 39)

In the film and radio industries, on the other hand, close miking, mixing of sound sources and signal processing became increasingly important as engineers strove to *simulate* sound in its notional place of origin. It was this approach which finally won through in the hi-fi market. As a contributor to *High Fidelity* magazine put it in 1958, 'the usual definition of hi-fi, by its exponents at least, is the illusion of being in one's favorite seat in the concert hall' (quoted in Keightley 1996: 153). Hi-fi illusionism was middle class, respectable and still nodded, as this quotation suggests, in the direction of source. However elsewhere in pop, illusionism was to become much bolder. In rock'n'roll the illusion involved the creation of a performance space that could never have existed without technological mediation. It is significant, then, that some of the engineers in rock'n'roll had worked in the Hollywood film studios where sound effects were widely used, while Sam Phillips, owner/producer at the pivotal Sun Studios, learnt his trade as an engineer at the WREC radio station in Memphis (Cunningham 1996: 31–5). The expansion of the recording industry in the 1950s thus brought a technical cadre into the studios which was much less bound by codes of phonographic documentation and much more willing to experiment than the old-school engineers.

Tape delay (2) – making space

Illusionism, or trickiness, represented an important aspect of what I have been calling ventriloquism too. Crooning, scat and saxophone neophonics were all forms of uncanny performance, premised on a profoundly unnatural throwing of the voice across the technosphere, away from the performer. Yet, at the same time, these performance techniques depended on an understanding that sound must emanate from the body. In effect, the aesthetic of ventriloquism was achieved through the perceived disjunction between human source and inhuman sounds, sounds which had to be *traced back* to the body by the listener.

With the advent of the electric guitar the degree of ambiguity at stake here was increased significantly. The loudspeaker cabinet could be seen in live performance: a dummy throat and mouth situated away from the performer. Moreover, the electric guitarist in rhythm and blues and rock'n'roll generated a new experience of sound-as-environment through a series of space-inferring effects: reverberation, echo, tremolo, thick overtones (Tagg 1999/1994). As we will see the electric guitar came to constitute a bridge between earlier ventriloquial practice and the virtual space aesthetic of popular music in the 1950s and after. How did this happen though?

Blues guitarists were solo or small group performers before the war. Against only one or two other voices their instruments could be heard quite easily in small venues or the studio. In big band swing, on the other hand, the guitar was limited to an almost subliminal accompanying role in the rhythm section. It seems that the first electric guitarists such as Eddie Durham, T-Bone Walker, Floyd Smith and Charlie Christian (all black musicians) turned to electronics during the mid-1930s in the search for enough volume to play single-note solos, like a saxophone or trumpet, above the sound of the band (Collier 1989: 262–5, C. Gill 1995: 148–51). In effect, then, the new apparatus was a simulating device. However it was quickly discovered that along with greater loudness the electromagnetic pick-up and amplifier system produced other sound effects. To begin with it enabled a much longer sustain envelope than could be achieved on the acoustic instrument. Moreover, by adjusting plucking style and volume, sound could be 'thickened', as overtones were added to the instrument's tonal profile. In Chicago and Memphis the blues guitarists who had moved up from the rural south after the war immediately adopted the electric instrument, apparently for the same functional reasons it had been taken up in the big bands. Quite simply it was loud, in this case loud enough to be heard over the drinking and talking clientele of the bars and clubs where the music was played (Palmer 1992: 19, Murray 1991: 182).

But even as it was introduced the electric guitar immediately transcended its designated function. There were two related aspects here. In terms of *performance* the extravagant use of echo and distortion represented new expressive parameters. Strangely, cultural tradition was reaffirmed in electronics. Take, for example, 'Smokestack Lightning' by Howling Wolf from 1956. The lyrics, unfolding the eerie drama of an electrical storm, together with the heavy echo on Wolf's voice and the plangent, overdriven valve amp sound used by guitarist Hubert Sumlin, translate the country blues into a city dialect which speaks simultaneously of past and future. Crucially, though, the appropriation of electricity in 1950s rhythm and blues was not just a symbolic trope, it also became an embodied one as the bands moved from the studio into the bar or street. Live blues was techno-theatre in which musicians for the first time appeared as appendages of the apparatus. Guitarists were effectively plugged into their amps, harmonica players cupped the microphone around their instruments. Bo Diddley makes this point. Touring the south early in his career he took to using a guitar lead that was 50 feet long so that he could prowl from one side of the hall to the other playing to the different sections of the segregated audience (White 1995: 65). There is a strange ambiguity about the spectacle. The players are empowered, using electricity to project their voices, fingers ... whole bodies; but they are also automatons, apparently controlled by the huge riffs and beats coming from the speakers.[8]

Along with the new performance mode a new kind of *space* was conjured up in electric blues and rock'n'roll. As the sound of the guitar thickened and got louder, so reverberation levels increased in the small venues where the music was played. This posed a problem in the recording studio since engineers could not easily balance or control 'excessive' volume levels. Robert Palmer suggests that the sound of the early Muddy Waters recordings at Chess, 'consciously creates the illusion of a cranked-up-to-10 juke joint guitar but is in fact an illusion, the guitar sound being modified not only by the amplifier but by the judicious application of both room acoustics and recording technology' (Palmer 1992: 20). If Palmer is right this represents something quite new: the ratcheting up of studio artifice in a quest to emulate 'dirty', live sound. Techniques tried out at Chess included using the studio's tiled bathroom as a reverb chamber, and then mixing the resulting sound with directly recorded 'dry' guitar as well as ambient sound from the studio (Palmer 1992: 21).

But the most important single method for creating the big rock'n'roll and blues sound was tape delay (or 'slapback' echo) which Les Paul claims to have invented (Cunningham 1996: 24–5), and which Sam Phillips pioneered at Sun. Tape delay involved using an extra playback head behind the recording head. As sounds were recorded some of the signal was fed back to the tape at an earlier stage producing an echo effect. Phillips used this technique more and more obsessively. On the first Elvis Presley recording sessions his voice is already beginning to proliferate. On 'Mystery Train', laid down seven months later in February 1955, the echo is heavier still. Scotty Moore's electric guitar resonates in and out of phase with the wobble on Elvis's vocal, while the dry click of D.J. Fontana's drum sticks marks off a nimble, syncopated metre in front of voice and guitar. Beneath this edifice the bass pumps out a two-step pulse, with acoustic guitar providing the mid-range, jangling ground. All the time Phillips 'rides the faders', bringing up the volume of one or other guitar at bridges, switching off the tape echo for Scotty Moore's solo, and then back on for the rhythm work.

With 'Mystery Train' the space of popular music starts to open up in an unprecedented way. The place that we are taken to as we listen is emphatically *not* a concert hall, bar, or lounge though. Rather this is a virtual architecture, one that is much 'larger than life'. It derives to a great extent from the echo and reverberation in which voice and certain instruments are soused. In everyday, unmediated listening the relationship between direct and reflected sound is a key index of space. The further a sound source is from the point of audition, the greater the amount of reflected sound we expect to hear (Altman 1992). 'Mystery Train' then takes us to a place with a *fantastic* dimensionality where the Presley voice is prominent due to its relative volume, yet, according to reverberation cues, far off; while the trap drum, which we know to be a loud instrument, has a crisp, 'dry' sound suggesting closeness. Such challenges to aural norms constitute an important historical shift. Whereas in the documentary mode of recording the ensemble had been a discrete, pro-phonographic entity in the studio, now the whole apparatus of band–tape–effects–engineer became a sound and space generating unit. In an important sense the construction of sound now prevailed over documentation, while the strict division of labour (musicians against engineers) and of function (sound-making against sound-recording) on which the earlier mode had been premised was swept away by a tidal wave of recalcitrant, electrified sounds. In effect, recording was absorbed into amplification.

But we also need to understand the new technological mode as a discursive formation. Sarah Thornton (1995) has traced the genealogy of speech about music in promotional materials, the press, Musicians Union memoranda and so. As she puts it:

> The term 'live' entered the lexicon of music appreciation only in the fifties. As more and more of the music heard was recorded, however, records became synonymous with music itself. It was only music's marginalised other – *performance* – which had to speak its difference with a qualifying adjective.
>
> (1995: 41)

I would want to add that the live/recorded binary which Thornton discusses encompassed quality of sound as well as context for listening. The emergence of a radically distinct recorded sonority in rock'n'roll reinforced the difference between the social institutions of live and recorded reception. For musicians a major consequence was that live performance became increasingly problematic. In a historic reversal sensory plenitude was now invested in the medium of the recording. Without the benefit of the studio-larynx it was musicians on stage who would struggle to emulate recorded sound rather than the other way around. The decision of The Beatles to stop touring in 1966 and spend all their time in the studio represented a public acknowledgement of this tendency. Perhaps, then, we can revise Charles Keil's (1994b) judgement about phonography being a means for perfecting popular music. Quite simply it needs a historical dimension. Before the 1950s the live concert was to a greater or lesser extent the site of the ideal performance; after that decade the locus shifted to recorded work.[9]

Something similar even happened in classical music with the introduction of stereo technology, although the norm of reproducing an ideal, live performance and 'its' space continued to have a greater momentum than in pop. Producer John Culshaw, for example, realized very early the potential power of stereo – its ability to suggest to the listener a lateral array of instruments, movement across an opera stage or separation of singing voices from an orchestra (Culshaw 1981: 156). Culshaw demonstrated these techniques in 1958 with a stereo production of *Tristan und Isolde* where the singers were placed 'forward' in the mix. It caused uproar in the classical music world (Culshaw 1981: 175).

Stereo thus offered a pretext for making virtual soundscapes in classical music in a way which paralleled, on a smaller scale, developments in monophonic pop. How can we account for this reconceptualization? I suggested earlier in the chapter that one reason why the spatial unity of the ensemble had been consolidated in the early period of recording was because the horn and loudspeaker yielded a radical impoverishment of musical presence. The loss, both of the visual image of musicians at work and also of heterogeneous live sound, led to an obsession with fidelity, that is truth to the prophonographic musical performance. What seems to have happened by the 1950s was that this need for an authentic moment behind the record, had lost its repressive hegemony. The record had became normalized.[10] Indeed, once the opportunities for artificially creating a musical environment had been glimpsed they were taken up enthusiastically. It is to the nature of this musical environment and the role of music makers in producing it that we turn next.

Aesthetics and politics in the Wall of Sound

Phil Spector's coinage, 'Wall of Sound', used to describe his own productions from the early 1960s, is misleading. The term 'wall' is too one-dimensional. In fact what Spector achieved was a significant extension and articulation of the sort of sonic architecture we can hear in 'Mystery Train'. Interestingly, Spector's use of tape technology was quite conservative. According to engineer Larry Levine he spurned stereo on the grounds that, 'you can never balance those channels precisely' (quoted in Cunningham 1996: 55); and although three- and four-track recorders were installed at

Gold Star, his preferred studio in Hollywood, they were used in real time as much as for overdubbing (Ribowsky 1989: 88). The key factor in Spector productions was precisely a lack of isolation between discrete sound sources. Basses, drums, guitars, pianos, and singers too, would be placed together in the cramped confines of the recording area. Sounds were grouped and microphones placed accordingly, but there was often a considerable amount of leakage between them. Spector also made a conscious effort to pick up ambient sound suffusing the whole studio space (Tobler and Grundy 1982: 48–58, Ribowsky 1989, Cunningham 1996: 53–9). Interestingly, this was in marked contrast to the shift towards spatial separation which Paul Théberge notes in multitrack recording during the 1960s (1989: 100–4). In fact what seems to have characterized production methods in early 1960s pop was a combination of methods: isolation of local sounds *and* the effecting of a sonorous nimbus around the whole ensemble.

Spector's Wall of Sound encapsulated some important contradictions in the popular music apparatus of the post-documentary period. It included progressive tendencies, yet it was deeply reactionary too. On the one hand the music represented perhaps the fullest development to date of an aesthetic proper to pop. The musician-ventriloquists played *across* the technosphere. They employed an aesthetic of ambiguity which depended on a degree of uncertainty in the audience about the status of the performed musical event and its position in relation both to the performer and the listener her/himself. In the case of the Wall of Sound, however, the listener is *immersed* in sound. The technosphere now extends out beyond the loud-speaker to envelop the audience. As Mark Ribowsky (1989) says of Spector's breakthrough record 'He's A Rebel' this was, '[a] sound that would pour out of a transistor radio like cake batter' (122). There is some-thing profoundly democratic about this: vast and opulent sounds available for everyone on cheap, portable listening machines.

On the other hand Spector was a tyrant in the studio. Musicians, singers and engineers constantly complained of his outrageous demands – for endless retakes, figures that were impossible to play or for a technical per-formance beyond the specification of the equipment being used (Ribowsky 1989). In one sense Spector productions represented a return to that world of divided labour and rational organization that we examined in the Hollywood studios in Chapter 1. Now, though, the situation was even worse with Spector throwing tantrums, flouting union contract terms (Ribowsky 1989: 119), and undermining the craft autonomy of musicians and engineers. Edward Kealy (1990/1979) notes the emergence of an 'entre-preneurial mode' in rock'n'roll production in the 1950s with sound mixers and musicians making technical – and therefore aesthetic – decisions together, on a mutual basis. Now Spector certainly made use of collabora-tors' ideas. Often he would just wait for a performance to emerge from the studio floor, offering little in the way of concept or direction. Whatever methods were used, though, he claimed authorial credit (Tobler and Grundy 1982: 48–58, Ribowsky 1989). Spector's arrogance, angst and indeed his success were untypical of entrepreneur producers in the period. The point is, though, that his methods represent the fullest development of the entrepreneurial mode, that is towards complete control of the production apparatus.

If I have so far been tracing a history of democratic, technological development and experiment from below, then such a tendency is undoubtedly compromised with the advent of the 'big production' in the early 1960s. For from now on the manipulation of sound increasingly becomes an aspect of a dominant approach to pop music-making in the major record companies and music-using media. This represents a significant shift in the apparatus away from *documentation* of a performed song to the *construction* of a song-sound, where production values are at the core of the aesthetic, and therefore exchange, value of the record commodity.

Multitracking and experimenting with time

Significantly, it was the attempt to translate the Spector mode of production in the context of a relatively undeveloped music industry in Britain which spawned the next phase in the development of the apparatus – the shift to multitrack recording. The Beatles (and other British beat groups) began their recording careers by attempting to ape the sound of American rhythm and blues and pop. But they had neither the technical means, nor the accumulated culture and expertise on which the big, transatlantic productions were premised. Among other factors we can note here that producer George Martin's experience had been mainly in light music or comedy (the antithesis of rock'n'roll); EMI expressly forbade the high bass levels needed to punch through to the front of a mix; and Abbey Road studios only took delivery of its first four-track tape recorder in October 1963 (Lewisohn 1994, Martin 1979).

As George Martin himself puts it, 'the boys were snapping at my heels. They could hear the difference in the US imports just as well as I could. "Why can't you get it like that, George?" they would chorus. "We want it like that"' (Martin 1995: 46). The Beatles and their producer began from a position of relative technological inferiority then. Certainly this was assumed by the group themselves. It explains to some extent why they were so determined to exceed any technologically inscribed barriers. Paul McCartney's motto was, 'louder, further, longer, more, different' (quoted in Lewisohn 1994: 13) – a cussed response to American techno-imperialism.

In the war of retaliation the most important tactic was an increasing use of sequential multitrack recording. We have seen how American producers treated the studio as a site for relatively homogenous, real-time performance. For George Martin and The Beatles, though, multitrack enabled an additive methodology: the accumulation of sounds by means of a virtual ensemble much 'larger' than the four-person unit of the real-time Beatles. This began early too. Mark Lewisohn points to the sophisticated, four-track overdubbing on 'A Hard Day's Night' from April 1964 (1994: 43), well before the self-conscious, art work of *Revolver* and the later albums. At stake here was a new temporal economy. For example, double tracking (the practice of adding a second unison voice to 'thicken' a vocal line) had been a laborious process which depended on accurate reduplication of the first performance, and often involved multiple takes to get it right. Then in 1964 EMI engineer Ken Townsend developed ADT, a variation on the tape echo idea, which enabled one voice to be doubled artificially with the use of a tape loop (Martin 1979: 155).

There was, then, as Paul Théberge (1989) has argued, a labour-substituting ideology at work here which fed experimentation. But Théberge surely goes too far when he says of multitracking that, 'technical mastery of musical time becomes inextricably linked with the technical mastery of labour relations' (1989: 106). For in an important sense multitrack recording restored a degree of control to musicians. True, the greater complexity of the studio apparatus strengthened the role of producer, but this was more than balanced by the fact that the rock band, or singer–songwriter, was a self-contained author–performer unit with a considerable degree of autonomy, conferred on it, as I argued in Chapter 1, by the emerging cult of rock authorship.

The Beatles provide the paradigmatic case in point here. Their working methods in the studio depended on collaboration and exchange between band members (with Lennon and McCartney providing the greatest input), producer (George Martin) and engineer (Norman Smith, then Geoff Emerick). This was in effect a *flexible* division of labour, one based on an exchange of cultural capital as much as strict, professional expertise. Crudely put, the Beatles contributed 'street' knowledge and 'feel', while Martin provided art music reference and the transferable skill of working with large arrangements and many voices. Smith and Emerick's role was important too, in enabling the array of tape and pro-phonographic effects that were used (Lewisohn 1994).

This collaborative regime in which the band had the last say (Edward Kealy (1982, 1990/79) usefully calls it the 'art mode') was by no means unproblematic though. Significantly, it could disempower musicians who did not feel confident in the high-tech environment of the studio. An account by Ian Hunter, of British rock band Mott the Hoople, paints a rather depressing picture of constraint and alienation during recording in the early 1970s:

Now the studio can make or break the song. Some twat engineer reading *Reveille* can put you off your stroke and he may not even try for a good sound on bass and drums – that pisses Pete and Buff off for a start. Having bumbled through this drama we then endeavour to get a back track down.

(Hunter 1996: 118)

Hunter's description of sixteen-track recording is strangely reminiscent of Gerald Moore's discussion of the acoustic process in the 1920s. As before, the apparatus stands in the way of communion with the audience; musicianship is at odds with the values of the engineer. Here is Hunter again. 'They talk about frequencies being too high or too low, of limiters and other technical contraptions of which I have no knowledge. I wish to fuck I had' (Hunter 1996: 119).

During the 1970s the rock production apparatus became ever more sophisticated. Hunter belonged to a tradition of live performers and showmen which could no longer afford the luxury of technophobia (although it might usefully be affected in certain scenes). As studios got larger, the number of tracks increased, and new kinds of sound processing equipment ('outboard') became available. Certainly this enabled flexibility – all kinds of music could be recorded in the same facility. Yet it also represented the dominance of the rock aesthetic; the quest to make a single, full sound by means of adding more.

The implications of this for the fabric of rock music were twofold. First of all, increasing separation, recombination and processing of sound sources yielded an ever-deeper sonic field. Rock albums from the late 1970s sound 'big' in comparison with records made ten years earlier. The spatial implications of multitracking are now much clearer. Sequential recording has been successfully rendered as a spatial ordering of sounds in which each separately recorded track is given a different treatment in the post-production, mix-down stage. So, the parameters of a single sound source – guitar say – can now be adjusted in at least the following aspects: overall volume, frequency profile ('Eq.'), to the right or left in the stereo array, amount and kind of reverberation and echo, attack and decay envelope ('gating'), dynamics ('compressing' and 'limiting'). The effect of this comprehensive control over sound quality on a recording can perhaps best be understood in terms of Allan Moore's (1993) heuristic model of the 'sound-box'. It represents a sort of three-dimensional freeze frame, or, as Moore puts it, 'a "virtual textural space", envisaged as an empty cube of finite dimensions, changing with respect to real time' (106). The box contains different textures of sound – 'strands' and 'blocks' – whose positions vertically, horizontally and front–back are determined not only by the musicians playing and singing but also by the application of effects and adjustments to the mix as a whole.

Critically, such control of texture and space became a compositional device – the big sound could now be articulated in order to inflect the musical narrative or time sense of a piece. This produced the conditions for the second significant aspect of what might be called the high rock studio mode, namely a shift towards 'hierarchically ordered discourse' (Middleton 1986). In a discussion of musical repetition Richard Middleton distinguishes two types:

> Musematic repetition is the repetition of short units; the most immediately familiar examples – riffs – are found in Afro-American music and in rock. Discursive repetition is the repetition of longer units, at the level of the phrase (defined as a unit roughly equivalent to a verbal clause or short sentence ...).
>
> (163)

Although both sorts may be combined in a given piece they nevertheless tend towards distinct modalities which 'may be tentatively characterised as "epic-recursive" and "narrative-lyric" respectively' (163). The latter is particularly associated with the developmental structure of European art music but also pop before African-American influence. It is characterized by 'discursive repetition, usually worked into hierarchical structures ... with a sense of "narrative closure"' (164). Now I want to suggest that, largely as a result of the multitrack additive aesthetic, certain areas of rock music took on an increasingly narrative-lyric quality in the 1970s. We can hear this particularly in heavy metal, progressive and what became known as album-oriented rock or AOR.

A good example from the last genre is 'So Good to See You' by Cheap Trick from 1977. It has an extended AABC form in which the cycle is repeated three and a half times. In each cycle the second of the eight-bar A sections can be distinguished by a 'thicker' mix – backing vocals are more prominent, the opening guitar chord is more sustained. At the same time successive cycles are themselves progressively mixed 'up'; extra sustain is used, and vocals and guitar are treated with more reverb. Now it is certainly the case that there are musematic devices here (particularly a boogie guitar figure in the A section). None the less, such small-scale repetition is actually varied and developed in a linear fashion by means of the addition of outboard effects, double tracking and so on. In this way technologically manipulated, musematic repetition serves to support the narrative-lyric structure of the song through the 'unfolding' of the mix.

Not only is such a linear structure typical of AOR, but the logic of multitrack recording – the articulation and separation of voices, differential processing of sound over the length of a piece – needs to be seen in a reciprocally determinant relationship to rock more generally. The aesthetic of rock in the late 1970s depended above all on highlighting a particular kind of production. Indeed the term 'production' now became a key term in rock discourse, with producers and engineers credited as co-authors on album covers and in reviews or media commentary (Straw 1990/1983).

How to assess this triumph of production? In terms of social relations, we can note the return of a more bureaucratic mode. True, the collaboration between technical personnel and band members that had characterized the emergence of multitrack recording in rock in the 1960s still remained. But the aesthetic of experiment, and especially the idea that technology was a domain of creative possibility, had been replaced by a highly routinized and centralized process of music-making. Paradoxically, this involved a loosening of the division of labour. As Will Straw (1990/1983) puts it,

> many of those formerly involved in support capacities (songwriters, session musicians, etc.) achieved star status because of the ease with which they could move between divisions or combine the production, composing, and performing functions (just as members of new groups now took it for granted that they could record solo albums).
>
> (99)

This 'rock elite' of aesthetically *and* technically competent music makers was reinforced in its position by the onward development of technology. As the complexity of equipment increased so too did the cultural and financial capital required to gain access to the means of production. In effect the record industry had ceded control of the apparatus to a coterie of established rock-masters. As for the relationship between technology and musical form, more than 50 years after the maturation of 'classical Hollywood style' (Bordwell *et al.* 1985) in the cinema, a comparable process of fragmentation and recomposition of time–space for narrative effect had finally been realized in popular music.

Programmed beats in the new age of dance

The most determined resistance to the centralized and technocratic rock mode of production came in the shape of punk with its do-it-yourself approach and privileging of technological simplicity (Laing 1985). More important in the longer term, however, was the development of a new generation of electronic instruments and music machines. These enabled the growth of a decentralized, yet technologically sophisticated, production culture in pop. In the new genres of electronic dance music which emerged in the mid-1980s the new technology has also been associated with a complete reconceptualization of the role of musicians and the nature of the technosphere.

In a highly persuasive study Paul Théberge (1997: 41–71) argues that the key factor in the development of electronic music in pop was a new breed of aggressively entrepreneurial electronics corporations. Until the mid-1970s synthesizers were expensive and hard to program. They had been designed mainly for avant-garde composers and advanced use in the recording studio. Then American companies like E-mu, Sequential and Oberheim translated the synthesizer into a 'user-friendly' musical instrument for performing musicians. By the 1980s high-volume Japanese manufacturers like Roland and Yamaha were producing electronic instruments too for what was now a huge market. Théberge suggests that in addition to the important technological component the key innovation here was the '"production" of musicians as consumers of high technology' (70–1). Amateurs and bottom-rung musicians, stars and session players – all constituted a single market where technological development and innovation were at a premium.

In an important sense this represents a new phase in what Bernard Miège (1989) calls 'the capitalization of cultural production'. For now, in a complete reversal of the situation pertaining during the documentary mode, capital outside the conservative music industries was driving technological development in music-making onwards. What have been the implications of this?

In order to answer the question we need first to review issues of technical facility. Along with the synthesizer the most significant device in the new generation of machines has been the sequencer. This is a programmable digital 'clock' which stores sequences of note on and off information (and now many other parameters too). Once programmed, the sequencer can then send these commands to a synthesizer, or other sound-yielding device like a sampler, for realization in sound. With its many programmable tracks, and input and output channels the sequencer resembles the multi-track tape recorder in important respects. The key differences are, first, that it 'records' music in an *abstract* form, as sequences of electronic commands which must then be assigned to voices produced by other machines. Second, as well as being able to record musical event information from a keyboard in real time, sequencers are 'step time' programmable. Introduced in 1977 the Roland MC-8 represented the paradigmatic device here. It enabled the entry of musical event information in short 'steps' which could then be chained to produce longer sections (Théberge 1997: 223–4). By the mid-1980s part and chain methodology was employed on the host of dedicated sequencers which were now on the market, so obviating the need for conventional keyboard skills and dexterity on the part of the programmer. One other development needs to be mentioned: the agreement between equipment manufacturers in 1981 on a common digital information code called MIDI enabled straightforward networking between different makes of machine. Within a few years sequencers could control any number of 'slave' devices.

There have been two major effects of this new technology (and market). First technical and musician functions, already imbricated in rock as we saw, have been completely elided. MIDI musicians are always programmers and technicians too. In fact the distinction between musicianship and technicianship has almost disappeared. In British dance music genres this is indicated by the term used to describe someone who makes dance music up to the stage of mastering, namely 'producer'. Second, the production apparatus has been decentralized once again. The cost of professional or near professional MIDI set-ups is considerably less than the big studios which predominated in the high rock mode of the 1970s.[11] Musicians can produce finished or part-finished work in their own home studios (Goodwin 1992: 89–90). Indeed, the bedroom has become a metonym for a new cultural politics of access and empowerment.

However, it is in particular genres – hip hop and dance music – that the most radical implications of the new music technology have emerged. Here aesthetics have converged with technics in significant ways. To understand this we need to return to the late 1970s for a moment and consider disco. Disco's characteristic features, like the alternating octave bass figure, 'four-on-the-floor' bass drum pattern and downbeat hi-hat lick, were quintessentially musematic and repetitive. In this context musicians had to play extremely precisely so that the small units were repeated without variation. The narrative inscribing facility of the multitrack studio was to a great extent superfluous here. No doubt all available tracks could be put to good use, laying down strings, brass or extra percussion for example. But there was little call for the topographically waymarked journeys of the sort found in rock. Equally, the instrumental virtuosity at a premium in rock was of little importance in disco or funk. There were virtuoso players, but whether live or in the studio, they tended to 'go to work' without accruing a cult following.[12]

These aesthetic and formal characteristics of dance musics at the turn of the 1970s were congruent with the emerging new music technologies in several ways. First, step-time programming matched the intense musematic repetition at a constant tempo that was called for in dance. The unit of the step, generally a bar or half a bar, tended to correspond to the key musematic units of bass line, drum beat, short riff and so on. Thus programming methodology was (accidentally) conducive to musematic structure. At first the inflexibility of sequencing and drum machine programming made for a certain 'robotic feel' (Théberge 1997: 224): musematic units were uninflected and there was little sense of dynamics. Notes were sounded exactly in line with a strict but coarse-grained temporal value. Crucially, though, the machine connotation was then incorporated into the aesthetics of dance music. By a paradoxical turn, funk quickly came to include the antithesis of 'funk', namely cold, inhuman precision.[13] Second, and connected to this, the relatively impersonal approach to music-making of 1970s funk and disco found an echo in the studio-based nature of electronic music-making. The difficulty of rendering the recorded in live performance which we noted in rock, had now become almost insurmountable. Computers were notoriously maladapted to life and work 'on the road'. Even more important, live acts had ceased to be the main providers of dance music; by the 1980s record play in clubs had superseded performance by bands (Thornton 1995: 26–86).

In these conditions – deriving from a complex interaction of the technologically given and the culturally created – a new conception of the technosphere has emerged in the 1980s and 1990s. You will remember I proposed at the beginning of the chapter that the technosphere was an imaginary space of musical possibilities and constraints. The *relationship* between possibility and constraint has always been crucial here. In dance music – garage, house, techno and so on – it seems to have taken a new form. For now the very degree of technical facility and rational control over music-making is accompanied by sequestration, a hiding away of the site of production in the studio/bedroom. This marks, paradoxically enough, a return to the masquerade of earlier ventriloquial tropes where voices were thrown from hidden places. In its new guise, though, the 'trick' is performed by another agent, the DJ who stands in for the music maker her/himself. We will examine the DJ's role in a moment. First, though, I want to investigate the implications of this scenario for the producer.

The case of Larry (Mr Fingers) Heard, a key player in the mid- and late 1980s Chicago 'house' scene, is instructive here. In late 1984 Heard gave up drumming, frustrated that his ideas and compositions were constantly being turned down by the funk band with which he played. He bought a drum machine and a synthesizer, and on the same day made three tracks, all of which became highly influential house music sides. On the genesis of one of them, 'Washing Machine', he says:

> I had the clock out, I think, from the Roland 707 [drum machine] and hooked the wire into the arpeggiator clock in on the Juno 6 [synthesizer], and it just happened. I just hit a chord with two hands on the keyboard and the Juno 6 arpeggiated it. I never could recreate that, it was just something that happened in the midst of me experimenting, and I got it on tape. The sound was one I programmed, and while it was playing I was messing with the envelope and the frequency and resonance, to get that kind of effect where it was sweeping and what have you. I was just fooling around with the knobs. All those knobs are so tempting.
>
> (Heard, quoted in Trask 1996/1992: 36)

Several things strike one about this description. To begin with there is the solitariness. Heard is creating alone, or rather in the company of machines. The contrast with Charles Mingus seems immense. Yet at the same time this process involves the discovery of what remain *socially produced* possibilities. The arpeggiator, an on-board micro-sequencer for generating arpeggios, is a classical example of what electronic instrument entrepreneur Tony Gambacurta calls a 'selling feature ... something that sells the product but is not that important to the final user' (quoted by S. Jones 1992: 79). Here, though, Heard converts the 'selling feature' into something useful. He makes it sing again. This is nothing less than the expropriation of technology, the skilful misuse of equipment by a musician for creative ends: vernacular avant-gardism in fact.

The solitary experimentalism evident here also has a strong tactile element. One reason why early 1980s music machines have such a high resale value today is because of their (mythical) hands-on nature. It is the palpability of the knobs, their phenomenal roundness that counts. Something similar is true of the slider control, commonly found on old synthesizers. Like the slide on a trombone it is an analogue interface between the organic, free-moving body and organic, free-moving sounds.

Finally, we can note a strange mixture in Heard's discourse of pleasure in control, it is he who has 'had the clock out' and 'hit the chord', and delight at the mysteries of happenstance. The events he describes are then reported with that self-deprecating, low-key turn of phrase so typical of the popular musician: 'I was messing with', 'I was just fooling around'.

Heard belongs to a heroic age of advanced technology. By the end of the decade the removal of back panels, hooking wires in and so on were already becoming outmoded. For the sequencer now became a piece of software installed on the computer to which samplers and synthesizers could then be connected via a MIDI interface. Once this happened another aspect of its modality became apparent, namely the reinscription of music.

Generally, as we have seen, pop since rock'n'roll has used an oral/aural process of composition and song transmission between musicians, based on the empirical evidence of recordings, shared idioms and a specialist, if inevitably imprecise, vocabulary (on the last point see Vignolle 1980, Hennion 1990/1983). The sequencing programme, however, represents a radical return to the graphic representation of music. On screen every aspect of the musical performance is registered as it is entered or played back. All programmes use some form of matrix where one axis is temporal, showing diachronic position in the piece down to the smallest fraction of a bar. The other axis is synchronic. It carries musical event information at any specified moment – notes on, voice channels activated, volume settings and so on. In effect the linear narrative of the stave is rendered as a series of frames which may be frozen or scanned sequentially.

Now Paul Théberge (1997) suggests that this process represents a continuation of 'the fragmentation of the ensemble' (228) which he had already noted in the multitrack studio (Théberge 1989). I am not so sure. Certainly, sequencing programmes tend to simulate tape transport controls and indeed the whole functional system of multitracking in their interface – the way they appear to the user on screen. But the crucial difference is the visibility and graphical control represented by the 'editing window' in whatever particular form it takes. Here *all* tracks can be seen; and if only a segment of a whole song will be visible, this does not represent fragmentation of the ensemble but rather division of the piece into units. In other words the iterative-variative form of dance music in which short sections are 'bolted together' is privileged over linear, narrative development. It seems then that the original sequencer construct of step time, and so musematic repetition, have acquired an institutional weight and inertia in the technics of popular music.

What does the virtual inscription of music on the computer screen mean for the music maker? Above all it represents the fullest development yet in popular music's short twentieth century of the *non*-tactile, rational and abstract control of music. True, many musicians continue to use old machines or new 'retro' equipment which maintain a degree of tactility in music-making and a sense of the body engaged in performance. Generally, though, the trend is towards microscopic, musematic control in what is a radically dis-corporate mode of production.

The contrast, then, is with the work of the DJ. In the Introduction we saw how the institution of the disc jockey emerged in Jamaica in the 1960s and 1970s. Something similar happened in dance music in America and Britain. In disco, particularly, the disc jockey assumed a new importance as a live performer of records (Collin 1997: 10–24, Rietveld 1998: 99–120). Playing a continuous mix, often with long cross-fades between records and the addition of 'live' effects disco, and later house, DJs have effectively played two roles. First they are organizers of pleasure in the beat. In other words they do the functional work of gauging the mood of the crowd and adjusting the repertoire and dynamics of the mix to ensure that floors stay full.

Second, the DJ is a ventriloquist. This aspect consists in the performance of *marvelous* sounds (in the archaic sense of that adjective). On a nightly basis DJs throw voices – from the grooves on the record – so turning the whole club into a phonic sensorium which is a wonder to inhabit. Generally, the DJ is a semi-reclusive figure, and often hidden behind the booth. But even when visible to the crowd s/he always appears distracted, deeply involved in the arcane rites of mixing and making the dance floor shake. In this respect the DJ is rather like a cathedral organist: a small figure controlling a machine which makes awesome sounds in a spectacular environment.[14]

With the advent of the division of labour in dance music between record producer and DJ we almost come full circle, back to Tin Pan Alley. There are now two cadres of music maker again. One is a composer and writer of sounds, the other is a performer and interpreter. As we will see in Chapter 5, this may not represent unequivocal progress. The very separation of functions can produce a sense of alienation, particularly for producers cut off in their studios. None the less, what is striking is that at the end of popular music's short twentieth century, in dance music at least, the aesthetic constraints and possibilities of the technosphere continue to be reimagined and worked on in new ways.

Coda: technological determinism and gendered power

An important theme in cultural studies since the 1970s has been criticism of 'technological determinism', the idea that technology is an autonomous domain and a primary cause of cultural phenomena. For example Raymond

Williams (1996/1983) argues that 'virtually all technical study and experiment are undertaken within already existing social relations and cultural forms, typically for purposes that are already in general foreseen' (120). Furthermore, technical advances can only develop into practical technology through a process of economic and social selection. Technologies must serve profit-making strategies and have a broader cultural 'fit' if they are to succeed. This is a telling critique of crude technological determinism. However Williams still treats technology as a matter of function – technology simply *does* things. The issue for him is then how far technological factors are mediated by social ones, or where they should be ranked in a hierarchy of influences.

My approach in this chapter has taken a different turn. I have argued that technology and the social and cultural are always imbricated. Technology is never just selected, rather it is always already a discursive formation. We can see this in the work of marketing departments and copywriters who brand machines. The Fender Stratocaster, Ensoniq Mirage, Technics SL1000 and so on summon up (or attempt to) imagined worlds of technological potency. Even more important is the way new machines are validated within a specific, and usually genre-based, music makers' culture. Here counter-discourses of technology (as in 'fooling with the knobs') may prevail. In other words, technologies take off because they are congruent with an emerging aesthetic among musicians; they must literally be imagined into existence.

This does not mean that extrinsic determinants – above all the imperative of capital accumulation – are unimportant. The relatively slow development of music technology up until the 1960s, and a much faster rate of innovation since the late 1970s have much to do with the structure of the cultural industries and in turn their changing position within capital as a whole (Miège 1989, Garnham 1990c, Lash and Urry 1994). None the less, within this broad historical sweep the shape of technological innovation is very much a cultural phenomenon. One other point needs to be added here, namely that technological developments may be strikingly *un*foreseeable (Frith 1986). As we have seen, music technology is often misused by musicians, adopted for purposes other than that for which it was designed. To put it another way, there seems to be a historical uncertainty about the use value of the means of musical production as well as music products themselves (see Chapter 1).

So, I am arguing against both technological determinism and social selectionism on the grounds that they isolate technology and reify it. Yet having made this point, there is an immediate need to qualify it. For from the point of view of the social relations of gender, 'technology' does indeed stick out, appearing as a solid and impervious entity.

Throughout the chapter women have been notable by their absence. All the examples we have examined of technological development have been initiated by men. Indeed there is a strong case for saying that the whole process of the 'technification' of music which we have been examining in this chapter has tended to exclude women. Women continue to take up instruments and become performers in classical music. But in the world of pop, as music-making has taken a technological turn women have been to a great extent kept out. As Mavis Bayton succinctly puts it, '[r]ock is associated with technology, which is itself strongly categorised as "masculine"' (1997: 42). What applies in the case of rock, applies too in other genres and periods. For example, I have argued for the importance of ventriloquism as a trope over the whole course of popular music's short twentieth century. But ventriloquism (being tricky with technology) assumes precisely a masculine command and knowledge of technology.

There seem to be two ways of responding to 'techno-pessimism' in respect of gender. The first is to stress other, more salient aspects of popular music-making. Take the case of Phil Spector. Barbara Bradby (1990) points out the absurdity of lauding Spector as *auteur* and techno-visionary in a situation where production of 'his' work was actually social and many-faceted (342–3). But she goes further. Her analysis of girl-group songs, produced by men like Spector, reveals 'a structure of *feminine discourse* which offers positions for the speaking female subject' (343, original emphasis). Bradby suggests these songs show reflexivity on the part of girls about the ambiguity of romance and normative heterosexual relations. They are addressed to girls who are 'in the know' about boys. Bradby's analysis thus undermines any straightforward evaluation of the Wall of Sound. Her reading suggests that what is aesthetically valuable in girl-group music depends not on technology or authorship, but rather on mode of address and the way the audience is hailed.

The other response to the technological exclusion of women in pop is to look for and advocate change. Mavis Bayton's (1998) work on women in rock bands has been exemplary in this respect. Bayton shows how women musicians use electric guitars, amplifiers and effects with ease and adroitness. The point here is that being kept out of the technosphere is partly a matter of not being acknowledged or publicly represented as technically competent. From a policy perspective, recent work in the UK has suggested the need for much more proactive development of girls' skills in technology as part of music education. Clearly the engendering of music technology happens at an early age partly because teachers let, or even encourage, it to happen. Education policy and the school therefore have a key role to play in change (Comber *et al.* 1993, Green 1996). Finally, there are signs that in dance music – a genre in which technology is venerated in an unparalleled fashion – women have been able to make significant, if limited, inroads. Hillegonda Rietveld was an electronic dance music pioneer in the early 1980s with Quando Quango and continues to make tracks and DJ today. She also supplies critique and theory on music and technology (Rietveld 1998). On the British drum and bass scene DJ Rap, and Kemistry and Storm have made their own records as well as being key DJs and tastemakers.

Sister Bliss – keyboard player, programmer and successful remix specialist – has recently become an international star with her band Faithless.

Perhaps what arguments about technological determinism and gender in music-making suggest most of all, though, is that to make judgements on the political value of technological change is a difficult business. It needs to be considered in the light of developments in relations of power across the social and cultural fields more generally. For all that, as I have argued, what is extraordinary about popular music-making is its continuing technological reflexivity. This is a domain in which relations between the body and machines are reinvented in new and exciting ways. Everybody who wants to make music could and should have access to it.

|4|

Genre-cultures

Funk is something that one feels, and everybody has the ability to feel it. The irony is: the more one thinks about it, the harder it is to get the feel of the Funk. It's just done.

(Clinton 1996: xiii)

'Heavy metal' is a term that is constantly debated and contested, primarily among fans but also in dialogue with musicians, commercial marketing strategists, and outside critics and censors. Debates over which bands, songs, sounds and sights get to count as heavy metal provide occasions for contesting musical and social prestige. 'That's not heavy metal' is the most damning criticism a fan can inflict, for that genre name has great prestige among fans.

(Walser 1993: 4)

If anything can unfailingly accomplish an end, why not repeat it again and again, both for its effect considered singly and then as part of a growing chain.

(Meltzer 1987/1970: 73)

Why is genre so important in popular music? In Chapter 2 we examined how music makers work with historically bestowed possibles. At that stage in the argument the focus was on understanding creativity as a general process. Now, though, we need to move on and deal with the way creative acts are structured according to style. For, above all, those densely clustered possibles near the centre of the radius of creativity (the codes, traditions and musical traits most commonly selected by a music maker) are generic. I mean that they are shared among music makers who belong to the same culture of production, while other groups of musicians inherit quite different sets of possibles proper to their 'own' genres. Considered in this way the importance of genre is that it ensures alignment between habitus and the field of works, acting as a filter to allow some possibles in the field to be heard by the music maker while cutting out others. We might even say that the constraints of genre provide a basic condition for the productive ordering of sound in music. As Derrida asks rhetorically, '[c]an one identify a work of art of whatever sort ... if it does not bear the mark of a genre?' (quoted by Cohen 1986: 204).

This approach, primarily textual in that it treats genre as a set of formal attributes, is an important one, not least because as we will hear in the first section of the chapter musicians more or less consciously consider their music-making in such terms. But there are real limits to it. For no text will have all the traits of the genre to which it belongs. Particular texts are precisely not identical to the categories in which they are included. As a result genre is an elusive term, being neither a textual essence nor a comprehensive code.

Steve Neale offers a way out of this impasse in a discussion of film genre. He suggests that rather than being categories of text, genres are 'systems of orientations, expectations and conventions that circulate between industry, text and subject' (1980: 19). This notion of genre as a social process enables a much more flexible and comprehensive approach. For the present argument its importance lies in the suggestion that style cannot be the exclusive domain of musicians. Rather it will tend to be contested, becoming the subject of struggles for definition across the continuum from production to consumption.

In particular, communities of listeners lay claim to genres. In the 1970s researchers from the Centre for Contemporary Cultural Studies argued that musical styles might represent in a 'homological' fashion the social character of subcultures and ethnic groups (Willis n/d and 1978, Hebdige 1979). Later I will suggest (against a now dominant view in cultural studies) that we can usefully return to the idea of the homology. For the moment I simply want to observe that however one conceives the link between them, social formations often have a strong affiliation with musical genres and may invest them with intense cultural significance. This obvious, but vital, point complicates any straightforward conception of genre as the set of traditions with which the musician-*auteur* works.

There is one more factor we need to consider when we treat genre as social process: the role of the music industries. A case in point is the way radio stations in North America have, since the mid-1950s, 'formatted' the recorded music they play in order to segment audiences for delivery to advertisers. Historically, particular categories of music have been constructed by radio programmes and widely adopted across the industry in order to target particular kinds of listener; they include Top Forty, adult-oriented rock and contemporary hit radio. However, fears within the radio industry that these formats fail to reflect the taste of a national 'real' market make any typology of music a temporary fix, and in a forlorn attempt to map the taste of their audience in a definite way stations continuously reformat musical output (Barnes 1990, Berland 1993, Peterson 1994). It seems, then, that the very imperative to determine the audience through the construction of a style produces instability.

The radio format is effectively a secondary genre. It involves the repackaging of units originally divided into genres by the record industry. But this only serves to underline the contested nature of genre, its *intermediate* status at the nexus between competing interests and expectations. Over the course of the chapter we will explore this contradictory character of genre, the fact that it is on the one hand the focus for affiliation and continuity, while on the other being subject to dispute and displacement.

Actually, as we will hear in the next section, this tension in genre can even be detected at the production stage. In genres where there appears to be a large degree of coherence and solidarity, musicians are often unsure about practical questions of genre – to do with boundaries, the nature of rules and so on. This suggests that genres may be *inherently* unstable and not just riven by socially produced differences of interest and position.

The sound of genre

There is a tendency amongst popular music makers to idealize style. What seems to be at stake is a notion of the perfected genre made up of a set of sonic and musical attributes at the dead-centre of the class, so to speak. We can hear this in the account by Austin, Texas producer John Crosslin of his approach to recording local hardcore band the Wannabes.[1]

> The Wannabes are a band that really like Husker Du and the Replacements. They are people who love the guitar sound on the Husker Du records or the production on *Let it Be* [an album by the Replacements] or lack thereof. It kind of snuck up on them, then, when we went in the studio and started being real careful about the way things sounded. I think they were kind of going, hmm, well, shouldn't this be spontaneous?
>
> (quoted by Shank 1994: 185)

Clearly Crosslin is trying to persuade the musicians of the need for 'artificial' restraint in the studio. But he does so precisely because he wants to help the band realize an ideal hardcore sound. The Wannabes are not being cynical here, they have not simply run out of their own ideas. Rather Crosslin suggests that they *love* Husker Du's guitar sound. They hear it, with other attributes like 'lack of production', as part of a perfect form and sonority located at the heart of the genre.

Unusually, Crosslin provides a neutral description of genre and its attractions. More often the centripetal tendencies of a style are considered in a negative light by music makers on the grounds that they blot out the creative impulse. Mike Watt, bassist with fIREHOSE, makes this point.

> I remember when hardcore came. . . . In a way I was glad that it wasn't just old glitter people, you know from the burned-out Hollywood scene. But in another way, I was bummed out that they all wanted to play one song and they didn't have time to realize that it could be lots of different sounds.
>
> (quoted in Foege 1995: 84)

Coming from the member of an archetypal hardcore band this seems a little disingenuous. In fact Watt's comments are better read as the expression of a contradictory attitude commonly found among musicians. On the one hand there is the urge to make music deep within a style. Unlike the old Hollywood glitter scene hardcore is dynamic and coherent, and therefore desirable in aesthetic terms; on the other Watt feels repugnance towards what he hears as an unthinking drive in the direction of unity. He wants diversity as well.

If genre is a difficult term for musicians it also provides problems in critical analysis. A first sketch of the elements of hardcore might include these characteristics: 'noisy' guitar chords with many overtones, bass guitar played in a high register, a tendency towards monophony around the vocal line, declamatory vocal style, brisk tempo (circa 140 b.p.m.), dour or earnest overall sound. The analysis could be developed much further. Yet there is a sense in which increasing the amount of detail in order to specify hardcore only makes the definition more difficult. For as the number of required traits increases so the number of texts which conform to the resulting composite of genre attributes will decline. Take the issue of tempo. Where do the slower hardcore numbers fit in? Should they be excluded because they are the wrong speed? And if so what might be the cut-off point?

It is precisely this sort of difficulty which structuralist literary theorists like Tzvetan Todorov attempt to overcome. Arguing against the conception of literary genres as collections of traits, Todorov (1975) posits a system based on significant difference. Across a spectrum of genres from the 'uncanny' through the 'fantastic' to the 'marvellous' what matters in the classification of narratives is the extent to which natural or supernatural causation must be attributed in order to explain events. This is a classically structural schema in that it is organized by internal relations of difference. Yet ultimately, Todorov concedes, what guarantees the classification is external reference to the known world. As he puts it 'the fantastic requires . . . a reaction to events as they occur in the world evoked' (60). Such grounding in reference is, of course, impossible with music. We cannot talk about rational as against mystical causes of events in the case of, say, hardcore or cool jazz.

Franco Fabbri's (1982) approach to genre might then offer a way forward. It has the virtues of structuralist analysis, but does not depend on language or reference. This is a theory of *musical* genre. Fabbri proposes a matrix 'with rows of rules and columns of genres, in which each single element a_{ij} would indicate the value of the rule i for the genre j' (54). While a useful way of showing commonality and significant difference in coding across genres, as Fabbri himself argues, such a method leaves us with little idea of the relative importance of rules within a class. His response is to propose a hierarchical model of genre with a 'hyper-rule' or 'ideology' at the apex (55). The problem now, though, is that the 'hyper-rule' takes us back to a descriptive approach to genre. Instead of a collection of traits we have a predominating, even essential, genre characteristic in the guise of the 'hyper-rule'. It seems that despite having set up a system of difference based on the distribution of rules across classes, Fabbri cannot help but return to a notion of the characterful and singular genre.

For critics as much as for musicians, then, genre poses a conundrum. At one and the same time it seems to be constituted as an essence, as a collection of traits, and in structured opposition to other genres. Is there any way of getting over this dilemma? Perhaps the first step is to recognize that genre can never be a static system of classification. Rather, as Steve Neale (1980) argues, genre needs to be seen as a process in which the tension between repetition and difference fundamental to all symbolic forms is regulated. Neale deals with cinema, but the broad approach can be applied to music and the listening subject too. He begins by considering pleasure and desire from a broadly Freudian perspective. What is at stake in reading (but surely also in producing) a text is the desire to repeat a first experience of pleasure. However pleasure and its signifier, the mark made by that experience, are always separated since subsequent readings fail to reduplicate the initial experience of pleasure. As Neale puts it, this gap 'is the reason for the inexhaustibility of desire, but it also allows whatever satisfaction is attainable to be renewed. Hence pleasure lies both in the repetition of the signifier(s) and in the limited but none the less fundamental difference underpinning and separating such instances of repetition' (48).[2]

If this is true at the level of the text the same principles can be identified in genre. Genre functions to control repetition and difference in such a way that desire is maintained *across* texts within a certain range of variation. In this light the comments by John Crosslin and Mike Watt take on a new significance. Certainly hardcore musicians keep on going back to the 'same' music, but in doing so they inflect their sound as they strive, but fail, to achieve an ideal, original aesthetic effect. Whether or not this is a conscious process we can hear it – and this is true of all genres, not just hardcore – in the material practice of music-making. What seems to be at stake is an exploration of the limits of repetition within a spectrum of musical parameters.

In hardcore, and later in grunge, repetition is most clearly audible in the thick-buzzy timbre of the overdriven electric guitar. This takes the form of chords which provide a musical ground, but also ostinati, solos and even lines played behind the vocal. What then directs attention to such a grossly ubiquitous sonic field is melody or tunefulness. We might say that thick-buzzy guitar textures are *tested* in the varying motivic contexts of the individual song. This is one reason why original compositions are so important in the ideology of hardcore. They are a key component of generic method, a tool for producing small variations along a bed of iterated texture. To put it another way, it is from the vantage of different listenings in the different songs that we can hear the full, engulfing sameness of the hardcore sound. Conversely with a genre like be-bop there is considerable repetition at the level of the song. A relatively stable repertoire of standard tunes, as well as newer 'classics' written within the genre, provide a set of melodies and chord changes which are then subjected to variative testing by improvising soloists.

The schema I have outlined for hardcore is selective. It excludes important musical parameters like metre or harmony, and it does not deal with words. However the aim here is less to produce a complete analysis of the genre than to suggest its most salient dimensions of repetition and variation. In the case of hardcore the thick-buzzy guitar sound does not so much define the genre as become the object of its aesthetic practice. It is held tenuously in place as a generic signifier by the competing imperatives of returning to and moving on from the one sound. We will come back to the important question of how this process of excursion and return contributes to generic change in the last chapter.

The inevitability of genre – the case of free music

In the meantime, though, we ought to ask if such an approach can be applied to other kinds of music. Maybe it works in the case of hardcore because that genre is so manifestly repetitive, showing a high level of 'intensional development'. Andrew Chester (1990/1970) uses this term to characterize popular music emerging from the African-American tradition which depends on 'inflection' and 'modulation', in other words multi-parametric development of materials over quite basic and repetitive musical structures. It can be contrasted with the 'extensional' mode found in western classical music. Here '[t]he complex is created by combination of the simple, which remains discrete and unchanged in the complex unity' (315). Now, as Alan Moore (1993: 21–3) argues, it is a mistake to treat these two modes as mutually exclusive. Indeed, all music involves a mixture of the two. My point, though, is that in cases of extensional development as much as in more obviously intensional texts, the genre function of regulating repetition and variation is critical. To make that argument I want to examine free improvised music, a form which shows both intensional and extensional tendencies. What makes free music particularly significant, though, is that practitioners tend to deny that it belongs to any particular genre. It therefore provides a limit case.

Guitarist Derek Bailey describes free improvisation in this way:

> diversity is its most consistent characteristic. It has no stylistic or idiomatic commitment. It has no prescribed idiomatic sound. The characteristics of freely improvised music are established only by the sonic-musical identity of the person or persons playing it.
>
> (1992: 83)

Something similar is proposed by the saxophonist John Zorn.

> I don't think I'm capable of doing any kind of objective music where everybody feels the same way when I play it. I'm not really interested in that. The plurality is more important to me. Everybody gets something different and everybody experiences it in a different way. As far as the audience is concerned, I have nothing whatsoever to do with them when we're performing . . . I'm concerned with the music itself.
>
> (Quoted in Such 1993: 158)

These comments are typical of testimony from freely improvising musicians. We can identify at least three themes here. The first is an extreme version of the expressive individualism we noted in Chapter 2 in discourse by and about popular music *auteurs*. Zorn seems to be suggesting that the fabric of the music directly manifests his persona. Second, innovation is emphasized – the music should avoid iteration and tend towards absolute diversity. Third, there is a refusal of orientation towards the audience on the grounds that, lacking any idiom, free music cannot be channelled towards a particular receptive sensibility.

Jacques Attali (1985) also argues that free jazz represents liberation from idiom, but appeals to Bakhtin and cultural theory to make his case. As Attali has it the music arises from a historically new mode of music production called 'composition' where the anarchic-grotesque production 'of differences, of the rediscovery and blossoming of the body' is at stake (142). Reflecting on what this might mean for conventional notions of communication Attali suggests that free music is 'a labour on sounds without a grammar', that is to say an uncoded process where one 'hear[s] the noises of others in exchange for one's own' (143).

It seems to me that Attali and the musicians are wrong to construe free music in such a way. Certainly the form's aesthetic *goal* is an unhinged affirmation of the body, the spirit (see Such 1993: 112–44) or the particular player's persona. The claim being made here is for a break through into a space beyond the normative confines of the code. Yet the *practice* of free music cannot be exempted from what I now want to call the inevitability of genre. This is sometimes acknowledged by players themselves. For example, describing the improvising percussionist's equipment Bailey says, '[t]he usual basic stuff ... is supplemented by gongs, saucepans, gunshells, handbells and all the other early Cage paraphernalia' (1992: 100). What we have is an assumption that the listener can recognize the sound of both 'the usual basic stuff' and 'early Cage paraphernalia'; in other words two highly idiomatic approaches to music-making. There is also an air of whimsy about the term 'paraphernalia', it suggests a cosy world of percussive disorder.

In fact acknowledgement of the generic aspect of free music can be found throughout Bailey's discussion. He talks about 'the vocabulary widely used by improvising trombonists' (109), 'the continuity of involvement which is available in solo improvisation' (111), and the way in which his experience as a dance band musician feeds into judgement of 'overall balance and pace' while he is improvising (109). What makes these reflections so interesting is that, just like the hardcore musicians, Bailey reveals both a desire for maximum variation, and the urge to ground his playing in what is known and shared, in other words that which tends to remain the same. In this connection it might be useful to return to Andrew Chester's (1990) distinction between intensional and extensional modes of musical organization.

A few years ago I heard an arts administrator use the phrase 'squeaky bonk' to describe free music. It strikes me that, despite the pejorative tone, squeaky bonk is a useful epithet. It points to the *vocalization* of the music. I use that term in the same way that I did in Chapter 3, to suggest a concern with inflecting, even transforming, the given sound of the instrument. Free musicians deploy a range of instrumental tropes such as thinning (to produce squeaks) or coarsening of timbre (to make bonks), pitch bending (slides from high squeak to low bonk or vice versa), and the playing of flurries of notes (squeaky bonk tone clusters or licks). What we have here is the intensional mode *par excellence* since these tropes involve an 'inward' (Chester 1990/1970: 316) development of materials within, as it were, the larger musical structure. But free music also shows clear extensional tendencies. That larger structure is actually derived from the syntagmatic recombination of (always permutated) licks in long, extemporized strings. Such strings tend towards what Richard Middleton (1986: 161) calls 'the *infinite set* (the linear, the "narrative"; most nearly approached by pieces whose aim is that nothing is heard twice)'. Thus in free music the regulation of repetition and variation shows some unusual characteristics. We have musematic repetition in the shape of instrumental tropes, but neither rhythmic groove nor recursive form. Rather, as in the case of western classical music, the structure is additive with patterns and dynamics emerging over the duration of a whole piece.

One last point needs to be made. I said just now that 'freedom' is an aesthetic goal rather than a form of musical practice. There is a further implication here, namely that the very notion of 'freedom' is constituted in dialectical opposition to the work-a-day demands of idiom. Talking about postmodern art Terry Threadgold puts it this way: 'What, after all, *is* "freedom" from generic norms but a recognition of the existence of the "ground" against which "freedom" is possible?' (1989: 111, original emphasis). The implication for the genre called free music is that *most* of what is played will be highly conventional. Ultimately, a reflexive and critical thinking practitioner like Derek Bailey understands this. As he explains, musicians 'come to [free music], not because it's an open space, but because they think there's some structure there they can use for their musical ends. So they're likely to take what is useful for their purposes. It's inevitable and I don't think it matters' (in Corbett 1994c: 241).

Community, subculture and the structural homology

So far I have been arguing that despite problems in defining particular cases it is impossible to do without a concept of genre at the level of the text. Even a music maker like Derek Bailey who is strongly opposed to the normative pull of idiom will concede that, as well as being constrictive, genre provides a necessary point of departure for creative action. But whether treated as burden or as opportunity the assumption has been that genre is part of the production environment, that it is something for the musician–creator to negotiate.

Clearly, though, in order for it to function beyond the backstage world of the musician genre must be recognized by the audience. To put it another way, there has to be a link between text group and social formation. In popular music, unlike other media, this link has often been conceived in quasi-political terms as a form of representation. Genre is seen to express the collective interest or point of view of a community.[3] One reason has to with the technologically determined scale of the production apparatus in different media. Whereas film and television are inevitably *provided* by a remote and large-scale industrial apparatus, popular music may be owned and produced *within communities*. The institution of the proto-market (see Chapter 1) is crucial here, enabling small-scale production and reception in bounded social–geographical spaces. This material possibility then under-writes a deeply embedded discourse which states that the validity of a musical style will be measured by the extent to which it is an expression of grass-roots values and identity. Now Simon Frith (1983) argues that such a position is developed most completely in rock ideology. This is an ideology because it fetishizes community while refusing to acknowledge the thoroughly commercial nature of popular music.

However the question I want to ask is whether the notion of style as the expression of community *is* invariably ideological. If this has been a key theme in popular music studies since the mid-1980s, it seems to me that behind it there lies a certain loss of faith. 'Community' has an air of naive collectivism about it which appears to many commentators to be out of kilter with the prevailing climate of political pragmatism. In this section I am going to argue against such a position, and suggest that there are good reasons to return to the idea of style as an expression of community. That groups of people may be represented in musical genre is not only empirically defensible, but also to be argued for on political grounds. For the big idea which underpins the community basis of style is that of solidarity from below, or the expression of common identity and interest against dominant social relations. Although this notion is susceptible to ideological distortion, such distortion is not inevitable, and each case ought to be examined on its merits. In order to make the argument we will examine criticisms of the community-style approach one by one.

The first objection is that it reduces music to an index of the social and fails to account for the specificity of the process by which sounds are produced and consumed (Bennett *et al.* 1993). Now of course it is the case that there are excessively 'sociologistic' analyses of popular music (similar charges can be made against 'economistic' or 'formalistic' work). But to talk about style as the expression of community does not necessarily lead to the abstraction of music's social function. For a highly persuasive analysis which avoids such problems and relates social process, specific production cultures and textual form we can turn to an essay by Charles Keil (1994b). His subject is the historical emergence of polka and the blues in America. Keil offers a general description of the community-style relationship. 'The presence of style indicates a strong community, an intense sociability that has been given shape through time, an assertion of control over collective feelings so powerful that any expressive innovator in the community will necessarily put his or her content into that shaping continuum and no other' (202). This is about as bold a statement of style in terms of collective expression as one is likely to find. Immediately, though, Keil qualifies it. The shaping of both Polish-American polka and African-American blues involves the 'acceptance and transcendence of the dominant culture's stereotypes'. The figures of the 'happy polack' and 'nigger', for example, are actually taken up and transformed by exponents of the respective styles. Keil also notes that the development of these 'people's musics' depends on borrowings from high culture and the polite popular mainstream (206–8).

Keil's community-derived styles are thus impure. Not only are they reframed from outside the culture, but these external factors then become internalized and used as tropes within the styles. Ultimately, though, what guarantees their communal, participative character are 'immediate and constant feedback loops in a habitual, tightly patterned form' (205). In the case of polka, Keil talks about intense band–dancer interaction with musicians developing new licks in order to keep dancers dancing. In blues, feedback takes the guise of shouted responses from the audience. We could add the contemporary example of the dance club DJ who recomposes the generic mix in response to dance floor lulls and surges. The process here is dialogical, based on a process of mutual seduction by DJ and dancers.

Keil's is one among many cogent analyses of community-style interaction which tease out the complexity of the social process at stake. Other examples found in the literature deal with music and African-America (Small 1987b, George 1988, Jones 1995/1963), cities or regions (Gillett 1983/1970, Guralnick 1986, Shank 1994) and gay men and women (J. Gill 1995, Smith 1995). These have different emphases, but none could be described as sociologically reductive. The second problem has to do with the constitution and composition of musical communities. More or less explicit in community-style approaches is the idea that communities are primary social formations. Such communities also tend to be seen as subordinate, with their musical activity involving symbolic resistance to dominant social forces. Two key concepts are usually invoked to account for the formation of communities in this way: class and ethnicity. Both have been the subject of considerable argument.

In cultural studies the most influential account of how class comes to organize communities, and in turn their symbolic practice, can be found in the work on British youth subcultures which came out of the Centre for Contemporary Cultural Studies during the 1970s. In a seminal essay Clarke *et al.* (1976) argue that members of youth subcultures 'experience and respond to the *same basic problematic* as other members of their class'. What then differentiates them is a *double articulation* – 'first to their "parent" culture (e.g. working-class culture), second, to the dominant culture' (101, original emphasis). On a general level the double articulation can explain the complexity and diversity of subcultural styles. Specifically it accounts for how a large, homogeneous but culturally quiescent working class can yield symbolically rich, and at least potentially, resistant youth subcultures. It is a Marxist theory of culture which 'fits' the post-war period in Britain.

However sociologists have been pointing to changes in class structure over recent years. Lash and Urry (1987 and 1994), for example, suggest that the enlargement of the service sector in the West and the development of information technology has led to the emergence of a huge central stratum. Most of the old working class has either been absorbed into it, or dispersed to its margins as an excluded underclass. Does this mean that the conditions of possibility for vibrant class-derived subcultures have been eliminated?

I would argue not. If it is indeed the case that a large, homogeneous working class spawned 'classical' British subcultures such a model was never universal in capitalist societies. In America, as Mike Davis (1980: 82) points out, the working class has 'continued to find its social identity in fragmentary ethnic and racial communities'. Hence the importance of Keil's essay; quite simply he shows how class subordination has been historically tied up with various forms of racialized othering. The result has been the development of musical style-communities which are both representative of subordinate interests and inventively hybrid at one and the same time. If we consider the case of post-industrial Britain in the mid-1990s it seems that class subordination intersects with regional and ethnic identity to produce musical genre-cultures in a similar kind of way. Two examples: the working class 'laddishness' of northern-English rock bands like Oasis, and the black underclass identity forged in south London housing estates from which hardcore rave, and, more recently, 'jump-up' jungle styles have emerged.

We encountered ethnicity, the other disputed concept which comes up in accounts of community formation, just now in the context of Keil's (1994b) discussion of blues and polka. It is worth examining this in more detail. One of the strongest arguments against the notion of music being categorized according to some sort of 'ethnic' criterion comes from Phillip Tagg (1989). Tagg objects to the term black music which he suggests is more honestly translated as the music of 'Afro-Americans'. Tagg goes on to enumerate the historical diversity of the lived experience and musical activity of this broad category of people. Given such diversity, he suggests, the term black music has no analytical use; rather it serves as an ideological device which essentializes racial difference and obscures the role of class subordination. I am sympathetic to Tagg's position here, but it seems to me that he does not pursue the argument far enough. The new 'politics of identity' (see for example Hall 1991, West 1993) also challenges the notion of an essential black ethnicity. Instead it seeks to show the complexity of African diasporic identities, forged as they are by the othering gaze of white culture and the experience of migration as well as autochthonous histories of ethnic origination in Africa (Gilroy 1993).

Ultimately, though, such a complexity should not be equated with the absence of community. As bell hooks puts it, '[t]here is a radical difference between a repudiation of the idea there is a black "essence" and recognition of the way black identity has been specifically constituted in the experience of exile and struggle' (1993: 426). This experience is a fully material one which is inflected by class structure, but is by no means reducible to it.

To sum up, then: both class and ethnicity continue to generate communities. We can define these as groups of people with a strong sense of solidarity forged in subordination over time. Musical genres may then develop from within these communities which identify or represent them in some sense. This brings us to a third problem raised in connection with the community-style idea, that is, how the social experience of community is translated into the aesthetic practice of style.

Again, this has been most thoroughly theorized in the CCCS literature on youth subcultures. The key term here is the structural homology. For Paul Willis (n/d and 1978) musical styles adopted by a subculture 'reflected', 'resonated', 'expressed' or 'extended' the primary class character of the group. Thus, in his study of Midlands motor-bike boys, he suggests that they 'were exploring and extending versions of "rough" working-class themes' (1978: 8). In terms of musical preference the driving beats and 'the suppression of structured time' (Willis seems to be getting at the absence of narrative, linear development) in the 1950s rock'n'roll preferred by the motor-bike boys match their 'restless concrete lifestyle' (Willis 1978: 78).

There is a pair of problems with this formulation. Dave Laing suggests that 'homological matchings between "self-consciousness" and object-meaning are too rationalist and voluntarist' (1997: 119). This is one possible criticism. The trouble is that a writer like Willis sometimes appears to propose the converse, namely that the production of subcultural style is an unreflexive response to social positioning. For example, although the motor-bike boys' use of rock'n'roll involves the development and application of a complex system of knowledge, it seems that they have no consciousness of the homological nature of their practice. Ultimately, the lack of clarity about what kind of cognitive or perceptual process is at stake undermines the concept of homology.

Richard Middleton (1990: 162) then identifies another flaw – the circularity of homological cause and effect. The problem can be described like this: class produces subcultural position which produces style which in turn affirms class character. But how then to account for the diversity of subcultural styles and their liability to change over time? Why, in the short period from 1956 to 1978, and from the same national working class, should such a variety of youth subcultures as the teds, mods, skinheads, Bowie boys and punks, not to mention motor-bike boys, emerge? Clarke *et al.*'s (1976) 'double articulation' hints at a way forward here. Instead of the homology's single point of origin and return, symbol systems associated with different social formations (the 'parent culture' and 'dominant culture') are recombined over time to yield syncretic subcultures. Of course as it is used by Willis the homology is a totalizing theory, one which the concept of articulation threatens to undermine altogether.

But suppose we dethrone the homology. If the constitution of style-making communities can be said to be derived from a complex of social relations, including not only class and racial positioning, yet also a much looser bundle of associated symbolic resources and traditions, then the homology is hardly tenable as a general theory of cultural productivity. It is simply too crude and one-dimensional. However it can take its place instead as just one kind of link between community and musical practice. From this perspective the homology is best thought of precisely as an 'authentic' expression of social being in musical style. Homological tropes will tend to be bold, naturalistic and built out of intra-communal forms of knowledge. Take the case of rap. According to Tricia Rose, '[h]ip hop replicates and reimagines the experiences of urban life and symbolically appropriates urban space through sampling, attitude, dance, style and sound effects. Talk of subways, crews and posses, urban noise, economic stagnation, static and crossed signals leap out of hip hop lyrics, sounds and themes' (1994: 22).

It seems to me that this is a highly appropriate description of the way young black music makers make quite conscious use of communal experience in the post-industrial city. The directness of the relationship between such experience and the fabric of rap music is very much of a kind with the homological relations which the CCCS subcultural researchers delineated. But there is a crucial qualification: hip hop homologies constitute just one level of articulation in the symbolic practice of rap. As Rose points out we need to consider other important levels. For example stylistic continuities within African-American musics over the whole post-war period feed into the hip hop repertory (25), and there has been a synchronic 'internal cross-fertilization between rapping, breakdancing, and graffiti writing' too (35). Rose also shows how images and devices from mainstream, white media are imported into rap and parodied, as in Public Enemy's invocation of horror movies in the 'Night of the living baseheads' music track and video (115).

This discussion of intertextual elements in hip hop takes us a step beyond the homology towards a position which recognizes the autonomy of the aesthetic in the development of genres. What I hope to have done, though, is suggest that the two approaches are not mutually exclusive. Clearly, some sorts of community do have a social constitution which is 'reflected', 'extended' or 'resonated' in musical genre. In other cases the fit between community and style is less direct, or genres may encompass huge areas of social and geographical space which can hardly be described as communities at all. To understand these variable relations we need to examine another factor, the role of the music industry.

Commodity form, or genres across time, space and race

It is true that well established stars sell records on the basis of a supra-generic aura. But for most of the popular music market, genre provides a vital form of packaging and a means of organizing audience expectation about the sound of music. In a medium where invisible sound has been sundered from the context of performance (see Chapter 3), the industry needs to make music knowable, to place that which cannot be seen and which has not yet been heard in the realm of the familiar. Above all identification depends on being able to read a generic signature right through the fabric of the music; indeed, a style will usually 'introduce itself' in the first few bars of a song. But genre is also constructed through the structure of record labels, the layout of bins in a record shop, in the constitution of music magazines or radio station formatting.

So, genre is central to the music apparatus. Despite this we should note a paradox about the record industry's ability to address audiences and market genres. In the first place the apparatus has an enormous reach. The suffusion of commodified music though everyday life and across the world derives partly from the specific effects of the electronic media which carry it. As we saw in the last chapter they have replaced direct performance by musicians to audiences in common time–space with an *extensive* process of production and consumption.

The point that needs to be emphasized for the present argument is the resulting mobility of popular music, and the fact that it is distributed far beyond its point of origin. If media technology provides the means of extension then the process is driven by music's translatability. Pop genres tend to cross cultural boundaries because they can be 'reframed' by new audiences relatively easily, more so at least than narrative forms which are based on national languages and codes of verisimilitude specific to particular cultures.[4] We also need to consider temporal extension, made possible by phonographic storage. Although pop genres have a short period of peak currency, this is generally followed by a much longer term of low-level popularity, nourished by record reissues and sometimes punctuated by revival or recombination.

Now, on the face of it, musical extension would seem to detach style from those communities which we examined in the last section. Marketing a genre beyond its home territory may subvert the original context of production as musicians learn to please a new and diffuse audience. Sometimes musical communities are eliminated altogether as hegemonic genres swamp the market and drive out locally made sounds; or authentic styles may be appropriated by musicians from outside and refashioned in a profoundly inauthentic way. All these tendencies are real, and well documented, especially in the context of what has come to be called world music (Robinson *et al.* 1991, Taylor 1997). However, the key point I want to make here is that musical communities none the less continue to provide the basis for genre markets. In fact the mapping of genres on to distinct social formations has arguably become even more intense with the advent of globalization. This paradoxical situation derives from another aspect of the musical apparatus – its disintegrated structure.

As we saw in the first chapter record companies are forced to hunt for content in subcultural proto-markets and talent pools outside their ambit. In other words they select rather than initiate styles. And they must rely on media organizations to market and disseminate their product, organizations which often have divergent economic interests. This relative lack of control over both origination and marketing can be contrasted with the situation in the film or broadcasting industries. Talking about American television, Ien Ang (1991) argues that the networks initially confront a *heterogeneous* audience which they attempt to transform into a coherent and controllable entity through market research. Programming is then developed so as to address this discursive construct. Significantly, the record industry has never attempted to control its conditions of existence in this way. There is no equivalent of ratings research or pilot shows; focus groups are never used in the development of content.[5] Instead record companies adopt a two-pronged strategy. On the one hand they release a large repertoire, in effect leaving a significant part of product development to the post-market stage and the vagaries of consumer choice. On the other hand record companies will tend to address socially constituted, and relatively autonomous constituencies which they use as a foundation for marketing.

The reflexive collectivity, or sense of 'us', which we discussed in the previous section in connection with race and class, actually provides an ideal focus for audience-building. There are interesting parallels here with the 'imagined community' of the nation which according to Benedict Anderson (1991) was fostered by 'print capitalism', and the creation of 'unified fields of exchange and communication' in the nineteenth century (44). Anderson suggests that people became conscious of their common national bond by reading the vernacular tongue in mass-produced novels and newspapers. In much the same way, I would argue, the music industry has helped to construct musical communities by commercially exploiting the desire to find a common identity in music. The point is that community is neither wholly manufactured, nor wholly authentic in this context. Rather it takes on both aspects as its form emerges through negotiation and the unpredictable career of technological development.

We can see this process beginning in the early twentieth century as people start to listen to music on the phonograph in the private sphere of the home. Listeners know that any record will play 'the same' in every household. Perhaps the next significant step, during the 1920s, is that radio audiences experience the live musical hook-up, broadcast from ballroom or concert hall in a common timeframe. Then from the mid-1930s, but especially since the advent of Top Forty format radio in the 1950s, popularity charts bind music fans into a 'democracy of taste' (Parker 1991: 210) by publicly displaying the aggregation (or purported aggregation) of individual market choices. Week-on-week change here provides a graphic indicator of the collective will over 'calendrical time'. Anderson (1991: 24–36) coins this term to point up a post-traditional time which is conjured by, amongst other things, the novelistic narrative and the quotodien march of the 'news'. But calendrical time is surely also measured by the rise and fall of pop stars, the progress of musical genres and, perhaps most important of all, a sense of belonging to a generation through musical affiliation.

Anderson talks about another important way that print capitalism advances national community, that is through the setting of national limits. For literate citizens a defining attribute of those others beyond the border is that they read a different language (1991: 7). Once again useful comparisons can be made with pop where music capitalism produces limited collectivities. Yet there are also important ways in which these diverge from Anderson's model. In the case of music, communities coalesce above and below the national level to a far greater extent. And whereas nationalism conveniently (from the point of view of capitalism) blots out inequality and domination with an appeal to the fraternity of the common tongue, popular music publics may (if only partially and provisionally) be articulated with social formations of class, race, gender and sexuality.

So far in this section, then, I have been describing a set of connected circumstances in the political economy of popular music. These are the extensiveness of musical genres over space and time, a (paradoxically) low level of control over repertoire and market by record companies, and a tendency, by way of compensation, to address the audience as community. Their cumulative effect is to force the music industry into accepting the social context of music as a *datum*, while at the same time it seeks to *manipulate* styles and map them on to new audiences so as to extend markets. It is the tension between these divergent factors, I will argue, which produces such a wide range of relations across genre, community and market. In what follows we will explore that range through four case studies: race music, crossover, mainstream and the remote canon. These are not so much genres as genre-cultures, which have taken shape as the industries have struggled to articulate style with market.

Race music

The American record industry began to address subaltern communities, particularly the African-American community, as a market quite early on. Using the same approach they had already adopted towards immigrant European ethnic groups (Spottswood 1992) the majors set up 'race music' labels in the 1920s to recruit African-American artists, and produce an ethnically identifiable repertoire for distribution to a segregated audience (Ogren 1989, Kennedy 1994). As Paul Oliver reports, something between five and six million records on race labels were sold in 1925 to a black population twice that size (1968: 6). This was, then, a clearly segmented market in which a high degree of penetration was achieved – conditions which suggest that making and selling race records was a very profitable operation.

Richard Peterson (1994) uses the term 'categorising constraint' to describe the music industry's approach to race in the 1920s. According to him it launched an 'artificial division between the blues and country music' (175) since until that time black and white rural southerners had 'shared a wide range of musical stylings' (176). Peterson argues that the new policy was implemented in order '[t]o simplify the marketing of records' (177). This seems an uncontentious conclusion. Still, the fact that the music industry found racialized marketing to be a profitable strategy does not necessarily mean that we should see it as 'artificial'. Indeed Kathy Ogren (1989) reproduces some contemporary accounts of the reception of race music in the 1920s which suggest the contrary. What comes through is not only intense enthusiasm for the music, but also the communal form which this took. For example, according to Clarence Williams, pianist and A&R man for the Okeh label, '[c]olored people would form a line twice round the block when the latest record of Bessie or Ma or Clara or Mamie [classic blues singers] came in' (quoted in Ogren 1989: 92). This public affirmation of community through record-buying takes on an extra significance when we consider that black music was almost entirely excluded from radio play in the 1920s.

Perhaps two conclusions can be reached about the evidence on race music we have been examining. First, musical identification by African-Americans was exploited by the record industry. An impoverished stratum bought relatively large numbers of records at premium prices, while black composer-performers, when they were paid at all, gave up the rights in their songs for at most a $25 fee and minuscule royalty (Sanjek 1988: 65). Second, and crucially, racialized marketing needs to be recognized as economic exploitation rather than ideological manipulation. What I mean is that the sense of communal affiliation derived from making and buying records was not a false one, but instead represented the lived experience of black people clustered in urban ghettos or dispersed across villages and homesteads in the rural south. In effect the market for race records produced a tight genre circuit in which musical texts and discourses of solidarity were passed around an *already* bounded community. In other words, on one level at least, the industry helped to amplify class and ethnic solidarity rather than imposing musical segregation.

After the Second World War racialized marketing was renewed with the advent of rhythm and blues. The important developments were that while specialist radio stations began to programme black music to target black audiences, the new rhythm and blues record chart provided a weekly log of the music's stylistic development. In Anderson's terms R and B radio and chart established a 'simultaneity of time' (1991: 25) across the black community.

Black radio is most often discussed in the literature as a factor in the evolution of rock'n'roll. It is argued that its growing white youth audience in the early 1950s was a key factor in the victory of syncretism over segregation and the separate development of musical cultures (among many sources for this position see Gillett 1983/1970, Kloosterman and Quispel 1990, Friedlander 1996: 26–61). Other writers, however, have stressed the vital importance of an autonomous rhythm and blues world in which music continued to provide a resource of identity and hope for African-Americans in a hostile world (George 1988, Jones 1995/1963). The disagreement between syncretists and separatists persists today (Cashmore 1997, Perry 1990). However I would argue that a parallel development of *both* 'race music' and 'crossover' has characterized the history of popular music.

Crossover

The term crossover seems to have been adopted in the mid-1980s to describe music made by African-Americans and originally intended for the rhythm and blues market which then 'crossed over' to a white mainstream market (George 1988: 150, Perry 1990: 51). Now according to an often stated view – it is perhaps best put by Nelson George (1988) – crossover is a latterday dilution of black culture. The argument goes that in order to make it more palatable for a white market the ethnic particularity of black music is toned down. I would suggest there are several problems with this.

In the first place crossover can be traced back at least as far as racialized marketing. In the mid-1920s clubs began to open in New York offering black entertainment to whites. Some were segregated, others had mixed audiences. Black bands like those of Duke Ellington, Fletcher Henderson and Cab Calloway flourished in this new environment (Collier 1987: 75–91). Ellington, for example, was broadcasting regularly from the Cotton Club on the new CBS national radio network in 1927, and by 1930 his orchestra had made a full-length feature film with blackface duo Amos 'n' Andy as well as a short entitled *Black and Tan Fantasy* which showcased the song of that name. Collier suggests that these broadcasts and films were crucial in breaking the Ellington band to a national, white audience (1987: 98).

The key point for the present argument, though, is that the orchestra developed an ethnicized 'jungle' style at precisely this moment of crossover. Richard Middleton (1996) concludes that Ellington was constructing a primitive and 'low other' musical form in the audition, as it were, of the white listening subject. Such an act of musical parody provided, at one and the same time, a basis for further stylistic development where 'growling' trumpet, 'Creole love calls' and so on were set off by increasingly complex coloration and extended form. In some circumstances, then, it seems that crossover may constitute a reflexive mode of music-making where parodic presentation of subaltern positioning is redeemed and converted into affirmative aesthetic practice.

At moments like these the question of the subaltern's relation to cultural dominance is posed idiomatically, that is in the *sound* of music. On other occasions crossover music will be defined by the race of the performers measured against the *absence* of ethnic signifiers in their music, in other words when black musicians play mainstream music. Significantly, this form of crossover has met rather more resistance from the industry. Another black orchestra, Andy Kirk's Clouds of Joy, provides a case in point. From 1929 the Clouds toured incessantly across the United States. Playing to black and white dancers on the ballroom circuit the band – with its repertoire of ballads and sweet dance music – was extremely popular amongst both segregated audiences. However during the 1930s Brunswick label boss, Jack Kapp, insisted that the band record only hot swing numbers in the studio, that is to say material which was clearly stamped as race music. Finally in 1936, having set up the new American Decca label and taken most of the Brunswick roster including the Clouds of Joy with him, Kapp agreed that the band release a ballad, 'Until the real thing comes along' (Kirk 1991). The record was a huge hit, bought by large numbers of white fans as well in the race market (Driggs 1959: 226–7, Kirk 1989: 72–88).

The success of 'Until the real thing comes along' presaged the break-through of Nat 'King' Cole who by the late 1940s had established himself, in the words of Nelson George (1988), as the 'sepia Sinatra'. Cole became a hugely important figure in the music business, and established, almost alone, the terms and conditions under which a black artist might achieve stardom in the popular music mainstream. Jimi Hendrix then did the same thing in the 1960s as a star in the new mainstream formation of rock. Even after Cole and Hendrix, though, there has still been enormous resistance in the industry to African-Americans producing material outside the supposed provenance of black ethnicity. For example in the late 1980s the singer and guitarist Lenny Kravitz had extreme difficulty in getting a record deal with his rock-pop style (Negus 1992: 109).

These problems of instutionalized racism in the record industry should not be gainsaid. None the less, what seems remarkable is how a spectrum of crossover forms has been constructed through the commercial logic of the market. At one pole are those artists like the Clouds of Joy, Nat Cole, Jimi Hendrix and more recently Whitney Houston, Neneh Cherry, Michael Jackson or Prince who posit an integrationist, multicultural model of black music. I would argue that black music makers in subcultural dance genres from house to techno – people like Carl Craig and Marshall Jefferson – represent the same urge. Here what seems to be at stake is the notion of a flat array of different styles which together constitute a larger 'federation' of popular music.

At the other pole stands the performer whose appeal to a white audience, whatever her/his intention might be, is precisely as primitive and hyper-racialized Other. Louis Armstrong seems to represent such a figure in the early 1930s, wearing a leopard skin and playing a stereotypical, absurd savage in the film *Rhapsody in Black and Blue* (see the discussion about this in Keil and Feld 1994). However its contemporary instance is surely gangsta rap. Bakari Kitwana (1994) makes this point in a discussion of develop-ments in rap since the late 1980s, although he takes a tough, condemnatory stance. His argument is that record companies have constrained artists to produce images of exoticized sex and violence for delivery to a suburban, white youth audience – 'emancipated "niggers and bitches" for sale' as he puts it (1994: 24). Whether or not Kitwana's aesthetic and political judgement concerning gangsta rap is adequate, he is surely right about the ratcheting effect of the white market on the evolution of the genre.

Crossover is, then, a complex phenomenon. Rather than constituting a simple dilution of ethnicity in the way that Nelson George (1988) suggests, or producing a vigorous hybridity as Steve Perry (1990) would have it, both these tendencies may be at work together. And we can add a third dynamic. Crossover always attributes *priority* to an original community – the rhythm and blues world, hip hop nation, or simply its performers' race (that is to say, ethnicity heard from the vantage of dominance). To put it another way the recording which crosses over must, by definition, be launched from elsewhere, and as such represents a cultural given which A&R and marketing departments can polish, but not fundamentally change. In this sense crossover, an extension of musical texts across social space, also maps style 'back' on to community.

Mainstream

I have suggested that crossover depends on the notion of a mainstream – the place which one crosses to. In the framework I am developing here the mainstream can be conceived as a hegemonic formation which strives to institute a universal music. Having said this, we immediately run into a problem. The mainstream has no name for itself, or more properly, the record companies and broadcasters which disseminate it do not deploy the term. Rather it tends to be used in a pejorative sense by fans and cultural critics who see the mainstream as a bland, undifferentiated non-style, one which is always counterposed to authentic and oppositional forms. Sarah Thornton (1995: 92–8) criticizes subcultural theorists who use the term in this way. She points to the incoherence of mainstream–alternative binaries which are inflected quite differently in the various studies by class, commerce, education or relationship to official culture. Her conclusion is that the mainstream cannot be sustained as an analytical category. It is, to the contrary, an ideological term, a means of shoring up the 'subcultural capital' of those who use it. Now I would agree with Thornton to an extent: the mainstream clearly plays a crucial part in strategies of musical distinction; none the less it seems to me it is also the best available name for a dominant institution in Anglo-American pop which has prevailed, in one shape or another, until the mid-1980s. What I am suggesting, then, is that we use mainstream as a substantive category, and not only an ideological one.[6]

We can approach it from two directions. The first is a political-economy perspective. Clearly, the music industry has tried to create mass markets which are standardized in terms of genre and mode of production. Economies of scale and the concomitant need to build widespread and relatively uniform expectations about musical commodities among the audience make this desirable. However, as we saw above, the precondition for a music market is a bounded and reflexive social formation which can serve as a prototype for the mediated audience. In the case of the mass market this is much harder to identify than for ethnic and class-based styles. Quite simply the mainstream has to transcend *particular* communities in order to reach the largest number of people possible. It follows that in order to produce a mainstream the music industries must find musical texts and generic discourse which 'fold difference in', and articulate distinct social groups together.

This brings us to a second approach. We are close here to Gramsci's concept of hegemony, the idea that dominant social formations consist in alliances which cohere on the basis of consent. It seems to me this is exactly what is at stake in popular music mainstreams. Each conjuncture in the mainstream is a temporary, hegemonic union which binds together different social groups and subsumes their distinct political and aesthetic values (Hall 1994/1981). Above all, this depends on the construction of a meta-community, and the propagation of *universal* values of mutuality and sincerity. The goal of universality also means opposition to exclusive music cultures: what might be seen as the 'pretentiousness' of official art music or avant-gardes within pop. But it may also lead to exclusionary strategies where other musics are held to be irredemably low and other. Thus most often the mainstream will be a middle ground. As such its incipient social character is entirely congruent with the music industry's construction of a centred, mass market.

The obvious choice for a case study in the mainstream is the inter-war period. This, after all, is when the modern popular music apparatus with its mass audience emerges in America. The period also sees the crystallization of the 'standard' popular song, perhaps the *locus classicus* of genre considered as a system of regulated repetition (see Hamm 1979). For all that, it seems to me that rock provides a better example. Rock represents the *mature* mainstream and a culmination of several tendencies that were already apparent in the earlier period. Let us examine them.

The most significant is the construction of community. Jane Feuer argues that as a genre the classical Hollywood musical perceives 'the breakdown of community designated by the very distinction between performer and audience. ... [and] seeks to bridge the gap by putting up "community" as an ideal concept' (1993: 3). The musical does this, Feuer suggests, by enshrining folksiness, and in particular by creating communities offstage and backstage. Rock, too, is engaged in the construction of community and for the same kinds of reason. However it takes a more sceptical form, and depends very much on protocols of authentication. We can see this most obviously in the live concert which constitutes a verifiable gathering of the clans. At gigs and festivals (and in screen 'rockumentaries') fans rally around performers. What is at stake here is recognition of community on the basis of 'direct' evidence from the senses: you *touch* the person next to you, *see* the band on stage hailing you, and *immerse* your body in the noise, a common noise which envelops everyone.

One of the most important ways in which these community values are then universalized is through the process of naming. The key term here is 'rock and roll' (see among many sources DeCurtis 1992, Friedlander 1996, but also an indefinite number of musician interviews or pronouncements from the stage). As a name, rock and roll has a powerful hegemonic thrust to it, gluing together rock'n'roll of the 1950s and post-Beatles album format music into a single mega-genre. This elision is ideological for a number of reasons. It proposes a cultural year zero, 1955 is often touted, and in that way suggests there has been a clean break with the bad old days of the entertainment industry of ·Tin Pan Alley and Hollywood. But the discourse of rock and roll also offers an internal periodization: a primitive yet vigorous 'folk' stage in the 1950s is succeeded first by a mature form in the late 1960s, and then a moment of primitive renewal which comes with the arrival of punk at the end of the 1970s. In the sense of it being a history which pays tribute to the vicissitudes of 'the people' (while tending to suppress difference and conflict within that same social bloc) this is a good example of 'cultural populism' (McGuigan 1992). Rock and roll also makes a highly effective brand: anyone born from the early 1940s onwards can continue to be an aficionado through buying its accumulated catalogue on CD.[7]

How does the mainstream cope with difference at its boundaries, above and beneath so to speak? If we consider the lower border, both the pre-war mainstream and rock were built on 'primitive' African-American styles: jazz turning to swing in the 1930s, rhythm and blues re-emerging as rock in the 1960s. Both mainstreams, baldly put, transform marginal black genres into universal styles. But whereas in the earlier moment this process was most often repudiated, or the recollection of it suppressed, in rock black roots have been treated as a well spring of authenticity by the mainstream's normatively white musicians and audience. Indeed, a key discourse binding together constituencies of youth otherwise divided by class, region and (finally as rock became international) language into an 'affective alliance' of rock (Grossberg 1984) has been the myth of an authentic sensibility handed down by black forefathers. From Eric Clapton to U2 white rock musicians have continued, as they see it, to pick up the torch of organic, folk expression from a dying breed of bluesmen.

The contrast is with *contemporary* black music. After The Beatles most rock artists turned their backs on current R and B styles.[8] Soul, funk and disco all fail rock's authenticity test to varying degrees. Partly this has to do with the discourse of the pleasurable life which runs through soul and its successors. Rock is extremely suspicious of pleasure (which it conflates with 'commercial' entertainment), and the pleasure of dancing in particular. Partly also there is the feeling that, in contrast to the folk purity of the blues, R and B styles have become insidiously hybrid, tainted with kitsch and laden with the threat of miscegenation. Perhaps the clearest manifestation of these tendencies was the 'disco sucks' campaign of 1978, orchestrated by American FM radio stations and which culminated in the public burning of disco records (Garofalo 1993: 242).

There is another execrable, low music against which rock distinguishes itself: white pop. The way in which rock has constantly reproduced itself by marking the difference between its own authenticity and the artifice of pop has been widely discussed in the literature (Frith 1983, Frith and Horne 1987). I would simply want to add that vital though the pop–rock opposition has been, we ought to consider rock's upper border too. Generally rock has defined itself in opposition to official art on the grounds that it was a conservative and elite form. After punk, however, an art version of rock emerged, capable of 'de-constructing' rock from above by showing up its rhetoric as normative, and exposing it as a coded rather than expressive form (Laing 1985: 128).

This auto-critique certainly contributed to rock's demise, but we ought also to note the emergence of a new *pop* mainstream in the early 1980s, built in America on the reformatting of pop radio and the emergence of MTV (Straw 1993b), and in Britain focused on independent labels and the music press (Toynbee 1993). In fact this has been a short-lived and partial phenomenon. Currently, it seems, there is no mainstream at all, but rather a patchwork of genres, communities and patterns of generational affiliation. Among contemporary youth, rock is one music culture option among several, while for the baby boomers rock is vestigial. Like a photograph album it provides a link with the past.

Canonical cultures

Unlike the pre-war mainstream, rock was quite heterogeneous in formal terms. Alan Moore suggests that this was the result of processes of fission and hybridization in the beat group idiom (itself a simplification of various R and B idioms), yielding a 'profusion of rock styles' by the end of the decade (1993: 104–5). Such formal heterogeneity, or lack of a clear genre structure, can be contrasted with the tight policing of texts which goes on in 'canonical cultures'. I use that term to refer to music scenes which produce a corpus and normative style retrospectively, from music which has ceased to circulate in its original context. The canonical culture is thus temporally distant from the moment of production. Most often it will be socially and geographically remote also.

It is worth noting that revivals are a closely related phenomenon: New Orleans and Dixieland jazz were revived in the 1940s and 1950s (America, Britain and Australia), post-war rhythm and blues in the 1960s (Britain and America), country music in the 1970s (America) and in the mid-1980s hard bop was resuscitated (America and Britain). But whereas these tended to involve the construction of a canon based on the work of known *auteurs*, or an established tradition, which was then reinterpreted by musicians, in canonical cultures the key role is that of the disc jockey who acts both as repertorial archaeologist and performer. The example I want to look at here is northern soul.

The northern soul scene developed at the end of the 1960s in dance clubs in the north of England. In its original form it lasted until around 1980.

Repertoire rules were strict, or at least ostensibly strict. Records had to be in the style of that mid- to late-1960s soul music, produced largely in northern US cities such as Detroit and Chicago.[9] Records which had already been successful in the British Top Forty were excluded – this meant most Tamla Motown material. Significantly, obscurity soon became an end in itself. A key player in the northern scene, Russ Winstanley, has described how he and other DJs would go to America in search of unknown records, including extremely rare acetate pressings. Back in England they would then use a white 'cover up' label to hide the record's provenance while proffering a false title and artist name, all to maintain exclusivity and control (Winstanley and Nowell 1996, see also Hollows and Milestone 1998).

Almost immediately a repertoire crisis developed in the northern scene. In part this was to do with scarcity of supply. Quite simply it became more and more difficult to discover unknown records of a suitable style. But the issue of repertoire also hinged on what Joanne Hollows and Katie Milestone (1998) call (after Appadurai) the 'regime of value' pertaining in the scene. DJs deployed cultural capital in the form of specialized knowledge about rare soul music in order to increase the exclusivity and value of their own record collections and performances. The limited-number copies of dance floor hits then meant that some DJs outside the elite resorted to bootleg pressings in order to get copies. The response of a purist wing suggests that there was more at stake here than the niceties of copyright infraction. Writing in the soul magazine *Black Music* Tony Cummings described the habitués of the largest club, the Wigan Casino, as '[t]he black bombing bootleg playing dull brained brothers from Wigan' (quoted in McKenna 1996: 71).[10] For Cummings bootlegging was a threat to the archaeological imperative, the desire to make new from old, at the heart of northern soul. It meant, instead, dumbing down and the ossification of the canon around a small number of 'stompers', guaranteed to fill the dance floor.

One way of coping with the repertoire problem was to make a clear distinction between 'oldies' and 'newies', sometimes with separate nights for each category (McKenna 1996: 118). As Katie Milestone points out '[i]f a record is an "oldie", it means that it has been played at a soul venue in the past, if a record is a "newie" it is a still a 1960s record, but one that has only recently been unearthed by an enduring DJ or collector' (1997: 162). The oldie/newie distinction was a functional response to the scarcity problem. It gave a longer lifespan to an existing repertoire by legitimating the high circulation of certain records, but it did not obviate the crisis.

Indeed it could not do so. For northern soul was founded on a dilemma. Implicit in the classical repertoire were certain authentic characteristics: a soul sound of the period 1964–68, an 'uptown' (Gillett 1983/1970) sound perhaps, and without too emphatic a gospel or southern US inflection. Immediately, however, we are at that difficult point discussed near the start of the chapter where it proves impossible to define essential genre traits without excluding genre members. This definitional problem becomes even more acute at the moment of canonization. For in an important sense northern soul only existed as a *remote* canon, a code imposed on a variety of texts which had never been asked to carry such a burden of coherence at the moment of production. To put it another way the very distance – temporal, geographical and cultural – of the scene from the original context in which these records were made and used produced a crisis of authenticity which DJs and taste makers could not resolve no matter how many records they discovered. Ultimately the authority of the DJ depended on a *charismatic* invocation of his understanding of that rare and mysterious artifact, the true northern soul record.

Once this had happened (and it seems to have happened very early) the repertoire became unstable and as a consequence bush warfare broke out within the scene over boundaries. According to Stuart Maconie (BBC 1998) some northern DJs played near-soul records by white rock bands like Mitch Ryder and the Detroit Wheels ('Break Out') and the Human Beings ('Nobody But Me'), as well as the soul offerings of older bluesmen such as Lowell Fulson. On the other hand a DJ like Ian Levine, based at Blackpool's Highland Room, insisted that northern soul was essentially black, and was keen to play more contemporary funk and disco material as well as soul from the classical period (McKenna 1996: 72, Hollows and Milestone 1998: 87). These disagreements about repertoire became bitter, based as they were on the drive to accumulate subcultural capital, as well as the necessary response, a plebian counter-attack on pretension and decadence.

Northern soul is important because it heralds the rise of a new kind of popular connoisseurship (Straw 1993a). For all its problems the scene demonstrates an important way of sidestepping the hegemonic thrust of the mainstream by reframing sounds which had already been released – old commodities in fact. Interestingly, the music industry was never able to (re)commodify this potentially significant niche market – the Wigan Casino had 50 000 members at its height (RoDZ 1998). True, Pye did set up a label named Disco Demand which was intended to exploit the northern soul market, but it was short-lived (Milestone 1997: 162). A deeply ingrained anti-commercialism mitigated against corporate subvention. But the importance of the scene also lies in the fact that northern soul was a working-class, white subculture which, like the mod scene before it and rare groove after it (Melville 1998), affirmed its community by 'remapping' the music of oppressed African-Americans. What counts here is the solidarity expressed in common musical appreciation by one marginalized social formation for another (Hollows and Milestone 1998: 92–3).

The different kinds of alignment between genre and community which we have been examining – racialized music, crossover, the mainstream and the remote canon – are problematic. The trouble lies in the contradiction running through all of them between musical identities which are on the one hand partial and produced by exclusionary relations of power (this is notably the case with black music), and on the other falsely universal and inclusive (as in successive mainstreams). In this sense the social organization of popular music does no more than mirror an unequal and divided society at large. And yet the same contradictions, as they are represented in and through *music,* begin to take on a new meaning. The industries' role in mixing and matching markets is crucial here. We might say that the outcome is musical hybridity except that this term has rather too positive a connotation perhaps. Whatever term we use, though, it ought to refer to these tendencies: the turning of subordination to symbolic advantage, the mutual embrace of otherness, the expression of solidarity between subordinated groups, and the recognition that, none the less, power relations permeate textual and social collectivities in popular music.

Conclusion

Over the course of this chapter we have examined two distinct kinds of grouping in popular music, which despite differences in dynamics and field, have been articulated together historically in important ways. First there is text grouping or genre. What is at stake here is an impossible quest for a complete and original experience of music, that is to say a perfect text in the 'middle' of the genre. As we have seen the musician's urge to repeat produces difference just because that initial experience is irrecoverable, an aspect of the lack in which all human subjects are constituted. The point is that in trying and failing to repeat an ideal experience, variation creeps in. For this reason too it becomes impossible to define genre in terms of a complete set of rules. Exceptions keep cropping up. Still, genres do have rules. Repetition and variation are regulated and musicians, inevitably, follow convention in their creative practice. Such is the paradox of genre.

Meanwhile communities in modern societies may be represented by genres of music, and find identity in particular styles. This has something to do with music's quality of being voiced which yields a specificity, or specificity-without-reference (see Chapter 2). It is also facilitated by its small-scale mode of production (see Chapter 1) which means that music can be made within communities. Significantly, though, a counter-tendency, the extendibility of music across time and space, has led to ambiguity about who might appropriate particular genres. As a result the music industries have been able to adopt a range of strategies for marketing music both to broad and quite particular social formations. On balance, this has helped sustain people's musics – always contested and vulnerable though they are – throughout pop's short twentieth century.

As for musicians they are in an ambiguous position in the context of the collective organization of pop. On the one hand audiences (and industries) grant them authority and legitimacy as creative agents. On the other they are constrained by generic codes and the expectations of communities. The notion of minimal creativity which I have been developing in this book copes with this situation quite well. Musicians make incremental changes inside the variative bounds of a genre. Or they incorporate the expectations of audiences outside the primary community into their practice. Yet in an important sense this simply postpones the question of innovation. For genres, and community-genre relations *do* change, often in a fundamental way. And so, at some point, creative agency will be associated with radical changes in idiom. In the next chapter we take up this question of generic transformation and the role of the musician in it through a case study of contemporary British dance music.

|5|

Dance music: business as usual or heaven on earth?

While the music matters, it matters in not quite the same way. Rather than being the affective center and agency of people's mattering maps, music's power is articulated by its place on other mattering maps, by its relations to other activities, other functions. Rather than dancing to the music you like, you like the music you dance to.

(Grossberg 1994: 56)

Let the music use you.

(Nightwriters 1987)

Lawrence Grossberg (1994, 1997) has been arguing that rock is dead. More, he has suggested that popular music in the post-rock era is less empowering and more diffuse in its emotional effect. Let me say straight away that I disagree. First, rock is still alive as I suggested in the last chapter, but as one of a series of possible youth musics, rather than, as Grossberg puts it, a 'formation'. Evidence for this comes from record charts which show records by rock groups selling well, or from the presence of rock groups on MTV and radio. Second, but more importantly for the present argument, new not-rock music *has* been able to mobilize people.

In this chapter I want to explore how this might be so, and particularly what the role of not-rock musicians might be in bringing people together in and through music. Our focus will be on the electronic dance music genres which have developed in Britain since 1988. Like earlier music-based youth subcultures – psychedelic rock and punk most notably – dance music has proclaimed itself as a transformational social movement. Unlike them its ideology is relatively uncritical. Even in its most overtly political phase when it came into conflict with the state (1988–94), dance subculture never attacked dominant social relations in the way that the earlier musical movements had done. Its most militant demand was for 'the right to party'.

Yet from another point of view the full-tilt hedonism of dance subculture suggests an even more radical agenda. The music itself becomes a vehicle for the reintegration of the cerebral and the corporal, of modes of listening and dancing, of restraint and abandonment. In an important sense this reverses a dominant trend in popular music evident in genres as diverse as be-bop, country rock and rap. In these genres music has a *representing* function – it signifies on behalf of the subject and the community (Gilbert 1997). Dance music, however, presents itself as an *absolute* music which has immediate effect on mind and body. It hymns the very sense of being it produces, rather than referring to the world outside. If this is the case (and we will be considering just such a question shortly) then there are important implications for how the music is made and the role of its producers.

Throughout this book argument and evidence have been accumulating which point to the prevalence of slow change and common patterns between music-making in the first half of pop's short twentieth century and at its end. Dance music poses a challenge to this thesis and potentially undermines arguments about creativity and musician agency which I have been developing. These all assume, to some extent, a representative role for the music maker – for example as social author (Chapter 2) or bearer of community values (Chapter 4). The inward orientation of dance towards immediate subjective experience thus constitutes a shift not only in how popular music is experienced, but also in how it is made. That is the key reason for undertaking a case study of dance. We need to test earlier arguments about creativity in the light of the claims made within the subculture, but also by some academics, about dance music's break with the past.

With this in mind it might be useful to start by setting out a 'maximum programme' – an overview which emphasizes precisely the transformative character of dance music. There are five main planks to it.

1 There has been much discussion about the changing role of the music maker in the new genre. The rock *auteur* was always visible, the known creator of unique works and responsible for the whole production process – writing, singing, recording and performing live. Conversely the dance music producer tends to be anonymous. Hidden behind a changeable *nom de disque* s/he (but usually he) adopts an air of enigmatic accomplishment (Straw 1993a, Hesmondhalgh 1998). What's more the producer does not directly present musical works. Rather an extra stage is added to the labour process with the arrival of the disk jockey who 'performs' recorded sound in the dance club. In an important sense the DJ belongs to the apparatus, and so does not have a status so much as a function – to make bodies dance.[1] This utilitarian division of labour makes a sharp contrast with rock's expressionism, inscribed in stage performance and the 'great work' format of the album.

2 Corresponding to the shift in mode of production commentators have argued that a change can be heard in the sound of the music (Eshun 1998a, Reynolds 1998). Dance music seems to be a perfect postmodern form, rehearsing many of the features that are taken to characterize cultural artifacts in the contemporary era (Hebdige 1988a, Harvey 1989, Jameson 1991). For example, pastiche; we hear spoken phrases, sung passages, drum patterns and bass lines that, whether or not they are immediately recognizable, seem to come from sources outside the song. It is not at all clear which is the original motif, the one not enclosed in quotation marks. This contributes to another postmodern feature indicated in all the sub-genres of dance music – depthlessness. Voices are scattered over the surface of a tune, and often seem to be randomly assigned to musical function. Rhythm-making may be done by sounds (for example, bleeps, squeaks or sub-bass 'parps') not normally associated with the traditional rhythm section, while apparently melodic motives like synthesizer riffs or vocal lines have an ambivalent character; pitch is often less important than rhythm. Phillip Tagg sees this flattening of hierarchies which have traditionally organized musical form, including that of rock, as a democratic manifestation. As he puts it dance music 'contains plenty of small figures, constituting plenty of ground, plenty of "environment"' (1994: 218).

3 Dance subculture proposes a transformation in the subjectivity of initiates. The phrase 'loved up', widely used in the early 1990s, means to be under the influence of the drug Ecstasy (or MDMA). But it suggests, too, a state where the mind–body duality which underpins post-Enlightenment consciousness has imploded under the impact of repetitive beats and abandoned dancing. As we saw in Chapter 3, developments in technology have been extremely important for dance music. I said then that a new, graphic method of composition on the computer screen was contributing to a paradigm shift in popular music structure. Its most significant aspect for the present argument is the way that 'part' repetition and inflection have tended to replace narrative development with rhythmic articulation. Arguably, it is this intensely iterative structure which interpellates the subject-in-dance, producing trance-like states and dissolving individual identity.

4 Associated with the claim about changes in subjectivity is the suggestion that dance music has its own form of social organization: a flat subcultural network of clubs and micro-genres. In the 'heroic' period of British dance (1988–94) state repression generated an oppositional politics. People took part in direct action to defend the right to party (McKay 1996: 103–81, Collin 1997). While explicit politicization is still evident in some parts of the scene, what has more often been emphasized about dance music in recent years is its 'good vibe', a determination amongst members to act sociably in the pursuit of pleasure. The key things here are the democratic nature of the subculture – the fact that it is accessible

to many, and its connectivity – people spread out across the country are linked in a network for conviviality.

5 Finally, the distinctiveness of dance music has been identified at the economic level. On the one hand the anti-author aesthetic and high rate of innovation mean that the record industry cannot use its traditional strategy of establishing star-commodities. On the other the relatively low cost of access to the means of production (bedroom–computer–keyboard) enables high participation in production. The same factors which tend to keep major companies out encourage flexible independent record companies and distributors with low fixed costs to enter the market (Hesmondhalgh 1998). Executives from major record companies have regularly complained about this in the pages of the trade press, stating that the volatility of dance music is 'bad for' the industry.[2]

This five-point programme for dance music is optimistic, even utopian, in its tenor. The question is, how far is it accurate and, to the extent that it is, in what ways are musicians implicated in the changes?

Dance music: context

The histories of British dance music now being published broadly agree that its origins are to be found in the adaption of black American styles, styles which were themselves only crystallizing in the mid-1980s: in particular Chicago 'house' music, and Detroit 'techno' (Kempster 1996, Collin 1997, Garratt 1998, Reynolds 1998, Rietveld 1998). Both were largely black scenes. But whereas house music had a strong gay constituency and developed in large clubs, Detroit 'techno' was a small, mostly straight and more self-consciously experimental musical culture. Despite these differences a good deal of exchange went on between the two, as well as with New York DJs and producers from the so-called 'garage' scene. In terms of style all three were amalgams of post-disco dance music, and the electronic sounds of European avant-garde pop.[3] A highly reductive description might point up these features: electronic mode of production using sequencer, synthesizer and drum machine technology; 'four-on-the-floor' bass drum pattern inherited from disco; little or no harmonic development; staccato riffs often with 'discordant' intervals such as the minor second; a high level of musematic repetition.[4]

House music arrived in England in 1986. One route was through club DJs like Mike Pickering and Graeme Park who had experienced the last days of northern soul at the start of the decade and were quick to pick up on the new records coming out of Chicago. The music then gained some circulation in mainstream media through the release of compilation albums, and the breakthrough of a few singles into the charts. But house only became the soundtrack to a fully fledged subculture during the spring and summer of 1988. The critical new ingredients were the drug Ecstasy and a psychedelic sensibility that eschewed the monochrome cool of 1980s 'style' culture. In London the scene coalesced around a small group of DJs and their friends who had spent the previous summer in Ibiza using the drug and absorbing the musical eclecticism of the dance clubs there. As 'acid house' took off, new clubs opened up, at first largely in Manchester and London. Warehouse parties (already well established in London) also proliferated under the new aesthetic regime. But its most spectacular manifestation was a series of outdoor events called 'raves'. By the turn of the decade this subculture had become a mass phenomenon with hundreds of thousands of young people participating each week (Collin 1997, Anthony 1998).

The rapid expansion of rave subculture had a delayed effect on musicmaking in Britain. Initially, in 1988 and 1989, acid house was a remote canon (see Chapter 4), consisting of a largely imported repertoire (Reynolds 1998: 55). More and more, though, demand for records to play at clubs and raves outstripped supply (Garratt 1998: 82, Rietveld 1998: 49). One important factor was that the Chicago house scene was going into decline precisely at the moment British DJs needed an increasing amount of music. True, there was a considerable back catalogue but this was quickly used up. And although Detroit techno did contribute to the flow of imports after its 'discovery' in 1988, output from the city was relatively low.

Clearly, then, dance music production in Britain was stimulated by the combination of voracious market and declining availability of new material from the US. What enabled a response by producers was an emergent tradition of electronic music-making; first synthesizer-pop in the early 1980s, and then a variant of hip hop. The year 1987 saw a rash of so-called DJ singles, including an extended remix of Eric B and Rakim's 'Paid in Full' by the DJ duo Coldcut (Eric B and Rakim 1997/1987). With its wilfully eclectic use of 'drops' from a dazzling array of sources this record placed hip hop in a distinctly British-cosmopolitan frame.[5] Back in New York Eric B certainly recognized the extent of the transformation, dismissing the remix as 'girly disco music'.[6]

DJ culture in Britain fed directly into the development of house, techno and their descendent forms as we will see in a moment. It typifies the sort of connoisseurship which Will Straw (1993b, 1997) has suggested is one of the defining characteristics of the new dance music. For unlike rock, whose aesthetic rationale lies more in its claims to express community values, dance music is legitimated and directed by the musical expertise of player–collectors. Indeed, that intense hybridity and innovation which characterizes British dance after 1988 could only have occurred because of the production and exchange of rich knowledge about the recent history of transatlantic popular music. We will return to this factor later on. For now, though, I want to argue that important though it has been for providing the conditions of change, expert culture can hardly explain the direction or intensity of innovation in dance music. To understand these factors we need a fuller theory of generic change.

From house to drum and bass: two kinds of generic change

In the discussion of genre and form in the last chapter the emphasis was on stasis. Both the structuralist approach and Steve Neale's (1980) repetition/difference principle attempt to explain generic coherence, or to put it another way, the limits to divergence over time. So how can the sort of hyper-innovation which we encounter in dance music be accommodated in these theories of genre?

Franco Fabbri (1982) suggests that the principal cause of change in genres is *transgression* of existing codes. In the case of 'poor' codes, which are capable of generating a relatively predictable range of texts, musical communities soon become 'analytically competent'.[7] Not only do members acquire an understanding of the rules of the genre, they then lose interest as the texts which conform to them become predictable. At this point transgressions of the norm occur that restore interest by contradicting expectations about generic form. If these transgressions are repeated they will be codified and so yield a new genre (60–2). In the development of house and techno the most important transgressive change was in rhythmic coding.

The mainstream transatlantic dance style of the mid-1980s might be described as up-tempo soul, an African-American form with occasional British simulations. 'Till my baby comes home' by Luther Vandross from 1985 provides a good example. The common time rhythm of this record is brisk (152 b.p.m.) with a regular snare hit on second and fourth beats. The crotchet bass drum pattern is low in the mix, with a slight emphasis on the beats which coincide with the snare. Articulation of the rhythm section does occur – snare fills at the end of choruses, occasional slap bass runs, an eighth-note bongo figure – but the general feel of up-tempo soul is jerky and angular. In contrast dancers were moving to slower but more rhythmically supple musics in underground scenes: either hip hop or (only in Britain) the 1970s funk canon known as rare groove. Both these forms use a 16-beat drum pattern at a median tempo of around 90 b.p.m.

We can usefully consider these rhythms in the light of what Richard Middleton (1990) calls 'accentual hierarchy'. For Middleton rhythm depends on the relationship between strong and weak or long and short moments (1990: 212). In 1980s up-tempo soul we can hear a clear binary division between weak first and third, and strong second and fourth beats. The effect is almost of a duple time signature – an 'R and B two step'. There is a pronounced accentual hierarchy in funk/hip hop too, but it takes the form of heavy bass drum stress on the first beat (known in the funk community as 'the one' (Vincent 1996: 8)), typically followed by snare taps on second and fourth beats with an irregular, bass drum figure (often gesturing towards a triplet) around the third beat of the measure. In addition there is often a 16-beat hi-hat tap in the left hand.

Significantly, house music suppresses both sorts of accentual hierarchy. Above all it represents a return to disco pulsiveness. The key aspect here is the 'four-on-the-floor' kick drum pattern at around 120 b.p.m. This is often accompanied by a clipped, open hi-hat which sounds between the even, on beat bass drum strikes. (Because I want to refer to it quite a lot I will call this combination the basic disco rhythm or BDR.) For present purposes the most important attribute of the BDR is the way accents are flattened. This has considerable implications for how temporality is constructed. In house the continuous bass drum pulse gestures, as Richard Middleton says of the walking bass line in mainstream jazz, 'beyond the possible, to an undifferentiated flow of time' (1990: 212).

From the point of view of generic change the achronic pulse in house music constitutes a prime case of rule breaking. That is to say for a particular group of music makers and dancers, first in Chicago and Detroit and then in Britain, 'analytical competence' (Fabbri 1982: 62) in the rhythmic codes of existing dance genres made the patterns sound predictable. Conversely the apparent simplicity of the BDR was exciting precisely because it ignored 'cheesy' accentual hierarchies, evened out the beat and offered the sublime prospect of endlessness in the 'pumping' pulse of the bass drum. We will explore the connection between temporality and rhythm in more depth shortly. First, though, I want to examine another kind of change which has actually been much more important in dance music than transgression.

One reason why the structure–deterioration model is so useful in explaining change is because it accounts for the role of boredom, a perennial reaction to all sorts of music. However innovation may take a second form where, on the contrary, change follows from the obsessional pursuit of pleasure rather than from tedium. This form has been very important in dance music, sometimes compounding or interacting with transgressive change. The most appropriate name for it might be *intensification*. In order to understand the concept we need first to return to the proposal that genre is a process for regulating repetition and difference (Neale 1980 and Chapter 4). You will remember the argument went that the musician–subject tries to repeat an initial pleasurable experience in music by producing another, similar text. However the new work inevitably fails to yield pleasure in the same way as that first realization, and thus a gap opens up between a generic imago, or ur-text, and the actualized work that follows. The genre process then consists of the folding back of difference generated by (hopeless) attempts to recover the original moment.

Clearly change is latent in this model. Sometimes, as in the case of American hardcore rock in the 1980s (see Chapter 4), there may be little variation for a number of years because the existing form continues to offer the promise of bliss. However at other times a genre will mutate very fast if a particular aspect (or aspects) of the imago becomes aesthetically salient.[8] In effect what was previously an undifferentiated and small-scale epiphenomenon is subjected to micro-phonic audition, and so assumes increased musical significance. If such an 'aesthetic zone' is heard again in the next generation of text then generic stability may break down altogether. I want to examine how this occurred on an almost unprecedented scale in the first distinctly home-produced strand of dance music to emerge after the acid house revolution, a strand which runs from 'hardcore' rave to 'jungle'.

As Simon Reynolds points out (1998: 96–7) hardcore embraced quite disparate tendencies as it developed between 1989 and 1993. Right at the start the hyper-convivial effects of Ecstasy and inclusive 'one nation' discourse bequeathed by acid house ensured that a range of previously hermetic subcultures and musical genres were thrown together. The sound that everyone listened to was, of course, American house and techno. But many rave producers also had a background in what Andy Basire (1999: 39) calls the 'failed British hip hop scene'. Basire is right to suggest that hip hop never took off as a home-produced genre. However, flourishing hip hop sound systems and a vogue for break dancing did bring black and white youth together in a subculture that spread across the UK during the mid-1980s (Garratt 1998: 261). In London the multi-ethnic and cross-class 'rare groove' scene constituted another remote canon with its own lore and expertise – this time 1970s funk and jazz (Melville 1998). Finally, black DJs and music makers added a further ingredient to the resource bank: ragga. Ragga is a rap/reggae hybrid in which MCs 'chat' over digitized up-tempo 'dancehall' rhythms.

All these elements fed into hardcore. Whereas house music, garage and certain kinds of techno cleaved to the BDR – that 'four-on-the-floor' thump – British hardcore producers adopted the breakbeat. A breakbeat is the section of a funk or reggae track where pitched instruments drop out, leaving drums and percussion to play unadorned for a few bars. The first hip hop DJs used breakbeats in their live mixes at the end of the 1970s (Toop 1991: 60–2). Then from around 1986 breakbeat samples of one or two bars were 'looped' together to produce a continuous drum track. These quickly replaced drum machine sequences on hip hop records (Toop 1991: 163). 'Paid in full', referred to above, uses breakbeats. In the post-acid world, however, the breakbeat represented a scandalous return of the accentual hierarchy. In the increasingly glamorous house music scene DJs and clubbers abhorred breaks, hearing them as regressive and a messy corruption of the pure aesthetic of the BDR. For erstwhile B-Boys and ragga-muffins, however, the breakbeat was an article of faith, and the rhythmic nucleus of the style known as hardcore.[9]

Figure 5.1 shows how parts from that genre pool I have been describing were selected, assembled and intensified – first in hardcore and then in the transition to jungle. There are two timelines. The year 1992, the high water mark of hardcore, is represented by Nebula II's 'Explore H Core' (1998/1992). In the first place the tune can be heard as a synchronic structure of distinct stylistic components. These are arrayed across the time line. But, crucially, it also represents a moment in a continuous, diachronic process of intensification along several dimensions: bass, timbre, polyrhythms and tempo. As far as that first dimension is concerned frequencies are dropping on the bass line while at the same time its timbre is becoming 'dirtier'. At the top end of the frequency spectrum bleeps, squeaks and speeded-up vocal samples provide an hysterical, treble perimeter to the sound. They also serve to intensify another key aesthetic zone in hardcore – velocity. From the classic house tempo of 120 b.p.m. which had prevailed only a few years earlier, crotchet value on 'Explore H Core' has increased to 142.

In hardcore the principle of the addition of components prevails. From 1989 to 1992 we hear an increasing number of voices, parts and variation in general. The shift to jungle, or drum and bass, then depends on a paring away of parameters, and the intensification of those which are left. The jungle mode is represented in Figure 5.1 on the lower timeline of 1994 by Randall and Andy C's 'Feel It' (1995). There is still some melodic/harmonic movement in this tune in the form of a modal synth-string figure in the breakdown section of the tune from 2'27" to 3'0". A lone three-note riff also appears briefly at 4'42", but attention is now focused almost entirely on drums and bass. A breakbeat has been literally chopped up with 32nd-note snare figures, assembled from samples of a single hit, constantly erupting across surging bass drum riffs and irregular single-note 'bombs'. (The latter are strangely reminiscent of be-bop.) Drum sounds are still recognizable, although the 'kit' is being operated at an inhuman level of articulation. Not only does a virtual bass drum pedal execute impossibly fast runs, but several pairs of hands play polymetric patterns on snares tuned to discrete pitches, and all with a robot-like precision.

As for the bass line we can note two zones of intensification. The dirty, low-frequency sound (with so called sub-bass overtones) which can already be heard on 'Explore H Core' reaches an even lower point here. Individual notes are also articulated in a very complex fashion with variable attack and decay envelopes, pitch bending and sharp fluctuations in dynamics; the bass sonority is sculpted, as it were. There is also a very wide interval between highest and lowest bass notes (perhaps two octaves), although it is difficult to be precise about the pitch of sounds with so many overtones and such extreme portamento. The other development is the slowing down of the bass line. If a 'slow' bass line is implied in places on the hardcore tune, on 'Feel It' the bass line is half-tempo throughout, with a spare and open quality in the manner of dub. The result is profound temporal ambivalence. One can dance slowly to the bass at 80 b.p.m. or 'go mental' to the 'top end' of the tune at a breakneck 160 b.p.m.[10]

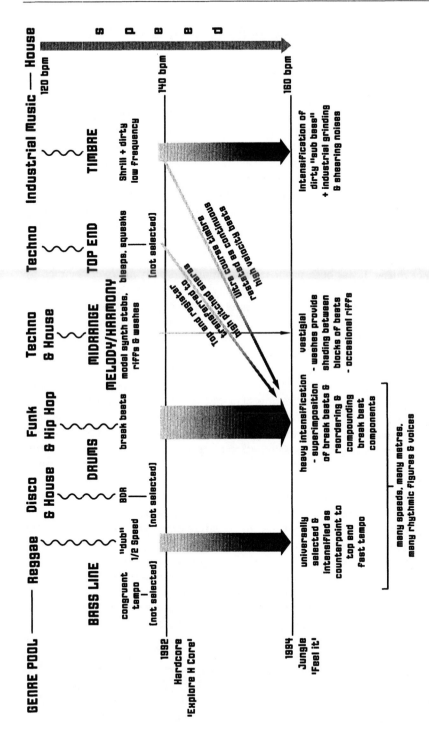

Figure 5.1 Selection and intensification of genre elements from hardcore to jungle

Agency, creativity and the aesthetics of dance

Jungle represents an extraordinary leap forward in popular music form and sonority. Its rich polymetre and textural syntax, together with the low salience of melody and harmony, mark a radical departure from earlier styles – even from hip hop or dub which had already begun to move in a similar direction. The sheer *speed* of the successive moves from house, to rave, to jungle in the period 1988–94 is also unprecedented. Such intense innovation raises important issues about the role of the musician. I argued in Chapter 2 that musicians work within a radius of creativity, or range of possibilities, determined by the prevailing discourses and practices in their field. The problem is that when musical practices are changing this quickly the whole notion of field, depending as it does on relatively stable structuring, becomes difficult to sustain. Another challenge to the model of creativity I have described arises from the much-vaunted immediacy of dance music. It has been proposed that mind and body are overwhelmed by music, and that repetitive beats send the dancer into a timeless state of bliss (Hughes 1994, Gilbert 1997). But how can this be squared with the idea of the music maker as reflexive designer or social author? It sounds, on the face of it, as though music-making now becomes a form of psychedelic programming, designed to obliterate thought.

Let us begin with the question of innovation. In fact the two sorts of change discussed above, transgression and intensification, have quite different implications for the musician–agent. Transgression is very much a reflexive process. That is to say, music makers recognize generic deterioration as such, and break existing codes as part of a conscious aesthetic strategy for renewal. This combination of rationality and violation of norms has made transgression the paradigmatic mode of change in popular music since 1945. It represents a kind of 'thoughtful deviance' and is central to the popular negative aesthetic which informs a range of musics from be-bop to punk. Popular conceptions of authorship also depend on transgression but emphasize its generative powers: the creative musician is precisely the one who breaks with convention.

However transgression has been less significant in dance music than in most post-war styles of pop. True, the early adoption of the BDR in house and techno represented a vital transgressive break with tradition. But since then dance music has diversified and change has become so constant that transgression is now almost beside the point. Instead the emphasis has shifted, as Jeremy Gilbert puts it, to 'pleasure – as much as possible – *entirely* for pleasure's sake' (1997: 17). Likewise, Simon Reynolds suggests that 'at the heart of rave lies a kernel of tautology: raving is about the celebration of celebration' (1997: 104). The emphasis from both these writers on pleasure adds weight to the idea that transgression has largely been replaced by a process of intensification in dance music. For intensification supposes a desiring as well as a thinking subject. In the language of Lacanian psychoanalysis the subject, constituted in lack, desires an imaginary, full experience of genre: 'same as the first time I heard it' (Lacan 1979: 53–64, Bowie 1991: 162–3). It is the pursuit of this generic imago which, paradoxically, yields difference through a cumulative process of selection and intensification of aesthetic zones.

However that does not mean intensification is 'dumb', that it represents a victory of the impulsive Imaginary over the disciplinary Symbolic order. Rather in those dance music genres like drum and bass where innovation has been particularly fast a highly productive meeting of reason and desire can be detected. How does it occur? We can usefully turn to Umberto Eco's concept of 'under-coding' to address this question (1976: 129–33, 135–6). Eco poses a situation in which a reader encounters symbolic material which s/he takes to be significant but cannot decode; a piece of music in a new idiom for example (135). One response is to infer, or 'abduct', coding which will give meaning to that material.[11] This is a necessarily tentative, even messy, process which depends on intuition, trial and error but also reasoning. Now it seems to me we can detect a similar process in the development of jungle. Beyond abductive reception, though, what's at stake here is the *production* of new musical forms abductively.

One of jungle's characteristic features is its use of high velocity, repetitive percussion patterns, of 32nd- or even 64th-note incidence, which skip around the measure. Often voiced by a notional snare drum, these patterns may be multiple, polymetric and tuned to different pitches. Sometimes pitch is bent to produce a sort of percussive melisma. As well as being extremely funky, these jungle tattoos have a textural dimension. Hits may come so quickly that we hear them as striated belts of sound, rolling across the surface of the music. This characteristic is picked up in drum and bass discourse where a 'roller' can be a track, a producer (E–Z Rollers) or an epithet (as in the form 'rollin(g)').

How did music makers conceive this radically new sound, or to put it another way, why did intensification take this form? We know that the funk breakbeat was a direct source (see Figure 5.1). The archetypal break, used on countless jungle tunes, is from James Brown's 'Funky Drummer'. Its irregular series of snare drum ruffs and drags provide rich material for sampling, editing and rearranging. Yet the breakbeat contained no genetic code which could have *caused* the hyperactive, interlocking tattoos of jungle.

The same thing is true of similar percussion figures in other genres which jungle producers were listening to: for example the dense semiquaver 'handclap' riffs heard on early house and techno records or the delay line snare figure from dub reggae. In retrospect it is tempting to hear these 'influences' teleologically, as though they were always already gesturing towards the jungle sound. However my suggestion would be that earlier figures constituted a field of desirable sound images, an inchoate aesthetic zone of rattle and roll which producers then had to *make sense* of. We can hear this happen in the critical period of 1992–94 as hardcore tips over into fully fledged jungle. Recalling his experience of that moment, leading producer of drum and bass, Goldie, explains:

> I was thinking a lot about various theories and this idea of dimensional sound but it was still quite a barbaric process. I just went in there and tried throwing nu-skool samples against old-skool stuff and then pulled other things in. It was just experimenting and trying things out. The name I came up with was Rufige Kru: 'rufige' was the way you described things that were left lying around on the surface – more or less scum – which you collected together and turned into something new. I was using fourth or fifth generation samples, just trash sounds, but they had a grittiness and a roughness which identified with the feel of the street.
>
> (Quoted by Barr 1996: 148)

Goldie's dual emphasis on dirt *and* theory is telling. It seems to me to be entirely congruent with the concept of intensification which I have been outlining. The 'things left lying around' are scraps and traces of a breakbeat imago, which can only be made to signify through the application of theory. But this theory is not a perfected system of knowledge. Rather it involves 'trying things out' and 'pulling other things in'. In Eco's terms codes are developed abductively. The reference to texture is important too. On the one hand Goldie proposes a homological relation between rough-grained sounds and 'the feel of the street'. This is a realist code which directs musical gesture outwards towards the world. On the other hand, grittiness and grain are desirable in themselves as musical attributes. They are 'trash sounds' generated, paradoxically, by a *careful* process of degradation.

A widely used term in the drum and bass scene suggests that other producers think about their work in the same way, as though it depended on a mixture of chance and logic. The word 'science' has been employed, among other things, as a *nom de disque* – Dropping Science, as an album title – 'Haunted Science', and as a description of music-making – 'breakbeat science'. It refers to the producer's methodology, and in particular the theory and practice of re-engineering sounds, whether samples or synthesizer voices. It is clearly not science in the officially consecrated sense of producing positive, verifiable knowledge. Nor does it imply domination as in the critical account of science by the Frankfurt School (Adorno and Horkheimer 1979). Instead it is a benign research and development process which works at a microphonic scale to change the way people are *subjected* to music. Such a science tends to take an arcane form precisely because it is an abductive process. In other words intuition and the constant recourse to musical pasts are integrated with systematic thought.

Intensification, abduction and science all suggest an inflection of the sort of social authorship discussed in Chapter 2. What I mean is that creative agency is not superseded so much as contextualized. The reflexive work of designing music has to accommodate both happenstance and a certain autonomic flow of genre. This suggests the need to think about the radius of creativity in a rather different way. It now becomes a space in which powerful, but widely dispersed exigencies, circulate. These 'packages of desire' tend to supplant the more densely woven practices and discourses of production found in earlier music cultures which we have been examining.

If the intense *innovation* of jungle calls for the revision of approaches to musician agency set out earlier, the much-vaunted *immediacy* of dance music threatens to abolish the notion of creativity altogether. In order to discuss this factor we need to move away from production for a moment and consider end-use, in other words, dance. A long tradition of criticism running from Plato (James 1995: 58–9) to Adorno (1991c: 46) has been extremely suspicious of music as a sensuous medium. In particular, rhythm is judged to be dangerous because it acts on the body and demands surrender of the thinking mind. In contemporary dance music culture, rhythm is also attributed with a direct, motor effect on mind and body but the normative judgement is reversed. Rhythms are good if they make you dance. We will examine this notion because it has radical implications for the present argument. Quite simply, I want to suggest that dance music makers' creative agency comes to the fore here, precisely where it would seem, prima facie, to be most absent.

First of all the idea that rhythm is immediate in its effect *does* have a phenomenological basis. Because it consists in 'regular recurrence, esp. of stress or of long and short sounds' (*Chambers Concise Dictionary* 1988: 854) rhythm is carried along two sense channels: we hear rhythm but also feel its accents, durations and intervals on the surface of our bodies. This combination gives it a plenary force, which, certainly in the West, has been institutionalized through discourse on dance. Traditionally, a single name is used to signify a dance style, a metre and a genre of music. Well-known examples include the waltz, the polka and the tango. However the vernacular tradition of correlating dance and music in the West starts to break down with rock'n'roll. Dances like the mashed potato and the jerk proliferate without a musical style of their own, while Motown is notionally social dance music but is mostly listened to at home on radio or record. In the early 1970s progressive rock repudiated dance altogether. Idiot dancing is the pejorative term applied in Britain to a kind of abandoned dancing at gigs. Only people who are abjectly 'out of their heads' – an uncool intoxication if ever there was one – do the idiot dance. In more recent times the pogo in punk, and its indie rock descendent, moshing, represent a partial rehabilitation of dance in rock culture, albeit on a rigorously functional basis. Dancers repress sensuousness and body articulation in favour of one-dimensional movement: up–down (and, every so often, fall over).

The shift to 'dance music', represented by disco, house, techno and other musics which claim lineage from these styles, then consists in dance once more becoming the *primary* orientation of production and reception.[12] Since disco in the mid-1970s, music for dance has been realized in two stages as we saw in the last chapter. First the producer assembles a master recording and gets it on to disc. The club DJ (sometimes the same person) then completes the process by 'playing out' the record as part of a continuous long mix or sequence of records. The DJ is utterly directed towards getting people on to the floor. In effect s/he has to construct dancers, by playing music which will articulate bodies in dance. It ought to do so with maximum force – one wants to be carried away by the music – but also without prescribing *how* one moves.

This paradoxical quality of dance music, as a form of programming and as a free zone, has been noted by several writers. It is often connected to the idea that dance music produces a trance-like state in which the passage of time is suspended. For example Walter Hughes (1994) talks about the 'empire of the beat' in disco. He argues that lyrics are often no more than simple imperatives to move, or else consist of

> counting, a repetitive enumeration that signifies only a precipitancy of succession without teleology or terminus ('five, four, three, two, one, let's go' or 'one, two, three shake your body down'). . . . The mixing of the music by the producer and the remixing of it by the club DJ shatter, rebuild, and reshatter any architectonics a disco song might ever have possessed, making it difficult to identify its beginning or end.
>
> (149)

Hughes further suggests that disco involves 'a free fall from rational self-mastery' (153) and a submission of the subject to the rapture of the beat. In a similar vein Jeremy Gilbert argues that rave 'doesn't have time to occupy itself *with* time. We hear this in the music; techno, trance, jungle and garage are all about creating a pleasurable moment rather than telling a story' (1997: 18).

For both writers, then, dance music places the subject in an endless and undifferentiated present. I think such an observation is important, but calls for qualification. First, the sense of timelessness is never completely accomplished: often it is set up only to be actively subverted. Second, to the extent that it is successfully produced, atemporality depends on a complex organization of rhythm by producers and DJs rather than a shattering of architectonics. The general point is that rhythm is tricky. To explain this I want to return to the apparently simplistic BDR, or on-beat pulse, at the core of a whole family of dance styles including disco, house, garage and techno. Earlier I mentioned that aficionados attributed the BDR with a purity which they contrasted with the jumbled-up beats of funk, hip hop and jungle. On one level this judgement is ideological: 'purity' is invariably invoked as part of a strategy of distinction within club culture.[13] However the purity argument can also be considered from an ontological point of view, and linked with the approach of those critics who talk about atemporality. Pure beats call us into a realm of pure presence where time, and therefore subjectivity, threaten to disappear altogether (Melechi 1993: 33–4). If we are to take this sensation at face value, and I want to do so because of the sheer weight of testimony about it, we ought to ask how such a state of grace might be constructed.

The simple pulse of the BDR consists in the recurrence of one sound (same attributes and duration each time) at equal intervals. It is voiced by the bass drum. Crucially, the positive value of the bass drum pulse derives from the absence, or weakness, of sound in the intervals. In a classical case of binarism gaps constitute beats (and vice versa) through their mutual opposition. Now to understand how this might produce a sense of temporal suspension we need to examine, briefly, the ontology of time. Peter Osborne usefully characterizes the Aristotelean 'image of time as an infinite succession of identical instants, split in relation to any one instant into a before and an after' (1994: 4). It is this image which informs the common-sense understanding of time in the West. In the case of the simple pulse my hypothesis would be that the even beat of the BDR indexes the 'point-like instant' of the present (Osborne 1994: 5).

However, whereas in Aristotle's formulation instants are rendered successively as before, present and after, the musical pulse takes, as we have seen, a binary form. Thus, in its opposition to the present (indexed by the on-beat), the interval (or off-beat) is constituted as a not-now. We should note here, as Hughes (1994) and others have done, that dancers tend to perceive time as being driven. Beats issue from the sound system and dancers are impelled by the beats. Accordingly, the not-now of the interval will be heard as before-present. The total effect of this temporal structuration is that on-beat, off-beat pairs unfold in a 'now-back-now-back-now-back-now . . .' series, with each interval looping back before each beat so as to constitute it as a now once more. Like much musical decoding this experience is pre-conscious, I would suggest. We hear a series of after-less, thumping nows without reflecting on the logical impossibility of their constitution.

So, the first point to make about the BDR is that its 'immediacy' actually depends on a trope. Like all music it is a device, something put together by the musician–agent with a particular aesthetic end in mind.[14] However, the bass drum beat is only the beginning of rhythmic articulation. So far I have been talking about a simplified, heuristic model of the BDR. In practice there are many ways in which it will be complicated. Almost invariably there is a sense of four to the bar time. Often riffs and vocal lines run over two bars to produce what Brian Currid calls 'the basic two-measure building block' of house music (1995: 170); and sometimes tunes use a compound hypermetre of 16 bars, implied by harmonic change or 'verse' structure.

However the BDR is also inflected in quite a different way, and it is this figure, I want to suggest, which is actually the most salient. It is where the question of creative agency and the selection of possibles becomes most acute. At the interval between on-beats there is usually an alternative percussive sound. Its classical manifestation is an open (or opening) hi-hat tap which is sharply damped.[15] Structurally, of course, this off-beat is weak – a discreet motivator of the pulse. We hear its debility in the undemonstrative sound and low volume of the hi-hat, whether synthesized or sampled. However over the last ten years or so there seems to have been an insinuating reversal of the BDR. More and more, attention has been shifting away from the bass drum towards richly articulated hi-hat sonority.

We can bring in Charles Keil's (1994c) extremely suggestive notion of the 'participatory discrepancy' in order to discuss this. Keil identifies the power of music to move people in a certain lack of consistency or match. This has both textural and temporal dimensions. In the case of the temporal dimension he suggests that 'semiconscious or unconscious slightly out of syncness' [produces] 'groove' (96). Keil goes on to investigate this phenomenon in the 'Bo Diddley beat'. At one point he proposes that Diddley's 'mechanical guitar vibrato' works as a kind of micro-template for the famous rhythm. However, having established a role for what might be called discrepant technology, Keil is unhappy about the effects of its later development. As he puts it 'the engineers have already arrived in force and taken control of the central dance sector in ongoing Afro-American music' (107).

The problem with this extreme scepticism about the creative potential of contemporary technology is that it short-circuits analysis and consigns discrepant tropes to an irrecoverable past. In fact when we examine the digital beats of house and techno there are few grounds for techno-pessimism. Rather, hi-hat voicings show that participatory discrepancies are alive and kicking even in the purest of pulse cultures. What producers seem to be up to is subversion of the metronome beat. There are at least three tactics. One is to transform the sound of the open hi-hat – perhaps into something much rougher like a pair of hydraulic sheers, or maybe something softer, a splash or a sigh. Another tactic is to place the sound slightly behind or ahead of the off-beat (for a discussion of a similar figure in jazz see Chapter 2 and Keil 1994a). A third involves articulation of the sonic envelope, to produce 'unnatural' attack and decay, and changes in timbre over its length. Often used in combination these tactics have several effects.

For instance, there may be ambiguity about where to locate the on-beat. We can dance to the bass drum, or the hi-hat or even in between the two. Lag and anticipation then lead to questions about 'out of syncness'. Is it the hi-hat which is out, or is it the bass drum? Finally, we may be seduced by absurdly mannered hi-hat sounds. On 'Been A Long Time' by The Fog (1998), for example, the hi-hat is an industrial grinder which catches its work, slows slightly and then stops quite suddenly. It is placed just ahead of the true off-beat, giving an almost ska-like feel. At the turn of every chorus its pitch drops an octave in four disorienting lurches before recovering for the next verse.

Discrepant hi-hat tropes like this have a funky, carnivalesque quality about them, and that bears strongly on the argument about agency I have been developing. For even as the trance-inducing repetition of the BDR threatens to transport dancers to a timeless state of bliss, makers of house and techno subvert this disappearance into the now by 'scratching' it. On the floor discrepant beats make dissolving bodies rematerialize as muscles pull, and dancers step and turn *against* the pulse. This is not only a matter of record production. DJs have routines of discrepancy too. During an interview DJ and producer Kevin Mason (1994) showed me how he would 'funk up' the pure beats of progressive house music by cross-fading two copies of the same record playing out of synchronization. In the mix, mis-aligned bass drum on-beats from the two record decks produced, for a moment, a distinctly *im*pure, 'b'boom, b'boom, b'boom . . .' effect.

Participatory discrepancies in dance music represent a departure in the aesthetics of pop it seems to me. What's at stake is a new kind of structural ambivalence. On the one hand we have immediacy: the pulsing re-presenta-tion of the now which can induce trance-like states and a dissolution of subjectivity. This is like Keil's notion of participation *without* discrepancy. As everyone starts to groove collective identity subsumes individual consciousness (1994c: 97–8). On the other hand, and this is what redeems the BDR, we hear sharpness and turn of phrase. In effect music makers write agency back into the frame by *thinking through* bliss, so making possi-bilities stick out from its amorphous field. We are close here to Lyotard's formulation, after Burke, of the sublime.

> [A] very big, very powerful object threatens to deprive the soul of any 'it happens', strikes it with 'astonishment' (at lower intensities the soul is seized with admiration, veneration, respect). The soul is thus dumb, immobilised, as good as dead. Art, by distancing this menace, procures a pleasure of relief, of delight. Thanks to art, the soul is returned to the agitated zone between life and death, and this agitation is its health and its life.
>
> (Lyotard 1993: 251)

In dance music it is the discrepant and abductive moves of producers and DJs that 'distance the menace' of dissolution, so producing a liminal state which I will call the material sublime. The material aspect derives from the way dance music works on the body, and through the body the mind also. As Kodwo Eshun puts it, the 'body . . . is a distributed brain, it's a big brain in the sense that the whole body thinks' (1998b). This modifies Lyotard's formulation in a significant way and yields a popular manifestation of the sublime; much less solipsistic and abstract, and much more democratic, than the avant-garde art which Lyotard champions. Many clubbers 'think' their bodies in dance and many producers and DJs research new ways of inducting subjects into the material sublime.

I want to stop at this point and sum up the observations about agency and aesthetics I have been making. First, dance music *does* represent an emancipatory turn in the politics of popular music. On the one hand intensive beats and the drive to bliss dissolve the sort of surefire, authentic subject who has inhabited 'heartland rock' (Straw 1991) over the last 30 years or so. In as much as the subject of rock is archetypically male (macho or heroically failed macho) and buoyed up in his complacent view of the world by rock's unreflexive ideology of individual expression, then I judge this to be a positive shift. On the other hand, and more affirmatively, dance music calls up a new embodied subject – fleet-footed and quick-thinking. In particular, DJs and producers show how it is possible to act demurely yet to extraordinary effect by making sublime music. They make a difference through recognizing contingency and then building it into their practice. Of course this is an incomplete evaluation. So far almost nothing has been said about how dance music works *inter*-subjectively, at the level of reception. Without considering that issue the concept of musician agency seems rather abstract. I mean that we need to examine how the realm of the material sublime brings together DJs, producers *and* people on dance floors. In the next section this will be our focus. In particular we will be examining how these different actors are linked in a series of overlapping subcultural networks which extend over geographical space, yet produce communities of interest and identity. I would suggest a further issue is lurking here: the question of whether dance music subculture provides an alternative to dominant forms of cultural production.

Dance music networks: corporal and economic

For Manuel Castells the network constitutes the basic unit and organizing principle of contemporary, 'informational' society (1994). He defines it as a system which facilitates flows of 'purposeful, repetitive, programmable sequences of exchange and interaction between physically disjointed positions held by social actors' (412). Networks traverse a world where the flow of communication is not just a means of coordination, but actually structures societies and determines economic development across space. As Castells puts it, 'places do not disappear, but their logic and their meaning become absorbed in the network' (412). In other words what counts is how well a place is connected to the net and its power flows. Although the most important network is economic – global capitalism – there are other networks, including the cultural. Crucially, all networks tend to be interconnected and implicated in the meta-function of capital accumulation (192–5).

It seems to me Castells' conception of the network has wide applicability to various forms of social organization at the turn of the millennium.

However there is a problem. Castells appears rather ambivalent about the political implications of the network. While he recogniszes that it dissolves bonds of solidarity and leaves those places outside its ambit in a marginalized state of exclusion, he also enthuses about how the network initiates fully social relations across the world (477–8). This conclusion is reached despite the fact that while Castells spends a considerable amount of time discussing economic networks he scarcely mentions social actors at all.[16]

However there are networks where agency counts and where the instrumental logic of accumulation has been resisted. Dance music is organized in this way. With its geographical reach, dispersed nodes and flows of information and affect it is very much a network of the sort we have been examining. But, and this is the crucial distinction, we can define it as an *alternative* network. I use the epithet, after Raymond Williams (1981: 70–86), to get at the way that dance music subculture not only represents an alternative to established cultural institutions (for example the rock gig), but also, through its mode of sociality, to point towards new kinds of equitable and democratic social organization (Laing 1997).

We can begin to investigate this idea by looking at the primary site of dance, the club. The club itself takes the form of a network in that dancers interact with those around them in a 360° radius, using a rich paralinguistic vocabulary of bodily movement and countenance. This can be contrasted with the spatial organization of the rock concert where everyone faces forward, towards the stage. As Wendy Fonorow (1995) has pointed out, there is a hierarchy of engagement at gigs from the high-activity 'mosh pit' at the front to areas of more limited involvement at the back. In all cases, though, audience members are disposed as supplicants of the band on stage.

It has been suggested that the rock gig is now in the throes of an 'authenticity crisis' (Auslander 1998). This is partly the result of constant repetition. Depending for its effect on naturalistic performance, rock has become so encrusted with convention as to make expression extremely difficult; there is a limit to how many times the artist can make 'his "innermost" appear' (Bahr 1992/1916: 118) using the standard repertory of rock stagecraft. Moreover strategies for variation and renewal – such as the shock theatre of punk or the neurotic sincerity of grunge – now seem to be played out. To use a term from information theory, the rock gig has become highly redundant.

However dance music does not involve expression. Rather the DJ works *off* the crowd by picking up dynamics in collective gesture and affect, and then amplifying them. Techniques like the 'beat edit' in which two copies of the same tune are played a half-beat apart, or the 'reverse edit' where one record is played backwards for a couple of beats, hold back the move towards closure while at the same time heightening its anticipation. To reiterate a point made earlier, the suspension of time is richly articulated. But, and this is the theme I want to develop here, it is articulated in a network of flows, both between dancers, and between dancers as a group and the DJ.

Each of these agents interacts with others via feedback loops of action and response where mutuality is at a premium. The dancer who shows off does so *for* the other. The DJ plays out on our behalf – her tropes are our tropes. Generally, one makes oneself present for the other in proxemic dialogue. At its best this sort of club experience is not only democratic, but utopian in that it shows what democracy might be like if everyone wanted to help everyone else have a good time.

If I have emphasized voluntary interaction between agents within the club there is also an embrace of system here. One of the pleasures of dancing is to become part of the apparatus, to be plugged into a synaesthetic sensorium which delivers sound and light in huge, yet precisely controlled doses. From this point of view the dancer might be considered a cyborg. In a much-cited essay Donna Haraway (1991) argues that the cyborg, a human–machine hybrid, has become a key metaphor in western culture. She goes so far as to construct a new politics around the cyborg, a politics based on 'kinship with animals and machines ... permanently partial identities and contradictory standpoints' (154). I have doubts about whether the cyborg is quite as ubiquitous as Haraway suggests. In particular it seems to me that she does not always show how the fragmented figure of the cyborg is appropriable by marginalized groups – women, ethnic minorities, gay people – as a mode of resistance.[17]

While noting these limits I still want to borrow Haraway's notion of cyborg liberation because, in the case of dance music, it has an almost *literal* applicability. In the club dancers are spliced into a circuit whose other components are DJ, decks, speakers, lights and drugs. Critically, the transformation into cyborg dancer involves shedding what Wilhelm Reich (1975/1946) called the 'character-armour' of bourgeois individuality. As a part of the machine one is immediately collectivized; that intense sense of equality and mutuality I have been describing is realized by and through (T)echnics.[18]

One other point needs to be made about cyborg dancers. Connected to a network of other cyborgs and plugged into the club apparatus, dancers are like the habitués of cyberspace, or their archetype Case in William Gibson's (1995/1984) novel *Neuromancer*. But unlike cyberspace surfers who leave 'the meat', or body, behind when they enter the computer-mediated world of the Internet, dancers make their bodies appear. The tug between timelessness and discrepancy has an embodying effect.

So far I have been discussing the club as network, emphasizing connectivity between dancers, feedback around 'system' parts, and the flat, democratic structure. But not only is the club a network itself, it also forms part of another, larger network for the dissemination of dance music. To understand how this works we need to adopt one more term from Castells: the 'node'. According to Castells the node is a site of strategic importance on a network, organized around a key function. Communications pass around the node enabling flows to be switched in and out, or on and off (1994:

413). Castells has in mind cities or sub-regions in his discussion, but the concept also fits the dance club very well. On the one hand it is the primary site of reception, the place where consumption of dance music begins. On the other the club is a relay point for macro network flow, both of recorded music *into* the club-arena and of opinion (positive or negative) about particular records *from* DJ and audience back to the music industries.

Clearly this macro club network has an economic function: it valorizes capital. However in the economic realm, as much as in relation to performance, there is a pronounced contrast with rock music. Networks have changed the terms and conditions of entrepreneurship and the profit-making routines which developed in the rock era. In rock the album is the key commodity. It depends for its success on a complex and expensive marketing strategy consisting of more or less simultaneous radio play of a single taken from the album, media appearances and reporting, live tour by the band and national retail distribution of records in different formats. In dance music, conversely, the club DJ alone initiates the dissemination of just one sound carrier, the 12-inch single. Entrusted by the subculture with ensuring a high rate of innovation the DJ's key function is to play new records early and, if possible, exclusively.

This is a classical case of 'restricted production' (see Chapter 1 and Bourdieu 1993g) in that obscurity helps to build esteem both for record and DJ. It has several implications for the process of dissemination. In the first place the economic cost to a record company of achieving a dance floor hit is low. The disadvantage is that the amount of cultural capital expended in achieving success beyond the club market can be considerable. Quite simply, large-scale sales mean a loss of credibility to both record company and producer. In an important sense, then, successful marketing of dance records means negotiating contradiction (Hesmondhalgh 1998: 241–3). The aura of uniqueness generated by club play has somehow to be transformed into a mass experience. In practice there are several ways this can happen.

The first is a crossover route to the Top Forty. It begins when dance floor acclaim generates sales among cognoscenti as well as airplay on specialist and pirate radio stations. In some genres, notably house, record companies may then be able to use this subcultural recognition as a basis for promoting the record to national daytime radio and national distributors. In effect the club audience acts as a test market for national gatekeepers who adopt those records which have already demonstrated sales potential. Finally, if it reaches this stage, the record has a chance of crossing over into the Top Forty.

As David Hesmondhalgh (1998) has pointed out another, increasingly important, destination for dance music tracks is the CD compilation. Tunes which do well in clubs, or are recognized by record companies as likely to maintain their aesthetic value over a year or so, are reissued on CD. There are several types. Mix CDs, produced by well known DJs, simulate the club experience with continuous play and 'cross-fading' between tracks. They have become increasingly important over the last few years as DJs seek to realize additional value from their reputations.[19] Then there are label compilations which provide a repertoire showcase for independents (or 'faux-indies'), and an opportunity for them to build brand identity.[20] Some companies specialize in licensing tracks from other small labels for release on albums put together under a new sub-generic badge or concept (Hesmondhalgh 1998: 243). Lastly, compilations released by the majors concentrate on dance singles which have already been Top Twenty hits. These albums can be very successful commercially, selling in excess of 250 000 units (*Music Week* 1996: 18).

The significant thing about Top Forty crossover and CD compilations, it seems to me, is not that these secondary markets represent a 'sell-out' or the victory of commercial interest over subcultural autonomy, but almost the reverse. I say this to stress the extent to which the lucrative secondary markets for dance music depend on the cachet and predicting power of a relatively independent network of dance clubs, a network which is difficult for record companies to control. Will Straw (1990) makes some interesting comments in this connection in a discussion of the disco market in North America during the late 1970s. He points out that record companies found it very difficult to achieve success here for two main reasons.

First, the market was so volatile that immediate feedback of dance floor reaction to a record release was required 'in order that decisions concerning the appropriate levels of investment in its manufacture and promotion might be made' (Straw 1990: 150). Delay in responding to dance floor success might mean a lost opportunity for sales. Equally, building up stocks and investing in promotion before the acquisition of market information could prove to be a waste of resources. Second, and compounding this problem, the fragmented nature of the discotheque network and the turnover of club promoters and DJs meant that standard methods for monitoring channels of dissemination were inadequate. In other words in a situation where accurate market information was most urgently needed at an early stage, it was most difficult to obtain. The record companies responded to this situation by liasing with DJs in order to create 'record pools' which brought DJs together on a local basis so that they could be more efficiently targeted by promotion departments. In return for free promotional records DJs were asked to fill in reaction sheets to show audience (and DJ) response in the discos.

We can see some interesting parallels between the political economy of disco and of contemporary British dance music. The key figure in both cases is the DJ whose power derives from her/his nodal position in the club network, switching new repertoire into the club or keeping it out, and relaying positive or negative feedback to record companies and media. The difference between the two scenes has mainly to do with degree of institutionalization. Where record companies dealt with the short-lived disco phenomenon on an ad hoc basis, the British music industries now have well established arrangements for commercial exploitation of clubs and DJs. I want to look briefly at these now.

As in the case of disco, record companies supply major league DJs on the circuit with records free of charge. But instead of the record pool – halfway between a DJ co-op and record company agency – 'club pluggers' are hired to persuade DJs to play records. Club promotion has become a critical function for record companies, and a small specialist industry has grown up to cater for it (*Music Week: Promotional Feature* 1999). On the monitoring side British DJs, like their disco counterparts twenty-five years earlier, compile reaction sheets and playlists as a *quid quo pro* in return for the 'free' promotional repertoire they receive. Despite its unreliability (DJs tend to mollify their suppliers by giving an artificially positive reaction) this market information is extremely valuable and much sought after. The specialist dance music magazines like *DJ*, *Muzik* and *Mixmag* also publish DJ playlists. They have more of a subcultural agenda with an emphasis on cutting-edge taste. The key issue, though, is not accuracy so much as 'truth effect': in an important sense it is the DJ's role as knowledge producer which gives her/him so much power.

If record promotion and the eliciting of feedback from clubs have become institutionalized, so too has the distribution of records. The important development here has been the growth of a network of specialist record shops all over the country. These tend to stock titles from across the range of dance music styles so enabling extremely fast feedback from dance floor to record shop. Responsiveness to demand generated in clubs has been further boosted in recent years by independent distributors. They use vans to supply the specialist retailers at short notice (Hesmondhalgh 1996b: 165). The sales teams from these companies have a detailed knowledge not only of genre markets but also of regional variations. This small-scale and decentralized distribution system then provides a lead for the multiple retailers which tend to stock those dance music titles already selling well in the specialist shops (*Music Week: Distribution Xtra* 1997: 14–15).

The most recent step in the institutionalization of dance music has been the arrival of specialist radio: first former pirate stations like Kiss FM and then, since 1996, a considerable expansion of dance programming on BBC Radio 1. Major club DJs like Pete Tong, Danny Rampling and Judge Jules now have their own national shows. Interestingly, though, there is no sign that radio broadcasting will supplant the role of the clubs in presenting new repertoire as happened with disco (Straw 1990: 156–7). Instead dance radio is presenting itself as an adjunct – a means of reminding dancers of the last night out, or preparing for the next one.

We saw how the development of secondary markets in crossover and CD compilation, paradoxically, reaffirmed the primacy of the club. In the same way the growth of institutional arrangements for disseminating dance music argues for the autonomy of club networks rather than their incorporation. The key point is that the specialist sector of pluggers, distributors, retailers and radio stations acts as a 'transmission belt' between the mainstream industry and an intractable subculture. In effect the club network is kept at a remove. Two main factors account for this. The first is the sheer turnover in repertoire generated by the voracious appetite of dancers for new beats. As we saw in Chapter 1 large corporations have difficulty in coping with volatile markets (Peterson and Berger 1990/1975). They need intermediaries who can respond quickly to change. The second is the resistance of the dance club to conventional audience-building techniques. Club networks are hermetic, their avowedly subcultural character tends to make them resistant to the fraternal mode of address developed by the music industries in order to appeal to rock audiences.

I suggested earlier that dance music networks constitute an *alternative*. But as we have just seen in terms of economic organization, such a status is not actively chosen so much as granted by default. To put it another way, dance music networks are structurally, rather than ideologically, alternative to the mainstream music industries. For David Hesmondhalgh the lack of an alternative politics of production in dance music is a serious one. He points out that 'dance music has failed to produce an intellectual culture capable of a critical analysis of its position within industrial systems of commodified culture' (1996b: 150). Moreover, on a practical level dance music activists have not developed a counter-economy in the manner of the post-punk independent record companies with their profit-sharing schemes and equitable contracts. His conclusion is that whatever the radical thrust of dance might be in other respects, 'all of these innovations need to be set against the limited impact of dance music on the organization of musical creativity' (Hesmondhalgh 1998: 249).

Hesmondhalgh is surely right to emphasize the shortage of political economic analysis within dance culture and the lack of principled *animateurs* like Rough Trades' Geoff Travis. However given historical developments in society and economy since the early 1980s the depoliticization of alternative music cultures is perhaps unsurprising. Not only has the rhetoric of the market become hegemonic, but Thatcherite policies of 'rolling back the state' have enabled a thorough penetration of market relations into everyday life. Significantly, acid house emerged in Britain precisely at the moment when these major ideological and political shifts were being accomplished. For Mathew Collin this goes a long way towards explaining the character of the dance music scene. As he puts it:

> Ecstasy culture ran with the blue print [of Thatcherite Conservatism] but inverted the morality, firing a vibrant black economy not only in illegal drugs but cash-in-hand deals for all manner of ancillary services, from DJ careers to home-produced records.
>
> (1997: 7)

Collin's qualification – 'inverted the morality' – is important I think. For, quite emphatically, the dance music scene has not adopted Thatcherite values. Instead, the networking arrangements I have been describing represent a softening of market relations. Of course the profit motive drives the new cultural entrepreneurs, but the crucial point is that they operate in a domain where there is, at one and the same time, a multiplication of lateral transactions and an emphasis on trust and goodwill across networks. What we have, in effect, is regulation by subcultural 'vibe'. I am not suggesting that this is an advance over the critical approach to the music industry found in some of the post-punk independent record companies (Hesmondhalgh 1999). However, combined with the structural factors I have been describing it has produced a historical shift in the politics of musical production which needs to be assessed carefully. I will attempt this in the last section of the chapter.

Record companies, producers and the politics of production

In 1998, 61 per cent of all singles titles released in Britain belonged to the broad category of dance (Jones 1999). Significantly, though, dance music accounted for only 22.2 per cent of singles sold (Scaping and Green 1999). A similar pattern can be traced since the turn of the decade (Scaping and Green 1998). In no other genre is there such a disparity between relatively large repertoire and relatively low total output. Figures are not available to show dispersion of sales across this repertoire range. However it seems that there is a comparatively even spread. Evidence for this comes mainly from the specialist charts which show a fast turnover of records (including the biggest dance floor hits). Such a pattern stands in marked contrast to the standard cultural industries model, strongly evident in the era of the rock mainstream, where a few massive successes are counter-balanced by the failure of most titles (Frith 1983: 102, Miege 1989). I have already mentioned some of the factors which help to produce this situation, such as dance floor demand for high innovation and the prevailing anti-author/ anti-star aesthetic. We should also add supply side push in the form of low-cost access to the means of production which enables many music makers to enter the labour market (see Chapter 3).

Potentially at least, the large number of releases in dance music and relatively even dispersion of sales across this repertoire mitigate in favour of a democratic culture of production. More labels take on more artists than in the case of rock and more artist-producers have a chance of gaining some reward from their work. In addition the low (and probably declining) mean sales for dance music records tend to deter major record companies from getting directly involved (Solomons 1996).

In fact there is a range of dance labels in Britain from true independents, through joint ventures to the specialist divisions of major record companies – Sony's Deconstruction label for instance. It seems that a trend towards greater integration in the early 1990s, with majors buying into smaller companies, obtaining overseas licenses for their repertoire and undertaking distribution, may now be going into reverse. Some joint ventures have collapsed and several former independents have relaunched in the last few years (*Music Week: Business Affairs* 1998). The closure of Polydor's dance imprint Hi Life in December 1997 was perhaps the most dramatic confirmation of the trend (*Music Week: RM* 1997). These developments reinforce my argument about the structural autonomy of dance music networks. As much as they would like to, major companies find it difficult to directly control the key label functions of recruiting talent and commissioning music.[21]

In the first part of the chapter I argued that the radius of creativity has changed for music makers in the dance music scene. Aesthetic agency now manifests itself in and through the relatively anonymous process of intensification across the genre. Now, to close the chapter, I want to come back to the question of creativity, but this time discuss it in relation to the institutions of dance music, especially record companies. The questions are, where do music makers fit into the network and what are their relations with the labels which control their output? Indeed, *are* networks alternative from the point of view of production, and if so then how might this be manifested? In order to address these questions I want to examine the experience of Midlands drum and bass producers, the Guardians of Dalliance, as recounted in interview (1998). The two Guardians make an interesting case study because they are relatively long-term professional music makers who have been through the whole rave scene from the earliest days.

The Guardians of Dalliance are Mike and James, both 31. They got together in 1996. Mike was brought up in Sheffield. His only formal music education consisted of six piano lessons when he was on a Youth Training Scheme in the mid-1980s. When he was 16 he had a Commodore 64 computer and began making music on that; 'a Vangelisy type of style' as he puts it. In 1986–87 he was drummer in a rock band doing covers like 'Radar love' by Golden Earring. By the end of the 1980s Mike had moved to Derby and was working as an engineer in a local studio, Square Dance. During this time he visited the Hacienda club in Manchester. A number of people from the new Manchester dance scene recorded at the studio including DJs Mike Pickering and Graeme Park. Mike first met James when the latter recorded with him in Derby. After moving to Coventry and setting up a little studio in 1994 he met James again, by happy accident. Their collaboration started at this point.

James played the recorder when he was a child, but then got into music at school 'banging on saucepans' and 'twiddling on school keyboards'.

He made music with a friend who was a skilled pianist. In the early 1980s he listened to electro pop and particularly Depeche Mode who were a big influence on him. As 'a mod' he also liked northern soul although he was too young to have gone to any of the allnighters. Later he started a pop band called Clone after getting a loan for a keyboard from his father. In 1988 he got into the acid house scene by going to the Manchester club, Konspiracy. From 1988 to 1995 James played all over the country in live rave bands; first Hard Move and then Essence of Aura.

James is more outgoing than Mike, and has continued to be involved in the club scene: from rave and techno through to drum'n'bass. He listens out for trends, and 'watches what people react to' in the clubs. Both James and Mike look at reaction sheets from DJs and other industry sources (although these are supposed to be for the eyes of record company personnel only). Mike talks about the need to make singles with a club orientation, with heavier beats and clearly inside the 'intelligent' drum'n'bass subgenre they work in. On album tracks, or on the third track of a three track single, they can stretch out and do their own thing more.

Mike says, 'all DJs want a little niche in the market'. He clearly resents this and offers an example of the way DJs exert unreasonable influence on the scene. Recently drum and bass DJ Fabio has proposed a new subgenre called 'liquid funk'. Mike and James see this as an annoying distraction, and potentially a threat to the work they are doing. James also blames 'sloppy journalists' who are always 'making their own assumptions over things'. They express a certain amount of anxiety about the scene being steered by other actors. In the case of 'liquid funk' the new generic label might leave them sidelined.

They make a point about having to work in advance – a single is likely to be released for club play six months after a tune is completed, perhaps becoming a hit nine months or a year down the line. The tune might then be compiled on a CD two years later. This future orientation is seen as being a burden, as well as a challenge. One of 'the downs of being a producer' is that 'you never get any instant reaction', James says. Instead there is constant waiting for DJ feedback and reaction sheets. They both contrast this with live work (public appearances or PAs) where there is an 'adrenalin rush' and instant response. James has clearly enjoyed his earlier live performance – he talked enthusiastically about being surrounded by a raving crowd on stage.

They have a good relationship with their record company, Moving Shadow, which they describe as a legitimate record company and well respected in the music business and media. It took them a year to get a deal. James contrasts the reputability and professionalism of Moving Shadow (MD Rob Playford) with Creative Source, on which label he has released material under the name Carlito. This is run by 'The Queen of the Scene', an arrogant, exploitative and unreasonable boss.

Moving Shadow's reputation, James thinks, partly explains why the record company has been successful in getting licensing deals for synchronization of its producers' tracks on advertisements and television programmes. A Guardians' tune was played on BBC *Science Week*; another was heard on prime time soap, *EastEnders*: Bianca listened to it as she walked down the street. Clearly media use of drum'n'bass is increasing, and James and Mike see this as an important avenue too. Significantly, the Guardians have produced the soundtrack for a play, currently running in Birmingham (spring 1999).

They also made a soundtrack for a film called *Two Bad Mice*. Originally Bjork and Goldie were involved too, but then dropped out. The film seems to have been unsuccessful: 'art house – shit house,' as Mike puts it. Still, they would like more film work. For James, in particular, it is important to vindicate what they do as professional artists, and not as crude, 'second rate producers'. He credits Goldie with the distinction of making drum 'n' bass a respected style, and a usable sound in the sophisticated synchronization market.

The Guardians don't have a manager. Initially, when they signed to Moving Shadow they used a Musicians Union solicitor. The contract is for an exclusive ten-year deal with the company. They get regular accounts showing their earnings. James' wife does his books, which then go to an accountant. Mike keeps his accounts on his home PC. James thinks there's a 'need to get more business minded'. Certainly if they become more successful both think they will have to get a manager. But what comes across strongly right now is how much they trust Moving Shadow and the personnel they deal with.

As for the working relationship between Mike and James it seems to be excellent. If James talked more he still deferred to Mike on several questions. Although I did not probe too deeply into their working methods it is clear that there is a kind of intuitive cooperation between them, built up over the last four years. The partnership is based on a combination of 'my club experience and Mike's engineering experience,' says James.

It strikes me that there are two, dichotomous ways of reading what the Guardians of Dalliance have to say about making a living in the drum and bass scene. The first is pessimistic, the second more optimistic. Although I come down on the side of the second interpretation it still seems wise to keep the first in mind.

READING ONE

James and Mike are stuck in a digital sweatshop. On a constant night shift (they work 8pm to 4am, five nights a week), they knock out tunes with very little financial reward for all the hours they put in. Having raised the money themselves for their own studio set-up, the record company, Moving Shadow, takes the lion's share of income earned from their output. This comes in the shape of both record sales and revenue from synchronization and public performance of Guardians' music. What we have here is a classical strategy of accumulation, known in other sectors as the outwork system. Production takes place in the workers' premises at the workers' expense. Inured in the studio and isolated from co-workers, they are paid by piece and have to absorb fixed costs together with all the risks of an uncertain market. From this perspective the ideology of partnership and mutuality between label and producer is just that, an ideology which keeps these ragged-trousered ravers with their noses to the computer screen.

READING TWO

The Guardians are creative agents with a large degree of autonomy over what they do. Unlike rock bands which have to put together an expensive and complex package of live act, demo tapes and publicity just to enter the market, James and Mike can operate cheaply and efficiently from their own studio. Advances on royalties from their record company have enabled them to continuously update their equipment. If most of the time they work on their own they know, and have a strong comradeship with, other artists on the Moving Shadow label. Moreover, they are involved with a larger drum and bass club network which spreads out across the country, and now internationally too.

Relations with their record company are cordial and based on trust tempered by realism: they recognize that not all labels behave with the professionalism of Moving Shadow. They are able, in practice, to breach exclusivity clauses in recording contracts and produce for more than one label. This suggests there is some understanding by label bosses of the exigencies of the labour market and the need for producers to maximize their ouput by recording under different *noms de disque*.

Interestingly, it is not record companies so much as gatekeepers, in the form of DJs and journalists, whom the Guardians see as the major obstacle to creative autonomy and economic self-sufficiency. Whereas many producers on the dance music scene are also DJs, James and Mike's back-grounds in live performance and engineering respectively have not equipped them to take a direct role in dissemination. The contrast here is with someone like Moving Shadow boss, Rob Playford, who is an all-round entrepreneur, producer and DJ. Playford's career has been built partly on his musical skills. He produced classical early hardcore tunes as well as working with Goldie on the groundbreaking 'Timeless'. But it has also flourished because as a DJ he has a good grasp of the drum and bass networks in which he operates.

It appears that the Guardians recognize their vulnerability in this respect. Ironically, perhaps, they see the way forward as being to tap into other networks beyond dance music, and particularly the world of media sound-tracks and synchronization. If they can become successful here their long-term future as a production partnership will be assured, above, as it were, the cut and thrust of the drum and bass scene.

Conclusion – creating in small amounts

I want to use the conclusion to this chapter as a way of closing the book. This seems an appropriate way of ending because issues raised by contemporary dance music are important for the whole study. You will remember the chapter began with a series of questions: how different was UK dance music from earlier musical styles and subcultures and, if there was a difference, what might it mean for production practices and the creative agency of music makers? I think some answers to these questions can be provided now. Overall, there *have* been significant shifts, both in the nature of the music and in the way it is made.

One of the most important is a new aesthetic regime of hyper-innovation. Here the transformation of musical code and fabric takes place at such a high rate as to challenge the model of social authorship which I proposed in Chapter 2. I stressed then that the radius of creativity depends on a certain degree of stability. There need to be coherent strands of musical possibility in the field of works. Or to put it another way, there must be recognizable traditions which the social author can work with.

But the kind of hyper-innovation we encounter in dance music is associated with a much larger and more volatile field than in previous forms of pop. The genre pool which supplies possible voices is extremely broad, taking in dance styles from America, Britain and the Caribbean since the mid-1960s. Rock, easy listening and different kinds of 'world music' may also provide source material. This breadth of reference is matched by a new volatility as possibilities emerge in an unpredictable way from the intensification of micro-musical aesthetic zones deep within a particular style. We might say, then, that through extension in range *and* depth the musical field has been destabilized. Accompanying these changes has been a shift in emphasis in creative practice. One aspect of this is abduction: producers apply a mixture of intuition and reasoning to recode the materials which they recover from the field. Another development has been the increasing use of the 'participatory discrepancy' (Keil 1994c) as a means of disrupting the blissful immediacy of dance. It can be deployed 'live' by DJs as well as producers. Discrepant tropes invite the entire body to take on a cognitive function; as Kodwo Eshun (1998a) puts it, arms and feet 'think' in dance. Significantly, the discrepant trope is a small device – it depends on careful control of limited variables.

It seems, then, that producers and DJs are creating in smaller amounts than before. The limited radius of creativity which we examined in

Chapter 2 has in the case of dance music been constricted even more tightly. In dance music no individual artist or band makes aesthetic breakthroughs on the model of jazz or rock authorship in the heroic period of these styles (1940s and 50s, 1960s and 70s respectively). Instead many music makers contribute incrementally to a continuous flow of innovation across a given genre. Sometimes this leads to fission with new sub-genes splitting away from existing styles, or fusion, in other words the emergence of hybrid forms like drum and bass. But in all cases what is at stake is a much flatter distribution of innovation among a relatively large number of producers and DJs.

This democratic tendency in production and performance is driven by greatly increased feedback between music makers and audience. The key factor here is a new kind of sociality for which the model is the network. In the club dancers have a 'flat' 360° disposition rather then being oriented towards a stage. They dance for each other in connected clusters, while the DJ operates as network facilitator. S/he provides the optimum conditions for interaction and the mutual pursuit of dance-bliss. The DJ is also a relay in a larger, economic network of dissemination to clubs and between clubs. S/he has a nodal function, switching flows of music and information in and out of clubs, and between actors in the system.

From the perspective of the labour process dance music differs from earlier styles, especially rock, in that DJs 'finish' dance music by inserting records into a continuous mix in the club. This practice reintroduces a division of labour in popular music-making and leaves producers dependent on DJs as performers of their music. ('Live' performance by producers in concert or personal club appearance is exceptional.) These changes in the labour process limit the role of the producer further, and reduce the potential for the ascription of *auteur* status to either role.

The key issue, though, and one which I raised in the introduction to this book, bears on the extent to which these shifts mark a break with past practices in pop. It seems to me that the new forms of production and dissemination in dance music actually represent an *extension of social authorship* rather than a substantially new form of music-making. It is possible that the immediacy of dance music culture which has been noted by several commentators (Melechi 1993, Gilbert 1997, Reynolds 1997 and 1998) may throw us off the scent here. Certainly, we can identify an inward-looking pursuit of pleasure, an aesthetics of the body and an emphasis on the here and now. But there is a danger of over-estimating the significance of rhetoric within the dance music scene which emphasizes a rapturous break with the past and the inauguration of a new age.

For in an important sense contemporary electronic dance music marks a return to forms of society and pleasure-taking from an age before rock. The swing bands were dance bands, they provided beats for crowds on the dance floor. And, as we saw in Chapter 1, swing was organised in a relatively flat structure with bands being 'plugged into' a number of different outlets – the dance hall, radio, films, records. More generally, in the pre-rock era popular music was produced as a form of entertainment (Frith 1983). True, musicians sometimes aspired to be artists, that is to make music which was not oriented towards the audience but rather took the form of self-expression (Becker 1952). Yet it seems that for the most part popular musicians made music in good faith in order to please their listeners and themselves. Music-making was, then, a trade.

The major shift came with rock and its cult of authorship. Now creativity was conceived as something much more grandiose. Furthermore, the musician took on a representative function. He (I use the gendered form intentionally) sang *for* a better world on behalf of a community of youth. As I have suggested the rock mode did contribute to institutional autonomy in the music industries by endorsing the idea that musicians should be independent creators as well as performers. However this by no means redeems the popular music *auteur* in my view. For, far from being exemplary, rock authorship has constituted a fetish. In other words creativity has been falsely venerated as something extraordinary. The fact that the music industry was able to graft long-term stardom on to the institution of the rock *auteur* also limited innovation and produced an elite echelon of stars remote from the very proto-markets which rock had spawned.

Dance music has excised stardom and, to a great extent, the authorship cult. The new scene *does* have something in common with certain forms of rock, and that is an experimental aesthetic, a notion of music-making as avant-garde practice. But dance producers and DJs are also, even in the most esoteric genres at the fringes of the culture, makers of beats which must literally move people on the dance floor. The need and desire to please crowds thus connects dance musicians to their counterparts in earlier periods. Of course this imperative did not die out with rock. It is just that a whole extra-musical ideology (an excluding ideology as it turned out) was planted on top of musician practice.

In dance music that ideology has been swept away. In an important sense the social aspect of authorship, which always underpinned the creative practice of music makers, is now extended to take on a more inclusive and democratic form. For the 'inward' aesthetic of dance bliss has as its corollary a practical ethics of self-management and participation, realized in the new networks linking music makers, audiences, clubs and technologies across genres and national boundaries. If there are grounds for optimism about popular music as a form of social action (always potentially redeemable as *political* action) it is here that we should listen and look.

Endnotes

Introduction

1 For an analysis of musicians' magazines see Théberge (1997: 93–130), for discussion of the British music press see Toynbee (1993), and on the musician 'bio-pic' see Romney and Wootton (1995).
2 In the interest of variety and euphony 'pop' is used interchangeably with 'popular music' in what follows. As a result the term pop should be taken to include, among other genres, jazz and rock.
3 The other side of the coin of utopianism is a tradition of social critique in the form of songs such as 'Buddy Can You Spare a Dime', 'War in a Babylon', 'Masters of War'. These hold out the promise of a better life too, but only after the inequity of the present social order has been overcome.
4 I sketch out a critique of capitalism, after Marx, at the beginning of Chapter 1.
5 Classical musics with a similar composition and performance system, and social function exist in other societies as well as in the West – in India, Indonesia and China for example.
6 In fact British involvement in global pop only begins in the mid-1960s with the Beatles and the 'British invasion' of America.

1   Market: the selling of soul(s)

1 The quotation is Bowie's own translation from the essay 'Über das gegenwärtige Verhältnis von Philosophie und Musick' by Adorno.
2 See in particular Chapters 2 and 5.
3 In fact Adorno offers an alternative explanation for standardization which has nothing to with commodity form. This is a historical argument concerning the political economy of the music industry. Although production is still organized on craft lines at mid-century – there is no substantial division of labour – the advent of monopoly conditions has 'frozen' standards originally developed under competition (Adorno 1990: 306). Production techniques – the making of the hit song – now exemplify a new and distinctive phase in capitalist economic organization characterized by increasing concentration of ownership.
4 This approach was derived from organization theory, see Karpic (1978) for an overview of the field.
5 The concentration ratio is expressed in terms of the proportion of market share held by a given number of the largest firms. It is a measure of oligopoly.

6 Peterson and Berger also refer to lyrical content as a way of assessing degree of homogeneity (1972 and 1990/1975: 145). In my view this is an enormously contentious and complex issue and I do not have time to deal with it properly here. Suffice to say that analysis which presumes to identify invariant genres – the romantic love song for example – through content analysis of lyrics is unlikely to catch the extraordinary connotative complexity of even the most hackneyed lyrics in the voice of the singer.

7 It is clear from Cohn's account that he adores precisely what Adorno despised in pop – its 'fetish character' and the idealization of music as commodity.

8 Actually there are intense debates about the nature of economic causality within the current Marxist tradition. See for example Rigby (1987) and Clarke (1991).

9 The change to the adjectival form of 'culture' and the pluralization of 'industry' as signalled by Garnham (1990b) help to mark the break with Adorno and Horkheimer's (1979) 'culture industry'.

10 We can note a strong convergence with the production of culture approach here. The argument about use values in critical political economy could easily incorporate terms like 'turbulence' and 'innovation'. More points of agreement between the two approaches will become apparent as we continue.

11 For example, record companies have become worried recently about the MP3 digital compression format which has enabled fans and musicians to upload music files on the Internet. This technology enables direct dissemination, at very low cost and on a global basis, from producer to listener – even from the same hard drive on which a piece has been 'mastered'.

12 For an extremely interesting, but highly pessimistic, analysis from just this perspective see Colin Sparks's (1994) account of the independent production sector which has emerged in British television since 1980. Sparks documents the way in which a number of small companies now compete in a cut-throat market for commissions from Channel 4, BBC and ITV, often at prices below any margin of viability. He suggests these companies 'are the industrial equivalent of small peasants who work themselves and their families to death' when the rational step would be 'to sell up to a large capitalist farmer and move to the city to find paid work' (1994: 151).

13 In 1921 the sale of records broke the 100 million barrier for the first time and then hovered around this figure for the rest of the decade (Gelatt 1977, Sanjek 1988).

14 A&R stands for artists and repertoire. In a record company A&R personnel are responsible for a) recruiting musician–artists, b) supervising the development of their public image, c) coordinating record-making with record producers and artists (see Stratton 1982, Negus 1992).

15 Some forms of writing and journalism are also undertaken in a sphere outside the ambit of publishing institutions. However there is no equivalent for writers of the extensive small-scale or local proto-markets which characterize popular music.

16 Sarah Thornton, for example, argues that a Bourdieuian perspective on the use of popular music as a strategy of distinction should supersede naive culturalist approaches (Thornton 1995). My response would be that *both* strategies of distinction *and* a utopian desire for community may be at stake in any given music scene, or even in any given subject within that scene. Social subjects are rarely so rigorously reflexive as to eliminate incoherence in their own thinking.

2 Making up and showing off: what musicians do

1 I would place both self-consciously liberationist music like punk or counter-cultural rock (see Waksman 1998 for an excellent analysis of the MC5 and collectivism), and easy listening or 'exotic' jazz (for a discussion of Les Baxter and the later Duke Ellington in this connection see Toop 1995: 161–8), not to mention contemporary dance music (see Chapter 5) in the category of 'utopian communal music'. I mean by this, music intended by its makers to unite listeners in common rapture.

   Evidence of less intense, more quotodien communality in the making of pop is so abundant that it would seem arbitrary to select particular sources. However for ethnographic work which brings out this theme see Bennett (1980), Finnegan (1989), Cohen (1991).

2 I develop these ideas about music's relation to social formations in Chapter 4.

3 The division between objective and subjective domains in Bourdieu's usage is not straightforward. Both field and habitus are objective in the sense that they are socially produced. To put it another way, social structure consists in these two elements. However habitus generates subjectivity, a practical sense of being in the world, under the rules of the various fields the agent enters.

4 For a discussion of the conventionality of an apparently unconventional style – 'free music' – see Chapter 4.

5 There are a few exceptions to this. Humming and whistling are examples of the non-specialist production of music done outside the normal musical 'frame'. Occasionally they are incorporated into formal musical texts in a similar way to the incorporation of speech genres in the novel. For an unusual and extremely effective example of the citation of whistling hear Dr John's version of 'Big Chief' from the album *Gumbo* (1972).

6 Leonard Bernstein (discussed by Chanan 1994: 83) makes a related point. Whereas ordinary language is punctuated, music tends towards flow. For example, a cadenza may provide an introduction to the next section even as it completes the previous one. In linguistic terms it could be said that in music there are no clearly defined subordinate clauses, only a sequence of overlapping relative ones.

7 It is worth, rather quickly, responding to the attack made by Roland Barthes on the use of the adjective in musical criticism (1976c: 179–81). His objection seems to be that the adjective is facile and serves, in a reactionary fashion, to protect critic and reader from the irruption of *jouissance*, that radical sense of loss so highly valued by Barthes. The alternative to epithetic criticism which he proposes is a refocusing of attention on the 'grain of the voice'. My own feeling is that if grain is an interesting and significant aspect of voice, it no more repels adjectives than any other aspect. Indeed, the only way it might do so is through its acquiring a mystical ineffability, something which Barthes says he wants to avoid (180).

8 Frequently music makers re-voice old materials by *using* their nostalgic connotations. A gap is opened up between nostalgic site and contemporary voicing. This can be satirical and critical in its effects, but equally it may evoke empathy towards a past musical moment.

9 For analyses of African-American popular music which also take a dialogical approach, but via Henry Louis Gates (1988) and his notion of 'Signifying', see Monson (1994) and Brackett (1995).

10 Phillip Tagg (1999/1994) names this function of music imitating non-musical sound events the 'sonic anaphone'.

11 See Chapter 3 for a discussion of musicians, technology and acoustic space.

12 For a contrary argument about 'free' music see John Corbett (1994b). He says that players like drummer Milford Graves or alto saxophonist Evan Parker should be heard as an 'assemblage' producing 'the effect of multiple voices' (84). Such musicians burst open the traditional univocal function of the jazz instrumentalist through their use of polymetric and polyphonic techniques. I think Corbett's notion of voice is some way from the one I delineate though. Certainly free players can use a wide variety of techniques, but they are explicitly hostile to idiom, and therefore in our terms to socially locatable voices. What's more the free aesthetic is often *avowedly* univocal; either it has a spiritual dimension (Such 1993), or it is strongly expressionist (Bailey 1992). Finally (perhaps this point should have come first) I cannot hear the multivocality of the musicians treated by Corbett. For more on the conventionality of 'free' music see Chapter 4.

13 Although these were innovations in mid-century jazz other musicians were doing similar things at the same time. Thelonius Monk also dispensed with scores in recording and rehearsal, humming his compositions to collaborators, while Teo Macero, Miles Davis's producer, made extensive use of tape editing.

14 As we will see shortly, this separation has been much sharper in times past.

15 The exception to this is the *song-idea* which has tended to last (beside or even beyond the recording). The resilience of the song in the age of mediated music probably has to do with its currency in oral traditions. In an important sense performance as *mediated* process represents a logical development of an earlier mode of performance as *oral* process. In other words the folk song is already well adapted for mass communication and mechanical reproduction. One other reason for the continuation of the song-idea is the persistence of archaic copyright laws which enshrine the principle of the composed work, even when the melody and lyrics, which are subject to copyright laws, have been written down *after* recording.

16 I write here from experience (see Introduction). My abiding memory of performance, both at gigs and recording sessions, is one of fear. This was partly a matter of anxiety about competence – was the song I was writing good enough, would I hit the right notes, get the phrasing together? I was right to be frightened about these matters because sometimes I did not achieve a competent performance. However inside these fears, on reflection, I often felt a sense of terror before the *banality* of performance. The expressive intensity which I aspired to seemed to be utterly unrealizable precisely because I was performing, repeating, doing something which if it was to be recognized (having passed the threshold of competence) meant nothing at all. Conversely my most successful and intense performances consisted essentially in bluster and involved my blithely ignoring the impossibility of performance, in other words they were a con-trick perpetrated on the audience *and* on myself.

17 The masculine pronoun is used on purpose here – this is a strongly masculine, even macho, mode.

3 Technology: the instrumental instrument

1 However in Moscow in 1938 Prokofiev's score for the film *Alexander Nevsky* was realized by using three microphones and allocating sections of the orchestra to different studios. According to the composer's own account, he was attempting to emulate the camera angles used by the film's director, Eisenstein (Eisenburg 1987: 94).

2 It needs to be added that the quest for fidelity did not stop at the end of the documentary period. As we will see 'high-fidelity' emerged as a new, hyper-real technical mode in the 1950s and 1960s (Keightley 1996). It persists today: see Note 10 below.

3 See Chapter 4 for further discussion of race music as genre and as market.

4 It seems to me that this has been far and away the most significant impact of phonography in all popular music production cultures, including rock and jazz where records have been subject to a particularly strong process of canonization. The key point is that even where the intention has been to copy a 'classic' recording this most often generates variation, often due to a mismatch in technical resources, instrumentation and so on. In this connection see Moore (1993: 62–4) for a discussion of the translation of American rhythm and blues styles by British beat groups in the 1960s using the 'wrong' instrumental line-up.

A number of writers make the contrary point as well, namely that recording fixes music in a completely realized or finished form (Small 1987b: 396, Chanan 1995: 18), and in this sense represents the antithesis of orality (Middleton 1990: 83). The two observations are eminently compatible. It is because music is printed on record in its phenomenal fullness that processes of copying and variation occur. Musician listeners wanting to adopt a song or an idiom have to work empirically and abductively (see Chapter 5) from the sound of the music rather than, as in the case of art music, from a rational, integrated production code – the score with its basis in 'music theory'. The result is, inevitably, approximation.

5 *Encyclopaedia Britannica* (1946), Chicago: University of Chicago Press, 70–1.

6 Such segregation persists in contemporary electronic dance genres. A popular format in British dance music is the 'club mix' CD produced by and attributed to a particular DJ. This provides a replica of the kind of performance the DJ does 'live' in the club, including long cross-fades and a range of other editing tropes.

7 As we saw in Chapter 1, the other development in the popular music apparatus in the 1950s was Top-Forty-format local radio which played a key role in generating a market for rock'n'roll records.

8 It is likely that rock's appropriation of electric blues in the 1960s included an appreciation of the theatrical and ventriloquial possibilities of the idiom. Amplifiers, guitars and leads provided a new repertoire of props for live performance in which expressive power was combined with sorcery. In the ballroom or concert hall the monstrous sounds seemed utterly incommensurate with the merely human figures on stage.

9 There have been two main exceptions to this. In punk rough, unperfected live performance became an emblem of the style's distinction from conventional rock. In the case of jazz live performance and recording co-exist on an equal footing; recording should in any event do no more than document the 'live' performance of the jazz group in the studio.

10 This account of the reduction of phonographic anxiety, through a process of historical normalization, has a different emphasis from John Corbett's (1994a) psychoanalytic approach to audio-fetishism mentioned earlier in the chapter. For Corbett the obsession with high fidelity is driven by a persisting visual lack which is indeed constitutive of the mode of listening in the phonographic age as whole. (Thanks to Dave Laing for pointing this out.) Actually, one can agree with Corbett on this, while also taking the historical position. The change in the 1950s (an approximate date which varies according to genre and musical culture) was from desire for fidelity to an *actual pro*-phonographic performance, to desire for fidelity to an *ideal* phonographic event. Thus visual lack is not obviated, it is just that the fetish object which stands in for such lack tends to be pure and 'sonically

autonomous' music (Corbett 1994a: 41), rather than sonic evidence of people playing and singing.
11 Though see Goodwin (1992: 91–2) for a cautionary note about the limits of democratization. There is a large range in price and capability between home and professional equipment, while a cadre of professional engineers, producers and programmers still exists in recording studios and pre-production facilities.
12 The possible exceptions to this are the bass players Bootsy Collins and Larry Graham who became band leaders in their own right.
13 As Paul Théberge notes (1997: 224–6) 'naturalness' became an option again during the 1980s as sequencer design began to include the facility to programme humanizing 'feel' back in again.
14 For a discussion of DJ techniques and tropes see Chapter 5.

4 Genre-cultures

1 Hardcore refers to the post-punk genre which took root across America in the mid-1980s. However there is potential for confusion about this because the term has been adopted as a generic signifier elsewhere in popular music recently. In addition to the post-punk rock style referred to here, the phrase was used to signify a branch of rap at the turn of the 1980s, and also a British dance music style popular at the beginning of the 1990s (see next chapter). In each of these guises 'hardcore' has connotations of extremity deriving from its prior reference to the sort of pornography which depicts sexual acts. Extremity or distance from the mainstream establishes these hardcore genres' *cultural* credentials (dissident machismo), but also their *textual* identity. Hardcore is the sound of the search for essence, a zone of intensity understood as the 'core'.
2 Richard Middleton (1986, 1990: 285–91) also discusses repetition, in relation to musical syntax, from a Lacanian–Freudian perspective. He suggests that although repetition can be inflected and combined in a number of ways it represents 'the minimum step into the game of language and culture' (1990: 290). This notion of repetition as a condition of possibility of musical form is broadly similar to Neale's understanding of the function of repetition in genre.
3 In this section the term style will be used rather than genre. I take style to denote a similar concept, in other words a text group. However since most writers talking about groups of text in relation to community use the term style it seems sensible to do the same thing here.
4 I do not mean to suggest that music is a 'universal language' – see Phillip Tagg (1993) for a critique of this notion. Rather what I want to emphasize is the high degree of cross-cultural reusability in music. Of course narrative forms are transposable too. The issue is really the extent of music's mobility.
5 Keith Negus observes that systematic market research is the exception rather than the rule in the record industry. It is sometimes used for repackaging back catalogue, or for relaunching an established artist, but almost never to determine whether a particular new act should be signed (1992: 78–9).
6 This dual use brings potential problems. It means we will need to make it clear explicitly or in context how the term is being used. None the less this seems a price worth paying. After all there are many cases in popular cultural analysis where value-laden and often unstable terms are used. 'Rock', for example, can by no means be assumed to be merely descriptive – it may carry strongly affirming or pejorative connotations. We ought to use it none the less just because of its social currency, and therefore salience as a category. The point, surely, is to remember that all classifying terms are likely to be contested.

7 For an updating of his earlier arguments about the 'rock formation' see Grossberg (1994), while for a perceptive critique of rock/rock and roll discourse, including Grossberg's work, see Laing (1997).

8 David Bowie stands out almost alone as a rock artist interested in working with black forms and black musicians.

9 The epithet northern does not derive from the music's source but rather the site of its reception – the northern cities of England.

10 Black bombers were amphetamine capsules renowned for their strength.

5 Dance music: business as usual or heaven on earth?

1 In fact DJs do tend to acquire cult status. But my point is that this depends on their *utility* – whether they can deliver an intensely pleasurable experience – rather than originality, soul or other authorial attributes.

2 See the British music trade journal *Music Week*. For a sustained argument about dance music's lack of viability see the article by Mark Solomons (1996), 'Dance makes its mark, but can it make money?'.

3 Kodwo Eshun (1998a) argues, convincingly I think, that for the black techno pioneers in Detroit, the middle European group Kraftwerk take on the function that Muddy Waters had for white rock bands in the 1960s: an original source which is at the same time Other.

4 Actually, these musics were quite heterogeneous. Not only did styles become much more complex between the early and late 1980s, but there were strong variations within and between them. For example some, if not all, house incorporated 'soulful' vocals while most techno tracks did not have a singer. The presence of a singer, invariably female, is still a defining factor of much house, and all garage music.

5 To 'drop' here means to play a section of a vinyl record, originally in a live DJ mix, but in this case for real-time transcription on to multitrack tape. This linear editing technique produces a similar result to digital sampling but has a live element, depending on the DJ's dexterity in synchronizing the 'drop' with the desired track position on tape. Notable drops on the Coldcut remix include passages from a song by Yemenite singer Ofra Haza, and some voiceover from a British easy listening album of the early 1960s.

6 Source: (1996) *Mixmag special: the 100 greatest dance singles of all time*: 3.

7 The converse of the 'poor' code is the 'rich' code which consists of complex rules and will therefore retain interest for long periods (Fabbri 1982: 62). It seems Fabbri has in mind western art music as the locus of the rich code. However the problem with the rich/poor distinction is that it fails to deal with the radically different dimensions of coding across the spectrum of musical genres. Chester's (1990) argument about 'intensional' and 'extensional' development in music is precisely that this distinction cannot be reduced to a difference in kind, but is rather one of scale and vector. So, marrying Chester's terminology to a structural approach, one might say that intensional development is micrological depending on the articulation of many small codes, while in the case of extension, codes are fewer but larger – each has a greater generative range across musical parameters. With this in mind I would suggest that it might be more appropriate to talk about 'short' and 'long' codes rather than 'poor' and 'rich' ones.

8 As we will hear shortly the imago is an ideal form and cannot be directly apprehended. In Lacan's terms it is an 'imaginary' form. Lacan discusses the imaginary

in relation to the 'lure' of the painting whereby we look, through the image, into its gaze. We can only look through being looked at, Lacan insists (1979: 107–8). The genre imago I am talking about has a similar reflecting function to it, only we *listen* to it *listening* to us. In general terms, it seems to be a property of desire that it would animate the inanimate.

9 B boys were hip hop followers. Raggamuffin was the name used by people into the post-reggae Jamaican-British style called ragga, popular in the late 1980s and early 1990s. For discussion of uses of the term hardcore see Note 1, Chapter 4.

10 David Lidov (1987) suggests that in classical music polymetre has an affective function. As he puts it, 'subordinated slower beats, hypermetrical accents over predominant fast measures, also index an internal state, a relatively calmer framework in which the faster action is perceived' (82). I think this analysis can be applied to jungle too. It is just that dominant and subordinate beats constantly shift. In effect accentual hierarchy becomes accentual ambivalence. For this writer the effect after listening to jungle is that the rhythmic organization of most classical music seems extraordinarily pedestrian.

See below in the chapter for a parallel argument about rhythmic ambivalence in the basic disco rhythm.

11 As Eco (1976: 131) shows, this term was originally used by C. S. Pierce.

12 Though see Thornton (1995: 26–86) for the early history of dancing to recorded music at record hops and discotheques.

13 Here is an example from late 1992. Praising the 'clearer perspective' of German and Belgian house music producers, journalist Nick Jones writes: 'Not for them our breakbeat fuelled hardcore travesties. The continent is moving to the sound of "pure" techno, forsaking "Mentasm" [a hardcore track by Joey Beltram] noises in favour of more musical climes, beautiful cool house for the 90s' (Jones N. 1992: 40).

14 Although this will not necessarily be accompanied by a theory of why a particular device works like the one I have just provided.

15 This has its origins in early 1970s soul, notably Philadelphia soul. 'The love I lost' by Harold Melvin and the Blue Notes and released on the Philadelphia International label in 1973 is perhaps the *locus classicus* of hi-hat offbeats.

16 One sometimes gets the sense from Castells' case studies that networks are infinitely recessive: networks only connect other networks.

17 There is a further issue here. Sometimes a *more*, rather than less coherent subject, may be required in political struggles. Quite simply, unified subjects engaged in logocentric praxis can be very effective in fighting subordination in some situations.

18 For people who are not familiar with DJ equipment this sentence constitutes a pun: Technics is the brand name of the leading professional record deck, the SL1200.

19 The increasing status of the DJ has been matched by a rise in the entrepreneurial power of the club: 'superclubs' like the Ministry of Sound are now signing exclusive record deals with top DJs for mix CDs (*Music Week: RM* 1996).

20 In 1998 independent drum and bass label, Moving Shadow, issued two mix CDs of label repertoire entitled 98.1 and 98.2 at the rock-bottom price of 99p. These albums are clearly designed as tasters for the artist albums which they showcase. If the low price smacks of the mass market, Moving Shadow's reputation as an underground label probably counter-balances this factor. Certainly both albums have gained wide distribution and sold well.

21 We ought to add another, and increasingly important, function: branding. As David Hesmondhalgh (1998) points out, the label as brand assumes particular significance in dance music because of the prevailing anti-author aesthetic. Producers often change their *noms de disque* or only have one hit. As a result

identification by consumers is displaced from the artist to the label. This sort of identification acquires an extra urgency in a world where new sub-genres are emerging all the time. For example Sheffield's Warp label played a crucial role in the emergence of British hardcore techno. Moving Shadow had a similar part in the arrival of jungle, while during the mid-1990s Mo Wax became virtually synonymous with the sub-genre known as trip-hop. However it would be wrong to see this phenomenon only in terms of branding, that is to say as an attribute of the music's commodity form. Identity and image of dance labels can also be considered as an aspect of a 'signal system' (Williams 1981: 130–7) which enables subcultural recognition and brings together producers under one banner for common aesthetic ends.

Bibliography

Abercrombie, N. and Longhurst, B. (1998) *Audiences: A Sociological Theory of Performance and Imagination*. London: Sage.

Adorno, T. (1945) 'A social critique of radio music', *Kenyon Review*, 7, Spring.

Adorno, T. (1967) 'Perennial fashion – jazz', in *Prisms*. London: Neville Spearman.

Adorno, T. (1973) *Philosophy of Modern Music*. London: Sheed and Ward.

Adorno, T. (1978a) 'On the social situation of music', *Telos*, 35.

Adorno, T. (1978b) *Minima Moralia: Reflections from Damaged Life*. London: Verso.

Adorno, T. (1990) 'On popular music', in Frith, S. and Goodwin, A. (eds) *On Popular Music: Rock, Pop and the Written Word*. London: Routledge.

Adorno, T. (1991a) 'Culture industry reconsidered', in Bernstein, J. (ed.) *The Culture Industry: Selected Essays on Mass Culture*. London: Routledge.

Adorno, T. (1991b) 'The schema of mass culture', in Bernstein, J. (ed.) *The Culture Industry: Selected Essays on Mass Culture*. London: Routledge.

Adorno, T. (1991c) 'On the fetish character in music and the regression of listening', in Bernstein, J. (ed.) *The Culture Industry: Selected Essays on Mass Culture*. London: Routledge.

Adorno, T. and Horkheimer, M. (1979) *Dialectic of Enlightenment*. London: Verso.

Aksoy, A. and Robins, K. (1992) 'Hollywood for the 21st century: global competition for critical mass in image markets', *Cambridge Journal of Economics*, 16.

Altman, R. (1992) 'The material heterogeneity of recorded sound', in Altman, R. (ed.) *Sound Theory, Sound Practice*. New York: Routledge/American Film Institute.

Anderson, B. (1991) *Imagined Communities: Reflections on the Origin and Spread of Nationalism* (2nd edn). London: Verso.

Ang, I. (1991) *Desperately Seeking the Audience*. London: Routledge.

Anthony, W. (1988) *Class of 88: The True Acid House Experience*. London: Virgin Books.

Attali, J. (1985) *Noise: The Political Economy of Music*. Manchester: Manchester University Press.

Auslander, P. (1996) 'Liveness: performance and the anxiety of simulation', in Diamond, E. (ed.) *Performance and Cultural Politics*. London: Routledge.

Auslander, P. (1998) 'Seeing is believing: live performance and the discourse of authenticity in rock culture', *Literature and Psychology: A Journal of Psychoanalytic and Cultural Criticism*, 44/4.

Bahr, H. (1992/1916) 'From *Expressionism*', in Harrison, C. and Wood, P. (eds) *Art in Theory 1900–1990: An Anthology of Changing Ideas*. Oxford: Blackwell.

Bailey, D. (1992) *Improvisation: Its Nature and Practice in Music* (2nd edn). London: British Library, National Sound Archive.

Bakhtin, M. (1981) *The Dialogic Imagination*, Holquist, M. (ed.). Austin: University of Texas Press.

Balio, T. (1976) 'A mature oligopoly: 1930–1948. Structure of the industry', in Balio, T. (ed.) *The American Film Industry*. Madison: University of Wisconsin Press.

Barnes, K. (1990) 'Top 40 radio: a fragment of the imagination', in Frith, S. (ed.) *Facing the Music: Essays on Pop, Rock and Culture*. London: Mandarin.

Barr, T. (1996) 'Concrete jungle', in Kempster, C. (ed.) *History of House*. London: Sanctuary.

Barthes, R. (1976a) 'The death of the author', in *Image/Music/Text*. London: Fontana. Press.

Barthes, R. (1976b) 'From work to text', in *Image/Music/Text*. London: Fontana Press.

Barthes, R. (1976c) 'The grain of the voice, in *Image/Music/Text*. London: Fontana Press.

Basire, A. (1999) 'Secrets of drum'n'bass', *Melody Maker*, 23 January.

Baudrillard, J. (1988) *Selected Writings*. Cambridge: Polity Press.

Bayton, M. (1997) 'Women and the electric guitar', in Whiteley, S. (ed.) *Sexing the Groove: Popular Music and Gender*. London: Routledge.

Bayton, M. (1998) *Frock Rock: Women Performing Popular Music*. Oxford: Oxford University Press.

BBC (1998) 'All singing, all dancing, all night', Radio 2, 28 October.

BBC (1999) '16: Rhythm is our business', *Jazz Century*, Radio 3, 17 April.

Becker, H. (1952) 'The professional dance band musician and his audience', *American Journal of Sociology*, 57.

Becker, H. (1982) *Art Worlds*. Berkeley: University of California Press.

Bennett, S. (1980) *On Becoming a Rock Musician*. Amherst: University of Massachusets Press.

Bennett, T., Frith, S., Grossberg, L., Shepherd, G. and Turner, G. (eds) (1993) 'Introduction', in *Rock and Popular Music: Politics, Policies, Institutions*. London: Routledge.

Berland, J. (1993) 'Radio space and industrial time: the case of music formats', in Bennett, T., Frith, S., Grossberg, L., Shepherd, G. and Turner, G. (eds) *Rock and Popular Music: Politics, Policies, Institutions*. London: Routledge.

Berry, J., Foose, J. and Jones, T. (1992) *Up From the Cradle of Jazz*. New York: Da Capo.

Bloch, E. (1985) 'Magic rattle, human harp', in *Essays on the Philosophy of Music*. Cambridge: Cambridge University Press.

Bordwell, D., Staiger, J. and Thompson, K. (1985) *The Classical Hollywood Cinema Film Style and Mode of Production to 1960*. New York: Columbia University Press.

Born, G. (1987) 'Modern music culture: on shock, pop and synthesis', *New Formations*, 2.

Born, G. (1993) 'Afterword: music policy, aesthetic and social difference', in Bennett, T., Frith, S., Grossberg, L., Shepherd, J. and Turner, G. (eds) *Rock and Popular Music: Politics, Policies, Institutions*. London: Routledge.

Bourdieu, P. (1984) *Distinction: A Social Critique of the Judgment of Taste*. London: Routledge and Kegan Paul.

Bourdieu, P. (1990) *The Logic of Practice*. Cambridge: Polity Press.

Bourdieu, P. (1991) 'Delegation and political fetishism', in *Language and Symbolic Power*. Cambridge: Polity Press.

Bourdieu, P. (1993a) 'The production of belief: contribution to an economy of symbolic goods', in *The Field of Cultural Production*. Cambridge: Polity Press.

Bourdieu, P. (1993b) 'The market of symbolic goods', in *The Field of Cultural Production*. Cambridge: Polity Press.

Bourdieu, P. (1993c) *The Field of Cultural Production*. Cambridge: Polity Press.

Bourdieu, P. (1993d) 'Some properties of fields', in *Sociology in Question*. London: Sage.

Bourdieu, P. (1993e) 'The linguistic market', in *Sociology in Question*. London: Sage.

Bourdieu, P. (1993f) 'Field of power, literary field and habitus', in *The Field of Cultural Production*. Cambridge: Polity Press.

Bourdieu, P. (1993g) 'The field of cultural production', in *The Field of Cultural Production*. Cambridge: Polity Press.

Bourdieu, P. (1996) *The Rules of Art: Genesis and Structure of the Literary Field*. Cambridge: Polity Press.

Bowie, A. (1990) *Aesthetics and Subjectivity from Kant to Nietzsche*. Manchester: Manchester University Press.

Bowie, M. (1991) *Lacan*. London: Fontana.

Brackett, D. (1995) 'James Brown's "Superbad" and the double-voiced utterance', in *Interpreting Popular Music*. Cambridge: Cambridge University Press.

Bradby, B. (1990) 'Do-talk and don't-talk: the division of the subject in girl-group music', in Frith, S. and Goodwin, A. (eds) *On Record: Rock, Pop and the Written Word*. London: Routledge.

Brecht, B. (1978) *Brecht on Theatre: the Development of an Aesthetic*, Willett, J. (ed. and trans.). London: Methuen.

Brecht, B. (1980) 'Against Georg Lukács', in Adorno, T., Benjamin, W., Bloch, E., Brecht, B. and Lukács, G. *Aesthetics and Politics*. London: Verso.

Burch, N. (1981) 'How we got into pictures', *Afterimage*, 8/9.

Burke, S. (1992) *The Death and Return of the Author: Criticism and Subjectivity in Barthes, Foucault and Derrida*. Edinburgh: Edinburgh University Press.

Burnett, R. (1990) *Concentration and Diversity in the International Phonogram Industry*. Gothenburg: University of Gothenburg.

Burnett, R. (1996) *The Global Jukebox: The International Music Industry*. London: Routledge.

Callon, M. (1997) Keynote speech: 'Actor network theory – the market test', *Actor Network and After Workshop*, Keele University, July, accessed at http://www.comp.lancs.ac.uk/sociology/stscallon1.html, 6 June 1999.

Carr, I., Fairweather, D. and Priestley, B. (1987) *Jazz: The Essential Companion*. London: Paladin.

Cashmore, E. (1997) *The Black Culture Industry*. London: Routledge.

Castells, M. (1994) *The Rise of the Network Society*. Oxford: Blackwell.

Chambers, I. (1985) *Urban Rhythms: Pop Music and Popular Culture*. London: Macmillan.

Chanan, M. (1994) *Musica Practica: the Social Practice of Western Music from Gregorian Chant to Postmodernism*. London: Verso.

Chanan, M. (1995) *Repeated Takes: A Short History of Recording and its Effects on Music*. London: Verso.

Chapple, S. and Garofalo, R. (1977) *Rock'n'Roll is Here to Pay: the History and Politics of the Music Industry*. Chicago: Nelson-Hall.

Chatman, S. (1979) *Story and Discourse: Narrative Structure in Fiction and Film*. Ithaca NY: Cornell University Press.

Chester, A. (1990/1970) 'Second thoughts on a rock aesthetic: The Band', in Frith, S. and Goodwin, A. (eds) *On Record: Rock, Pop and the Written Word*. London: Routledge.

Christianen, M. (1995) 'Cycles in symbol production? A new model to explain concentration, diversity and innovation in the music', *Popular Music*, 14/1.

Christopherson, S. and Storper, M. (1986) 'The city as studio; the world as back lot: the impact of vertical disintegration on the location of the motion picture industry', *Environment and Planning D: Society and Space*, 4.

Clarke, J., Hall, S., Jefferson, T. and Roberts, R. (1976) 'Subcultures, cultures and class', in Hall, S. and Jefferson, T. (eds) *Resistance Through Rituals: Youth Sub-cultures in Post War Britain*. London: Hutchinson.

Clarke, J. (1991) *New Times and Old Enemies: Essays on Cultural Studies and America*. London: HarperCollins.

Clinton, G. (1996) 'Foreword', in Vincent, R. *Funk: The Music, the People, and the Rhythm of the One*. New York: St Martin's Griffin.

Cohen, R. (1986) 'History and genre', *New Literary History*, 17/2.

Cohen, S. (1991) *Rock Culture in Liverpool: Popular Music in the Making*. Oxford: Clarendon Press.

Cohn, N. (1989/1969) 'Awopbopaloobop Alopbamboom', in *Ball the Wall: Nik Cohn in the Age of Rock*. London: Picador.

Collier, J. (1987) *Duke Ellington*. New York: Oxford University Press.

Collier, J. (1989) *Benny Goodman and the Swing Era*. New York: Oxford University Press.

Collin, M. (1997) *Altered State: The Story of Ecstasy Culture and Acid House*. London: Serpent's Tail.

Comber, C., Hargreaves, D. and Colley, A. (1993) 'Girls, boys and technology in music education', *British Journal of Music Education*, 10.

Cook, N. (1990) *Music, Imagination and Culture*. Oxford: Oxford University Press.

Cook, P. (1985) 'Genre', in *The Cinema Book*. London: British Film Institute.

Corbett, J. (1994a) 'Free, single and disengaged: listening pleasure and the popular music object', in *Extended Play: Sounding Off From John Cage to Dr Funkenstein*. Durham NC: Duke University Press.

Corbett (1994b) 'Ex uno plura: Milford Graves, Evan Parker, and the schizoanalysis of musical performance', in *Extended Play: Sounding Off From John Cage to Dr Funkenstein*. Durham NC: Duke University Press.

Corbett (1994c) 'Derek Bailey: free retirement plan', in *Extended Play: Sounding Off From John Cage to Dr Funkenstein*. Durham NC: Duke University Press.

Culshaw, J. (1981) *Putting the Record Straight*. London: Secker and Warburg.

Cunningham, M. (1996) *Good Vibrations: a History of Record Production*. Chessington: Castle Communications.

Currid, B. (1995) '"We Are Family": house music and queer performativity', in Case, S., Brett, P. and Foster, S. (eds) *Cruising the Performative*. Bloomington: Indiana University Press.

Curtis, D. (1995) *Touching from a Distance: Ian Curtis and Joy Division*. London: Faber.

Davis, M. (1980) 'The barren marriage of American labour and the Democratic Party', *New Left Review*, 124.

Davis, S. and Simon, P. (eds) (1983) *Reggae International*. London: Thames and Hudson.

Debord, G. (1994) *The Society of the Spectacle*. New York: Zone Books.

DeCurtis, A. (ed.) (1992) *Present Tense: Rock & Roll and Culture*. Durham NC: Duke University Press.

Derrida. J. (1991) 'Signature, event, context', in Kamuf, P. (ed.) *A Derrida Reader: Between the Blinds*. Hemel Hempstead: Harvester Wheatsheaf.

Deutsch, D. (1992) Liner notes to *Bing Crosby: Sixteen Most Requested Songs*. Columbia Legacy, 472198 2.

DiMaggio, P. (1977) 'Market structure, the creative process and popular culture: towards an organizational reinterpretation of mass-culture theory', *Journal of Popular Culture*, 11.

DiMaggio, P. and Hirsch, P. (1976) 'Production organizations in the arts', in Peterson, R. (ed.) *The Production of Culture*. Beverly Hills: Sage.

Dixon, W. and Snowden, D. (1995) *I am the Blues: the Willie Dixon Story*. London: Quartet Books.

Dorr-Dorynek, D. (1987) 'Mingus', in Cerulli, D., Korall, B. and Nasatir, M. (eds) *The Jazz Word*. New York: Da Capo.

Driggs, F. (1959) 'Kansas City and the Southwest', in Hentoff, N. and McCarthy, A. (eds) *Jazz*. New York: Rinehart.

Dr John with Jack Rummel (1994) *Under a Hoodoo Moon: the Life of Dr John the Night Tripper*. New York: St Martin's Press.

du Gay, P. (1997) 'Organizing identity; making up people at work', in du Gay, P. (ed.) *Production of Culture/Culture of Production*. Milton Keynes: Open University/Sage.

Dyer, R. (1979) *Stars*. London: British Film Institute.

Dyer, R. (1987) *Heavenly Bodies: Film Stars and Society*. London: Macmillan.

Eco, U. (1976) *A Theory of Semiotics*. Bloomington: Indiana University Press.

Eisenburg, E. (1987) *The Recording Angel: Music, Records and Culture from Aristotle to Zappa*. London: Picador.

Eshun, K. (1998a) *More Brilliant than the Sun: Adventures in Sonic Fiction*. London: Quartet.

Eshun, K. (1998b) 'futurrhythmachine', *Crash Media*, 15 May: accessed at http://www.yourserver.co.uk/crashmedia/utn/8.htm, 17 December.

Fabbri, F. (1982) 'A theory of musical genre: two applications', in Horn, D and Tagg, P. (eds) *Popular Music Perspectives*. Göteborg and Exeter.

Faulkner, R. (1971) *Hollywood Studio Musicians: Their Work and Careers in the Recording Industry*. Chicago: Aldine Atherton.

Feuer, J. (1993) *The Hollywood Musical* (2nd edn). London: Macmillan/BFI.

Finnegan, R. (1989) *The Hidden Musicians: Music Making in an English Town*. Cambridge: Cambridge University Press.

Fiske, J. (1989a) *Reading the Popular*. Boston: Unwin Hyman.

Fiske, J. (1989b) *Understanding Popular Culture*. Boston: Unwin Hyman.

Flinn, C. (1992) *Strains of Utopia: Gender, Nostalgia and Hollywood Film Music*. Princeton: Princeton University Press.

Foege, A. (1995) *Confusion is Next: The Sonic Youth Story*. London: Quartet.

Fonorow, W. (1995) 'Participatory alignment and spatial distribution at British indie gigs', paper presented at International Association for the Study of Popular Music conference: Issues of Performance, Glasgow: Strathclyde University, 2 July.

Foster, H. (1985) 'The expressive fallacy', in *Recodings: Art, Spectacle, Cultural Politics*. Port Townsend WA: Bay Press.

Fraser, N. (1992) 'Rethinking the public sphere', in Calhoun, C. (ed.) *Habermas and the Public Sphere*. Boston: MIT Press.

Friedlander, P. (1996) *Rock and Roll: A Social History*. Boulder CO: Westview Press.

Frith, S. (1983) *Sound Effects: Youth, Leisure and the Politics of Rock'n'Roll*. London: Constable.

Frith, S. (1986) 'Art versus technology: the strange case of popular music', *Media, Culture and Society*, 8/3.

Frith, S. (1988a) 'The industrialisation of music', in *Music For Pleasure: Essays in the Sociology of Pop*. Cambridge: Polity Press.

Frith, S. (1988b) 'The real thing – Bruce Springsteen', in *Music For Pleasure: Essays in the Sociology of Pop*. Cambridge: Polity Press.

Frith, S. (1988c) 'Playing with real feeling – jazz and suburbia', in *Music For Pleasure: Essays in the Sociology of Pop*. Cambridge: Polity Press.

Frith, S. (1990) (ed.) *Facing the Music, Essays on Pop, Rock and Culture*. London: Mandarin.

Frith, S. (1996) *Performing Rites: On the Value of Popular Music*. Oxford: Oxford University Press.

Frith, S. and Goodwin, A. (eds) (1990) *On Record: Rock, Pop and the Written Word*. London: Routledge.

Frith, S., Goodwin, A. and Grossberg, L. (eds) (1993) *Sound and Vision: the Music Video Reader*. London: Routledge.

Frith, S. and Horne, H. (1987) *Art into Pop*. London: Methuen.

Furtwängler, W. (1989) Notebooks 1924–1954. London: Quartet.

Gammond, P. (1993) *The Oxford Companion to Popular Music*. Oxford: Oxford University Press.

Garnham, N. (1990a) 'Public policy and the cultural industries', in *Capitalism and Communication: Global Culture and the Economics of Communication*. London: Sage.

Garnham, N. (1990b) 'Contribution to a political economy of mass communication', in *Capitalism and Communication: Global Culture and the Economics of Communication*. London: Sage.

Garnham, N. (1990c) *Capitalism and Communication: Global Culture and the Economics of Communication*. London: Sage.

Garofalo, R. (1993) 'Black popular music: crossing over or going under?' in Bennett, T., Frith, S., Grossberg, L., Shepherd, J. and Turner, G. (eds) *Rock and Popular Music: Politics, Policies, Institutions*. London: Routledge.

Garratt, S. (1998) *Adventures in Wonderland: A Decade of Club Culture*. London: Headline.

Gates, H. (1988) *The Signifying Monkey: A Theory of African-American Literary Criticism*. New York: Oxford University Press.

Gelatt, R. (1977) *The Fabulous Phonograph: 1877–1977* (2nd edn). London: Cassell.

George, N. (1988) *The Death of Rhythm and Blues*. New York: Pantheon.

Gibson, W. (1995/1984) *Neuromancer*. London: Voyager.

Giddens, G. (1985) *Rhythm-a-ning: Jazz Tradition and Innovation in the '80s*. New York: Oxford University Press.

Gilbert, J. (1997) 'Soundtrack to an uncivil socity: rave culture, the Criminal Justice Act and the politics of modernity', *New Formations*, 31.

Gill, C. (1995) *Guitar Legends: the Definitive Guide to the World's Greatest Guitar Players*. London: Studio Editions.

Gill, J. (1995) *Queer Noises: Male and Female Homosexuality in Twentieth Century Music*. London: Cassell.

Gillett, C. (1983/1970) *The Sound of the City: the Rise and Fall of Rock and Roll*. London: Souvenir Press.

Gilroy, P. (1993) *The Black Atlantic: Modernity and Double Consciousness*. London: Verso.

Goehr, L. (1992) *The Imaginary Museum of Musical Works: An Essay in the Philosophy of Music*. Oxford: Clarendon Press.

Goldmann, L. (1977) *Cultural Creation in Modern Society*. Oxford: Blackwell.

Goodwin, A. (1992) 'Rationalisation and democratization in the new technologies of popular music', in Lull, J. (ed.) *Popular Music and Communication*. Newbury Park CA: Sage.

Gordon, D. (1976) 'Why the movies are major', in Balio, T. (ed.) *The American Film Industry*. Madison: University of Wisconsin Press.

Gracyk, T. (1996) *Rhythm and Noise: An Aesthetics of Rock*. London: I.B. Tauris.

Grant, B. (ed.) (1995) *Film Genre Reader II*. Austin: University of Texas Press.

Green, L. (1996) 'Gender, musical meaning, and education', *Philosophy of Music Education Review*, 2/2.

Grossberg, L. (1984) 'Another boring day in paradise: rock'n'roll and the empowerment of everyday life', *Popular Music*, 4.

Grossberg. L. (1991) 'Rock, territorialization and power', *Cultural Studies*, 5/3.

Grossberg, L. (1994) 'Same as it ever was: youth culture and music', in Ross, A. and Rose, T. (eds) *Microphone Fiends: Youth Music and Youth Culture*. New York: Routledge.

Grossberg, L. (1997) 'Re-placing popular culture', in Redhead, S., Wynne, D. and O'Connor, J. (eds) *The Clubcultures Reader*. Oxford: Blackwell.

Guardians of Dalliance (1998) Personal interview, 1 December.

Guralnick, P. (1986) *Sweet Soul Music: Rhythm and Blues and the Southern Dream of Freedom*. New York: Harper and Row.

Hadju, D. (1997) *Lush Life: A Biography of Billy Strayhorn*. London: Granta.

Hall, S. (1991) 'Old and new identities, old and new ethnicities', King, A. (ed.) *Culture, Globalization and the World-System*. London: Macmillan.

Hall, S. (1994/1981) 'Notes on deconstructing "the popular"', in Storey, D. (ed.) *Cultural Theory and Popular Culture: A Reader*. Hemel Hempstead: Harvester Wheatsheaf.

Hall, S. and Jefferson, T. (eds) (1976) *Resistance Through Rituals: Youth Subcultures in Post War Britain*. London: Hutchinson.

Hamm, C. (1979) *Yesterdays: Popular Song in America*. New York: Norton.

Haraway, D. (1991) 'A cyborg manifesto: science, technology, and socialist-feminism in the late twentieth century', in *Simians, Cyborgs and Women: The Reinvention of Nature*. London: Free Association Books.

Harley, R. (1993) 'Beat in the system', in Bennett, T., Frith, S., Grossberg, L., Shepherd, G. and Turner, G. (eds) *Rock and Popular Music: Politics, Policies, Institutions*. London: Routledge.

Harvey, D. (1989) *The Condition of Postmodernity*. Oxford: Blackwell.

Head, S., Sterling, C. and Schofield, L. (1994) *Broadcasting in America: A Survey of Electronic Media* (7th edn). Boston: Houghton Mifflin.

Hebdige, D. (1979) *Subculture: The Meaning of Style*. London: Routledge.

Hebdige, D. (1988a) *Hiding in the Light: On Images and Things*. London: Comedia/Routledge.

Hebdige, D. (1988b) *Cut and Mix: Culture, Identity and Caribbean Music*. London: Comedia/Methuen.

Hennion, A. (1990/1983) 'The production of success: an antimusicology of the pop song', in Frith, S. and Goodwin, A. (eds) *On Record: Rock, Pop and the Written Word*. London: Routledge.

Hesmondhalgh, D. (1996a) 'Flexibility, post-Fordism and the music industries', *Media, Culture and Society*, 18/3.

Hesmondhalgh, D. (1996b) *Independent Record Companies and Democratisation in the Popular Music Industry*, PhD thesis, Goldsmiths College, University of London.

Hesmondhalgh, D. (1998) 'The British dance music industry: a case study of independent cultural production', *British Journal of Sociology*, 49/2.

Hesmondhalgh, D. (1999) 'Indie: the institutional politics and aesthetics of a popular music genre', *Cultural Studies*, 13/1.

Hirsch, P. (1990/1972) 'Processing fads and fashions: an organization-set analysis of the cultural industry systems', in Frith, S. and Goodwin, A. (eds) *On Record: Rock, Pop and the Written Word*. London: Routledge.

Hirschkop, K. (1989) 'The classical and the popular: musical form and social context', in Norris, C. (ed.) *Music and the Politics of Culture*. London: Lawrence and Wishart.

Hobsbawm, E. (1994) *Age of Extremes: The Short Twentieth Century 1914–1991*. London: Michael Joseph.

Hollows, J. and Milestone, K. (1998) 'Welcome to Dreamsville: A History and Geography of Northern Soul', in Leyshon, A., Matless, D. and Revill, G. (eds) *The Place of Music*. New York: The Guildford Press.

hooks, b. (1993) 'Postmodern blackness', in Williams, P. and Chrisman, L. (eds) *Colonial Discourse and Post-Colonial Theory: A Reader*. Hemel Hempstead: Harvester Wheatsheaf.

Horn, D. (1991) 'Review – *The Imperfect Art: Reflections on Jazz and Modern Culture*, by Ted Gioia', *Popular Music*, 10/1.

Horn, D and Tagg, P. (eds) (1982) *Popular Music Perspectives*. Göteborg and Exeter.

Hughes, W. (1994) 'In the empire of the beat: discipline and disco', in Ross, A. and Rose, T. (eds) *Microphone Fiends: Youth Music and Youth Culture*. New York: Routledge.

Hunter, I. (1996) *Diary of a Rock'n'Roll Star*. London: Independent Music Press.

James, J. (1995) *The Music of the Spheres: Music, Science and the Natural Order of the Universe*. London: Abacus.

Jameson, F. (1991) *Postmodernism, or, the Cultural Logic of Late Capitalism*. London: Verso.

Jones, L. (1995/1963) *Blues People*. Edinburgh: Payback Press.

Jones, M. (1998) *Organising Pop: Why So Few Pop Acts Make Pop Music*. PhD thesis, IPM, Liverpool University.

Jones, N (1992) 'France not French', *Mixmag*, 2/18 (November).

Jones, S. (1992) *Rock Formation: Music, Technology and Mass Communication*. Newbury Park CA: Sage.

Karpic, L. (ed.) (1978) *Organization and Environment: Theory, Issues and Reality*. Beverly Hills: Sage.

Kealy, E. (1982) 'Conventions and the production of the popular music aesthetic', *Journal of Popular Culture*, 16/2.

Kealy, E. (1990/1979) 'From craft to art: the case of sound mixers and popular music', in Frith, S. and Goodwin, A. (eds) *On Record: Rock, Pop and the Written Word*. London: Routledge.

Keightley, K. (1996) '"Turn it down!" she shrieked: gender, domestic space, and high fidelity, 1948–59', *Popular Music*, 15/2.

Keil, C. (1994a) 'Motion and feeling through music', in Keil, C. and Feld, S. *Music Grooves: Essays and Dialogues*. Chicago: University of Chicago Press.

Keil, C. (1994b) 'People's music comparatively: style and sterotype, class and hegemony', in Keil, C. and Feld, S. *Music Grooves: Essays and Dialogues*. Chicago: University of Chicago Press.

Keil, C. (1994c) 'Participatory discrepancies and the power of music', in Keil, C. and Feld, S. *Music Grooves: Essays and Dialogues*. Chicago: University of Chicago Press.

Keil, C. and Feld, S. (1994) 'Commodified grooves', in Keil, C. and Feld, S. *Music Grooves: Essays and Dialogues*. Chicago: University of Chicago Press.

Kempster, C. (ed.) (1996) *History of House*. London: Sanctuary.

Kennedy, R. (1994) *Jelly Roll, Bix and Hoagy: Gennet Studios and the Birth of Recorded Jazz*. Bloomington: Indiana University Press.

Kirk, A. (1989) *Twenty Years on Wheels*. Oxford: Bayou Press.

Kitwana, B. (1994) *The Rap on Gangsta Rap*. Chicago: Third World Press.

Kloosterman, R. and Quispel, C. (1990) 'Not just the same old show on my radio, an analysis of the role of radio in the diffusion of black music among whites in the South of the United States, 1920 to 1960', *Popular Music*, 9/2.

Kraft, J. (1994a) 'Musicians in Hollywood: work and technological change in entertainment industries, 1926–1940', *Technology and Culture*, 35/2.

Kraft, J. (1994b) 'The "pit" musicians: mechanization in the movie theatres, 1926–1934', *Labor History*, 35/1.

Lacan, J. (1979) *The Four Fundamental concepts of Psycho-analysis*. London: Penguin.

Laclau, E. and Mouffe, C. (1985) *Hegemony and Socialist Strategy: Towards a Radical Democratic Politics*. London: Verso.

Laing, D. (1985) *One Chord Wonders: Power and Meaning in Punk Rock*. Milton Keynes: Open University Press.

Laing, D. (1991) 'A voice without a face: popular music and the phonograph in the 1890s', *Popular Music*, 10/1.

Laing, D. (1997) 'Rock anxieties and new music networks', in McRobbie, A. (ed.) *Back to Reality? Social Experience and Cultural Studies*. Manchester: Manchester University Press.

Lash, S. and Urry, J. (1987) *The End of Organized Capitalism*. Cambridge: Polity Press.

Lash, S. and Urry, J. (1994) *Economies of Signs and Space*. London: Sage.

Lees, G. (1987) 'Pavilion in the rain', in *Singers and the Song*. New York: Oxford University Press.

Lewisohn, M. (1994) *The Beatles Recording Sessions: The Official Abbey Road Studio Session Notes 1962–1970*. London: Hamlyn/EMI.

Lidov (1987) 'Mind and body in music', *Semiotica*, 66/1–3.

Lopes, P. (1992) 'Innovation and diversity in the popular music industry 1969 to 1990', *American Sociological Review*, 57/1.

Lury, C. (1993) *Cultural Rights: Technology, Legality and Personality*. London: Routledge.

Lyotard, J-F. (1984) *The Postmodern Condition: A Report on Knowledge*. Manchester: Manchester University Press.

Lyotard, J-F. (1993) 'The sublime and the avant-garde', in Docherty, T.

(ed.) *Postmodernism: A Reader*. Hemel Hempstead: Harvester Wheatsheaf.

McGuigan, J. (1992) *Cultural Populism*. London: Routledge.

McKay, G. (1996) *Senseless Acts of Beauty: Cultures of Resistance since the Sixties*. London: Verso.

McKenna, P. (1996) *Nightshift*. Dunoon, Argyll: S.T. Publishing.

MacLeod, B. (1993) *Club Date Musicians: Playing the New York Party Circuit*. Urbana: University of Illinois Press.

McQuail, D. (1994) *Mass Communication Theory: An Introduction* (3rd edn). London: Sage.

Marcus, G. (1993) *In the Fascist Bathroom: Writings on Punk 1977–1992*. London: Viking.

Martin, G. (1979) *All You Need Is Ears*. London: Macmillan.

Martin, G. (1995) *Summer of Love: The Making of Sgt Pepper*. London: Pan.

Marx, K. (1976) *Capital, Volume One*. Harmondsworth, Middlesex: Penguin.

Mason, K. (1994) Personal interview, May 14.

Melechi, A. (1993) 'The ecstasy of disappearance', in Redhead, S. (ed.) *Rave Off, Politics and Deviance in Contemporary Youth Culture*. Aldershot: Avebury.

Meltzer, R. (1987/1970) *The Aesthetics of Rock* (2nd edn) New York: Da Capo.

Melville, C. (1998) 'Mapping nowheres: rare groove, warehouse parties and the poetics of journeys', paper presented at Popular Music – Past and Future, IASPM UK conference, Liverpool University, 12 September.

Mercer, K. (1994) 'Reading racial fetishism: the photographs of Robert Mapplethorpe', in *Welcome to the Jungle: New Positions in Black Cultural Studies*. New York: Routledge.

Middles, M. (1996) *From Joy Division to New Order: the Factory Story*. London: Virgin Books.

Middleton, R. (1986) 'In the groove, or blowing your mind? The pleasures of musical repetition', in Bennet, T., Mercer, C. and Woollacot, J. (eds) *Popular Culture and Social Relations*. Milton Keynes: Open University Press.

Middleton, R. (1990) *Studying Popular Music*. Milton Keynes: Open University Press.

Middleton, R. (1996) 'The aesthetics and sociology of "Otherness"', paper presented at Popular Music: Aesthetics versus Sociology, a conference organised by IASPM UK and Critical Musicology Group, Oxford Brookes University, 26 October.

Miège, B. (1989) *The Capitalization of Cultural Production*. New York: International General.

Milestone, K. (1997) 'The love factory: the sites, practices and media relationships of northern soul', in Redhead, S., Wynne, D. and O'Connor, J. (eds) *The Clubcultures Reader*. Oxford: Blackwell.

Miller, D. (1995) 'The moan with the tone: African retentions in rhythm and blues saxophone style in Afro-American popular music', *Popular Music*, 14/2.

Mingus, C. (1995) *Beneath the Underdog*. Edinburgh: Payback Press.

Monson, I. (1994) 'Doubleness and jazz improvisation: irony, parody and ethnomusicology', *Critical Inquiry*, 20.

Moore, A. (1993) *Rock: The Primary Text, Developing a Musicology of Rock*. Buckingham: Open University Press.

Moore, G. (1966) *Am I Too Loud? Memoirs of an Accompanist*. Harmondsworth: Penguin.

Mowett, J. (1989) 'The sound of music in the era of its electronic reproducibility', in Leppert, R. and McLary, S. (eds) *Music and Society: The Politics of Composition, Performance and Reception*. Cambridge: Cambridge University Press.

Murray, C. (1991) *Shots From the Hip*. London: Penguin.

Music Week (1996) 'Compilations battle it out in a crowded market', 14 December.

Music Week: RM (1996) 'George and Tong sign Ministry mixing deal', 20 April.

Music Week: RM (1997) 'The hi life is over as Polydor closes dance imprint', 13 December.

Music Week: Distribution Extra (1997): 14–15.

Music Week: Business Affairs (1998) 'Indies exploit major funds', January.

Music Week: Promotional Feature (1999) 'A decade of hits: Power Promotions', March.

Neale, S. (1980) *Genre*. London: British Film Institute.

Negus, K. (1992) *Producing Pop: Culture and Conflict in the Popular Music Industry*. London: Edward Arnold.

Ogren, K. (1989) *The Jazz Revolution: Twenties America and the Meaning of Jazz*. New York: Oxford University Press.

Oliver, P. (1968) *Screening the Blues: Aspects of the Blues Tradition*. London: Cassell.

Osborne, P. (1994) 'The politics of time', *Radical Philosophy*, 68.

Otis, J. (1993) *Upside Your Head! Rhythm and Blues on Central Avenue*. Hanover NH: Wesleyan University Press.

Palmer, R. (1992) 'The church of the sonic guitar', in DeCurtis, A. (ed.) *Present Tense: Rock & Roll and Culture*. Durham NC: Duke University Press.

Parker, M. (1991) 'Reading the charts – making sense with the hit parade', *Popular Music*, 10/2.

Perry, S. (1990) 'Ain't no mountain high enough: the politics of crossover', in Frith, S. (ed.) *Facing the Music, Essays on Pop, Rock and Culture*. London: Mandarin.

Peterson, R. (1976) 'The production of culture: a prolegomenon', in Peterson, R. (ed.) *The Production of Culture*. Beverly Hills: Sage.

Peterson, R. (1994) 'Measured markets and unknown audiences: case studies from the production and consumption of music', in Ettema, J. and Whitney, D. (eds) *Audience Making: How the Media Create the Audience*. Newbury Park CA: Sage.

Peterson, R. and Berger, D. (1971) 'Entrepreneurship in organizations: evidence from the popular music industry', *Administrative Science Quarterly*, 16.

Peterson, R. and Berger, D. (1972) 'Three eras in the manufacture of popular music lyrics', in Denisoff, R. and Peterson, R. (eds) *The Sounds of Social Change*. Chicago: Rand McNally.

Peterson, R. and Berger, D. (1990/1975) 'Cycles in symbol production: the case of popular music', in Frith, S. and Goodwin, A. (eds) *On Record: Rock, Pop and the Written Word*. London: Routledge.

Priestley, B. (1985) *Mingus: A Critical Biography*. London: Paladin.

Read, O. and Welch, W. (1976) *From Tin Foil to Stereo: Evolution of the Phonograph*. Indianapolis: Sams and Co.

Redhead, S. (ed.) (1993) *Rave Off, Politics and Deviance in Contemporary Youth Culture*. Aldershot: Avebury.

Reich, W. (1975/1946) *The Mass Psychology of Fascism*. Harmondsworth: Penguin.

Reynolds, S. (1997) 'Rave culture: living dream or living death?' in Redhead, S., Wynne, D. and O'Connor, J. (eds) *The Clubcultures Reader*. Oxford: Blackwell.

Reynolds, S. (1998) *Energy Flash: A Journey Through Rave Music and Dance Culture*. London: Picador.

Reynolds, S. and Press, J. (1995) *The Sex Revolts: Gender, Rebellion and Rock'n'Roll*. London: Serpent's Tail.

Ribowsky, M. (1989) *He's a Rebel*. New York: E. P. Dutton.

Rietveld, H. (1998) *This is Our House: House Music, Cultural Spaces and Technologies*. Aldershot: Ashgate.

Rigby, S. (1987) *Marxism and History: a Critical Introduction*. Manchester: Manchester University Press.

Robinson, D., Buck, E. and Cuthbert, M. (eds) (1991) *Music at the Margins: Popular Music and Global Cultural Diversity*. Newbury Park CA: Sage.

RoDZ (1998) 'Northern soul': accessed at http://users.zetnet.co.uk/RoDZ/rodz5.htm, 30 November.

Romney, J. and Wootton, A. (1995) *Celluloid Jukebox: Popular Music and the Movies Since the 50s*. London: BFI.

Rose, T. (1994) *Black Noise: Rap and Black Culture in Contemporary America*. Middletown CT: Wesleyan University Press.

Rosenthal, D. (1993) *Hard Bop: Jazz and Black Music 1955–1965*. New York: Oxford University Press.

Ross, A. and Rose, T. (eds) (1994) *Microphone Fiends: Youth Music and Youth Culture*. New York: Routledge.

Rothenbuhler, E. and Dimmick, J. (1982) 'Popular music: concentration and diversity in the industry, 1974–1980', *Journal of Communication*, 32/1.

Sanjek, R. (1988) *American Popular Music and Its Business: The First Four Hundred Years. Volume III: from 1900 to 1984*. New York: Oxford University Press.

Savage, J. (1996) *Time Travel: Pop, Media and Sexuality, 1976–96*. London: Chatto and Windus.

Scannell, P. (1996) *Radio, television and modern public life: a phenomenological approach*. Oxford: Blackwell.

Scaping, P. and Green, C. (1998) *BPI Statistical Handbook 1998*. London: British Phonographic Industry.

Scaping, P. and Green, C. (1999) *BPI Statistical Handbook 1999*. London: British Phonographic Industry.

Schoenberg, L. (1991) 'Benny and the band', liner notes to Goodman, B. *The Birth of Swing (1935–1936)*, RCA ND90601(3).

Schuller, G. (1986) 'The future of form in jazz', in *Musings: the Musical Worlds of Gunther Schuller*. New York: Oxford University Press.

Seltzer, R. (1989) *Music Matters: The Performer and the American Federation of Musicians*. Metuchen NJ: The Scarecrow Press.

Shank, B (1994) *Dissonant Identities: The Rock'n'Roll Scene in Austin, Texas*. Hanover NH: Wesleyan University Press.

Shapiro, N. and Hentoff, N. (eds) (1962) *Hear Me Talkin' To Ya: The Story of Jazz by the Men Who Made It*. Harmondsworth: Penguin.

Sidran, B. (1995/1971) *Black Talk*. Edinburgh: Payback Press.

Siefert, M (1995) 'Image/Music/Voice: Song Dubbing in Hollywood Musicals', *Journal of Communication*, 45/2.

Silverman, K. (1988) *The Acoustic Mirror: The Female Voice in Psychoanalysis and Cinema*. Bloomington: Indiana University Press.

Simon, G. (1981) *The Big Bands* (4th edn). New York: Schirmer.

Small, C. (1987a) 'Performance as ritual: sketch for an enquiry into the true nature of a symphony concert', in White, A. (ed.) *Lost in Music: Culture, Style and the Musical Event*. London: Routledge and Kegan Paul.

Small, C. (1987b) *Music of the Common Tongue: Survival and Celebration in Afro-American Music*. London: Calder.

Smith, R. (1995) *Seduced and Abandoned: Essays on Gay Men and Popular Music*. London: Cassell.

Solomons, M. (1996) 'Dance makes its mark, but can it make money?', *Music Week*, 14 December.

Sparks, C. (1994) 'Independent production: unions and casualisation', in Hood, S. (ed.) *Behind the Screens: the Structure of British Television in the Nineties*. London: Lawrence and Wishart.

Spottswood, R. (1992) Liner notes to Various Artists, *Authentic Recordings of Rebetika and Smyrneika Songs from 1917 to 1938: The Greek Popular Song in America* (compact disc), Lyra CD 0079.

Stratton, J. (1982) 'Reconciling contradictions: the role of artist and repertoire in the British record industry', *Popular Music and Society*, 8/2.

Straw, W. (1990) *Popular Music as Cultural Commodity: the American Recorded Music Industries 1976–1985*. PhD thesis, Montreal: McGill University.

Straw, W. (1990/1983) 'Characterizing rock music culture: the case of heavy metal', in Frith, S. and Goodwin, A. (eds) *On Record: Rock, Pop and the Written Word*. London: Routledge.

Straw, W. (1991) 'Systems of articulation, logics of change: communities and scenes in popular music', *Cultural Studies*, 5/3.

Straw, W. (1993a) 'The booth, the floor and the wall: dance music and the fear of falling', *Public*, 8.

Straw, W. (1993b) 'Popular music and postmodernism in the 1980s', in Frith, S., Goodwin, A. and Grossberg, L. (eds) *Sound and Vision: the Music Video Reader*. London: Routledge.

Straw, W. (1997) 'Sizing up record collections: gender and connoisseurship in rock music culture', in Whiteley, S. (ed.) *Sexing the Groove: Popular Music and Gender*. London: Routledge.

Such, D. (1993) *Avant-garde Jazz Musicians Performing 'Out There'*. Iowa City: University of Iowa Press.

Swiss, T., Sloop, S. and Herman, A. (eds) (1998) *Mapping the Beat: Popular Music and Contemporary Theory*. Malden MA: Blackwell.

Tagg, P. (1989) 'Open letter: "black music", "Afro-American music", and "European music"', *Popular Music*, 8/3.

Tagg, P. (1993) '"Universal" music and the case of death', *Critical Quarterly*, 35/2.

Tagg, P. (1994) 'From refrain to rave: the decline of figure and the rise of ground', *Popular Music*, 13/2.

Tagg, P. (1999/1994) 'Subjectivity and soundscape, motorbikes and music', accessed at http:/www.liv.ac.uk/IPM/tagg/articles, 15 May.

Taylor, P. (1997) *Global Pop: World Music, World Markets*. New York: Routledge.

Théberge, P. (1989) 'The "sound" of music: technological rationalisation and the production of popular music', *New Formations*, 8.

Théberge, P. (1997) *Any Sound You Can Imagine: Making Music/Consuming Technology*. Hanover NH: Wesleyan University Press.

Thornton, S. (1995) *Club Cultures: Music, Media and Subcultural Capital*. London: Routledge.

Threadgold, T. (1989) 'Talking about genre: ideologies and incompatible discourses', *New Formations*, 2.

Tobler, J. and Grundy, S. (1982) *The Record Producers*. London: BBC.

Todorov, T. (1975) *The Fantastic: a Structural Approach to a Literary Genre*. Ithaca: Cornell University Press.

Toop, D. (1991) *The Rap Attack: African Rap to Global Hip Hop* (2nd edn). London: Serpent's Tail.

Toop, D. (1995) *Ocean of Sound: Aether Talk, Ambient Sound and Imaginary Worlds*. London: Serpent's Tail.

Toynbee, J. (1993) 'Policing Bohemia, pinning up grunge: the music press and generic change in British pop and rock', *Popular Music*, 12/3.

Trask, S. (1996/1992) 'Jazz angles', in Kempster, C. (ed.) *History of House*. London: Sanctuary.

Tucker, M. (1993) *The Duke Ellington Reader*. New York: Oxford University Press.

Vignolle, J. (1980) 'Mixing genres and reaching the public: the production of pop music', *Social Science Information*, 19/1.

Vincent, R. (1996) *Funk: The Music, the People, and the Rhythm of the One*. New York: St Martin's Griffin.

Waksman, S. (1998) 'Kick Out The Jams! The MC5 and the politics of noise', in Swiss, T., Sloop, S. and Herman, A. (eds) *Mapping the Beat: Popular Music and Contemporary Theory*. Malden MA: Blackwell.

Wallerstein, I. (1995) 'Historical Capitalism', in *Historical Capitalism with Capitalist Civilization*. London: Verso.

Walser, R. (1993) *Running with the Devil: Power, Gender and Madness in Heavy Metal Music*. Hanover NH: Wesleyan University Press.

Warhol, A. and Hackett, P. (1990) *Popism: The Warhol '60s*. London: Harcourt, Brace, Javanovich.

Wasko, J. (1994) *Hollywood in the Information Age: Beyond the Silver Screen*. Cambridge: Polity Press.

Wenner, K. (1972) *Lennon Remembers*. Harmondsworth: Penguin.

West, C. (1993) 'The new cultural politics of difference', in During, S. (ed.) *The Cultural Studies Reader*. London: Routledge.

Whitcomb, I. (1973) *After the Ball*. Harmondsworth: Penguin.

White, C. (1985) *The Life and Times of Little Richard, the Quasar of Rock*. London: Pan.

White, G. (1995) *Bo Diddley: Living Legend*. Chessington: Castle Communications.

Whiteley, S. (ed.) (1997) *Sexing the Groove: Popular Music and Gender*. London: Routledge.

Willemen, P. (1980) 'Presentation', in Neale, S. *Genre*. London: British Film Institute

Williams, A. (1980) 'Is sound recording like a language?', *Yale French Studies*, 60.

Williams, R. (1965) *The Long Revolution*. Harmondsworth: Pelican.

Williams, R. (1981) *Culture*. London: Fontana.

Williams, R. (1996/1983) 'Culture and technology', in *The Politics of Modernism: Against the New Conformists*. London: Verso.

Willis, P. (n/d) *Symbolism and Practice: a Theory for the Social Meaning of Pop Music*. Birmingham: Centre for Contemporary Cultural Studies.

Willis, P. (1978) *Profane Culture*. London: RKP.

Willis, P. (1990) *Common Culture: Symbolic Work at Play in the Everyday Cultures of the Young*. Milton Keynes: Open University Press.

Willmott, B. (1998) 'Save our vinyl', *Muzik*, 41, October.

Willox, B. (1976) *James Last*. London: Everest Books.

Wilson, B. with Gold, T. (1996) *Wouldn't It Be Nice: My Own Story*. London: Bloomsbury.

Winstanley, R. and Nowell, D. (1996) *Soul Survivors: The Wigan Casino Story*. London: Robson Books.

Winston, B. (1995) 'How are media born and developed?' in Downing, J., Mohammadi, A. and Sreberny-Mohammadi, A. (eds) *Questioning the Media: a Critical Introduction*. Thousand Oaks CA: Sage.

Wood, N. (1984) 'Towards a semiotics of the transition to sound: spatial and temporal codes', *Screen*, 25/3.

Wolff, J. (1993) *The Social Production of Art* (2nd edn). Houndmills: Macmillan.

Wollen, P. (1993) *Raiding the Icebox: Reflections on Twentieth-Century Culture*. London: Verso.

Wurtzler, S. (1992) '"She sang live but the microphone was turned off": the live, the recorded and the subject of representation', in Altman, R. (ed.) *Sound Theory, Sound Practice*. New York: Routledge.

Zappa, F. with Occhiogrosso, P. (1989) *The Real Frank Zappa Book*. London: Picador.

Discography

Bridges, A. (1979) 'I Love the Nightlife', Various Artists, *Boogie Bus* (long player). Polystar 9198 174.

Cheap Trick (1977) 'So Good To See You', *In Color* (long player). Epic EPC 82214.

Dr John (1972) *Gumbo* (long player). Atlantic K40384.

Eric B and Rakim (1997/1987) 'Paid in Full (Seven Minutes of Madness – The Coldcut Remix)', Various Artists, *Hip Hop Don't Stop* (compact disc). Solidstate SOLIDCD6.

The Fog (1998) 'Been A Long Time' Original Mix, Various Artists, *Muzik Presents Summer Anthems* (compact disc). SACD.

Goodman, B. (1991) *The Birth of Swing (1935–1936)* (compact disc). RCA ND90601(3).

Kirk, A. (1991) 'Until The Real Thing Comes Along', *The Chronological Andy Kirk, 1936–1937* (compact disc). Classics 573.

Mingus, C. (n/d) 'What Love', *Charles Mingus Presents Charles Mingus* (long player). CS 9005.

Mingus, C. (n/d) 'Folk Forms No.1', *Charles Mingus Presents Charles Mingus* (long player). CS 9005.

Mingus, C. (n/d) 'Original Faubus Fables', *Charles Mingus Presents Charles Mingus* (long player). CS 9005.

Mingus (1956) *Pithecanthropus Erectus* (compact disc) Atlantic 81456.

Mingus, C. (1957) 'Haitian Fight Song', *The Clown* (compact disc). Atlantic 790142.

Mingus, C. (1960) 'Wednesday Night Prayer Meeting', *Blues and Roots* (long player). Atlantic 1305.

Mingus, C. (1960) 'Hog Callin' Blues', *Blues and Roots* (long player). Atlantic 1305.

Mingus, C. (1960) 'Cryin' Blues', *Blues and Roots* (long player). Atlantic 1305.

Mingus, C. (1962) 'Eat That Chicken', *Mingus – Oh Yeah* (long player). Atlantic 7567.

Mingus, C. (1962) 'Eclusiastics', *Mingus – Oh Yeah* (long player). Atlantic 7567.

Mingus, C. (1987/1962) *[New] Tijuana Moods* (compact disc) RCA ND85644.

Mingus, C. (1995/1963) *The Black Saint and the Sinner Lady* (compact disc). Impulse 11742.

Mingus, C. (1998/1959) 'Better Git It In Your Soul', *Mingus Ah Um* (compact disc). Columbia 065145.

Mingus, C. (1998/1959) 'Fables of Faubus', *Mingus Ah Um* (compact disc). Columbia 065145.

Mingus, C. (1998/1959) 'Jelly Rolls', *Mingus Ah Um* (compact disc). Columbia 065145.

Mingus, C. (1998/1960) 'Slop', *Mingus Dynasty* (compact disc). Columbia 065145.

Nebula II (1998/1992) 'Explore H Core', Various Artists, *Essential Old Skool Hardcore* (compact disc), DCID 004.

Nightwriters (1987) 'Let The Music Use You' (Frankie Knuckles Mix), Various Artists, *Jack Trax: The Second Album* (long player). Jack Trax JTrax 2.

Randall and Andy C (1995) 'Feel It', Various Artists, *Routes From The Jungle* (compact disc). Circa Records VTDCD 46.

Sims, Z. (1957) *Zoot Sims Plays Alto, Tenor and Baritone* (long player). ABC 155.

Vandross, L. (1985) 'Till My Baby Comes Home', *The Night I Fell In Love* (long player). Epic EPC 26387.

Velvet Underground (1967) 'I'm Waiting for the Man', *The Velvet Underground and Nico* (compact disc). Verve 823 290-2.

Velvet Underground (1969) 'White Light/White Heat', *White Light/White Heat* (compact disc). Verve 825 119-2.

Velvet Underground (1969) 'Sister Ray', *White Light/White Heat* (compact disc). Verve 825 119-2.

Weill, K. (1966) *The Threepenny Opera* (long player) Fontana SFL14077-8.

Index